Time and Realism

Representation and Mind
Hilary Putnam and Ned Block, editors

Representation and Reality
Hilary Putnam

Explaining Behavior: Reasons in a World of Causes
Fred Dretske

The Metaphysics of Meaning
Jerrold J. Katz

A Theory of Content and Other Essays
Jerry A. Fodor

The Realistic Spirit: Wittgenstein, Philosophy, and the Mind
Cora Diamond

The Unity of the Self
Stephen L. White

The Imagery Debate
Michael Tye

A Study of Concepts
Christopher Peacocke

The Rediscovery of the Mind
John R. Searle

Past, Space, and Self
John Campbell

Mental Reality
Galen Strawson

Ten Problems of Consciousness: A Representational Theory of the Phenomenal Mind
Michael Tye

Representations, Targets, and Attitudes
Robert Cummins

Starmaking: Realism, Anti-Realism, and Irrealism
Peter J. McCormick (editor)

A Logical Journey: From Gödel to Philosophy
Hao Wang

Brainchildren: Essays on Designing Minds
Daniel C. Dennett

Realistic Rationalism
Jerrold J. Katz

The Paradox of Self-Consciousness
José Luis Bermúdez

In Critical Condition: Polemical Essays on Cognitive Science and the Philosophy of Mind
Jerry Fodor

Mind in a Physical World: An Essay on the Mind–Body Problem and Mental Causation
Jaegwon Kim

The Mind Doesn't Work That Way
Jerry Fodor

New Essays on Semantic Externalism and Self-Knowledge
Susana Nuccetelli

Consciousness and Persons: Unity and Identity
Michael Tye

Naturalistic Realism and the Antirealist Challenge
Drew Khlentzos

Wittgenstein and the Moral Life: Essays in Honor of Cora Diamond
Alice Crary (editor)

Time and Realism: Metaphysical and Antimetaphysical Perspectives
Yuval Dolev

Time and Realism

Metaphysical and Antimetaphysical Perspectives

Yuval Dolev

A Bradford Book
The MIT Press
Cambridge, Massachusetts
London, England

MIT Press books may be purchased at special quantity discounts for business or sales promotional use. For information, please e-mail special_sales@mitpress.mit.edu or write to Special Sales Department, The MIT Press, 55 Hayward Street, Cambridge, MA 02142.

This book was set in Stone serif and Stone sans by SNP Best-set Typesetter Ltd., Hong Kong and was printed and bound in the United States of America.

Library of Congress Cataloging-in-Publication Data

Dolev, Yuval.
Time and realism : metaphysical and antimetaphysical perspectives / by Yuval Dolev.
    p.   cm.—(Representation and mind)
"A Bradford book."
Includes bibliographical references and index.
ISBN 978-0-262-04243-7 (hardcover : alk. paper)—ISBN 978-0-262-54194-7 (pbk. : alk. paper)
1. Time. 2. Metaphysics. I. Title.

BD638.D64   2007
115—dc22   2006037125

10 9 8 7 6 5 4 3 2 1

Contents

Preface and Acknowledgments   vii

1 Time and Philosophy   1
1.1   Time and *Zeit*   1
1.2   Tense and Tenselessness   4

2 Time's Supposed Illusoriness   17
2.1   The Logical Argument   18
2.2   The Metaphysical Argument   22
2.3   The Empirical Argument   25
2.4   The Relationship Between the Three Arguments   29
2.5   Tense in a Tenseless World   31

3 Time's Supposed Concreteness   37
3.1   The "Moving Now"   38
3.2   Solipsism of the Present Moment   44

4 Tense Beyond Ontology   59
4.1   The Emergence of Ontology   60
4.2   Incoherence of Joint Uses of "Real"   67
4.3   The Myth of Tenseless Relations   79
4.4   Delusions of Illusions   95
4.5   The Collapse of Dummett's Solipsism   102
4.6   The "Now" Moves to an Impasse   109
4.7   Transcending Ontology   113

5 Time—As Seen from a Post-Ontological Perspective   117
5.1   The Duration of the Present   117
5.2   The Presence of Experience   129

5.3   The Pastness of Remembered Experiences   146

5.4   Time's Passage   155

5.5   Tense-based Biases   171

5.6   The Future's Openness; The Past's Fixity   183

5.7   Relativity Theory   195

6   Post-Post-Ontological Epilogue   209

6.1   Retrospective Overview   209

6.2   Augustine's Confession   211

6.3   How to Continue   212

Notes   219

References   231

Index   235

Preface and Acknowledgments

One of the characters of Raymond Queneau's mesmerizing world, Valentin, the protagonist of *The Sunday of Life*, spends his days trying "to see how time passes."[1] A shopkeeper, Valentin finds that "It's especially in the afternoons that he is able to devote himself to following the movement of the clock-hand, with his mind clear of the pictures that everyday life deposits in it." The mornings are also suitable: "up at five o'clock, he opens the store at seven, thus gaining two hours in which to watch time, in the limpidity of morning, or the mists of daybreak." But, he discovers that, if following the clock-hand is easy, "to see how time passes is an undertaking as difficult as that of catching yourself fall asleep." This immediately invites the question: does time itself move, in addition to, or over and above, the movement of the clock's hand, or is time's passage merely an illusion?

I've posed this question to several shopkeepers myself, and then pestered with it colleagues from various university departments. I expected people to be outraged by the notion that time's passage is an illusion. And, although many were, to my surprise, here and there I ran into someone who vehemently insisted that, to the contrary, it was self-evident that time's passage has to do only with how we apprehend things from our subjective, human perspective, and not with how they really are. The question, at any rate, is a difficult one, even if it appears simple. And the semblance of simplicity too is deceptive—it turns out to be complicated to make sense of the question. But for those interested in time, it is well worth putting in the effort.

Philosophy makes, at times, for a hard read. Still, my conviction that Valentin represents a curiosity that is practically universal guided my efforts to render this book accessible to as wide an audience as possible. Indeed, I believe not only that time is something that might intrigue anyone, but that many of the insights philosophy has to offer on the subject can also be enjoyed by anyone willing to seek them, regardless of background.

Time's passage, naively, at least, consists of the becoming present of future events and then their becoming past. So the notion of time's passage is intimately implicated with the distinction between the past, present, and future. Analytic philosophers dealing with the above question tend to belong to one of two camps: the tensed camp, which defends the reality of time's passage within a framework in which the present is conceived as "ontologically privileged" with respect to the past and the future; and the tenseless camp, which denies the reality of the distinction between the past, present, and future and so of time's passage, holding instead that all events, irrespective of their temporal location, are on an "ontological par."

For defenders of either view, the position they espouse is supposed to be the definitive word on the nature of time. In this book, however, the debate between the tensed and tenseless camps is conceived as a first stage in the philosophical investigation of time, a crucial stage, but not a conclusive one. The next stage belongs to phenomenology. I will claim that phenomenology grows naturally out of the analytic enterprise, which is shown to, in itself, rely on phenomenological observations. I will also claim that although mature phenomenology takes the inquiry to places beyond the reach of analytic efforts, in doing so it should be supported by the kind of edifice the analytic arguments provide.

Time and Realism, then, has two related goals: to analyze, and then move beyond, the tensed/tenseless or presentist/eternalist[2] debate in the metaphysics of time, resolving along the way some of the central difficulties in the field; and to serve as a bridge between the analytic and the continental traditions in the philosophy of time, both of which I claim are vital to the philosophical examination of time.

Here's a brief rundown of the book's chapters. After the introductory chapter, the book turns to a presentation of the main arguments in favor of both the tenseless and tensed theories of time (chapters 2 and 3). One of the main theses educed (in chapter 4) from this presentation is that, contrary to the received view, the two rival theories have much in common, and in fact are generated and sustained by a joint metaphysical presupposition. The presupposition, referred to in the book as the *ontological assumption*, is, crudely, that tense concerns the ontological status of things, and that therefore the question the philosophical investigation of time ought to focus on is whether or not something's being "real" depends on its location in time. In addition to uncovering this joint assumption, I am concerned to establish (also in chapter 4) that this assumption and the questions it engenders emerge naturally and *inevitably* once time is posed as the subject of a philosophical inquiry. Hence the predominance and liveliness of the tensed/tenseless debate, which is underpinned by the assumption and concerns the questions derived from it. However, further examination of the ontological assumption shows it to be untenable, from which it follows that neither the tensed nor the tenseless view has the final word in the metaphysics of time. The investigation is then carried beyond the tensed/tenseless debate. Transcending the debate and leaving onto-logical theses behind creates a new viewpoint from which to study central topics in the metaphysics of time. Chapter 5 is devoted to such a study. The results obtained turn out to depend on the kind of meticulous atten-tion to our firsthand experiences that drives phenomenological investiga-tions. Realizing this sets phenomenology as the venue in which the investigation can advance. The transition from the analytic study to phe-nomenology is discussed in the final chapter (chapter 6).

I am indebted for advice and comments to Yemima Ben-Menahem, Ohad Nachtomy, Charles Parsons, Itamar Pitowski, Michael Roubach, Steve Savitt, Ori Simchen, Joseph Stern, Ruth Weintraub, and Noam Zohar. Joseph Almog urged me to rewrite parts that I regarded as finished, and thus helped bring about clarity to thoughts and passages I did not realize were blurry. Roger Teichmann's remarks were particularly poignant and useful. Derek Parfit's criticisms forced me to think much harder about some arguments than I would have otherwise. Micha Weiss provided logistic support and good company. The philosophy department at UBC was a wonderful abode for working on the final version of the manuscript. I'm also grateful to MIT Press, and Judy Feldmann in particular, for seeing this project through.

Above all I am indebted to Hilary Putnam, whose guidance and friend-ship have accompanied this project's every step, and much more.

Finally, thanks to Yona, my tenacious and faithful partner in learning from that great teacher—Time.

1 Time and Philosophy

1.1 Time and *Zeit*

Perplexity seems to be an inexorable companion to time's passage. Novelists such as Agnon, Borges, Sebald, to name but a few, have studied it relentlessly; poets have stretched language beyond its limits in their attempts to penetrate its secrets; and scientists, in their more philosophical moods, have deployed their heaviest ammunition striving to eradicate the confusion that it is wrapped in. For philosophers there is initially one question: does time really flow or is time's passage merely an illusion? This is at once the most serious and the least comprehensible question in the metaphysics of time. The intention of this book is to separate meaningful from meaningless formulations of it, and to address the former and transcend the latter.

There are many perspectives from which time can be studied. Since the events that make up the natural history of the universe occur in time, time enters into the work of anyone concerned with this history—from physicists to geologists and social scientists. In another way, however, time's dwelling place is the human subject and is therefore foremost among the concerns of existentialists and phenomenologists, as well as artists and religious thinkers. One can ask whether time truly divides into a past, a present, and a future, or whether it is continuous, linear, and so on—questions that seem to pertain to "physical reality." Or one's fascination may revolve around the present's intimacy with eternity, or time's role in carrying one toward one's death—questions that belong to the human realm.

It is a fact about contemporary philosophy that these two faces of time, let us call them its "physical" and "human" faces, are dealt with separately. They are separated to such an extent that it is not always evident that these are two faces of one thing. Those occupied with "human" time often write as though there is no reality outside of human reality. And those writing about "physical" time tend to write as though there are no human beings. This split traces quite accurately the rift running between so-called analytic philosophy, done mostly in English, and continental philosophy, the centers of which are located in France and Germany. Judging by the differences, not only in style and method, but also primarily in subject matter, the English word *time* as it is used by philosophers has little to do with the French *temps* and the German *Zeit*.

This dualism is bogus: There is only one time. There aren't two objects for philosophical investigations. Einstein's famous assertion that "the distinction between the past, present and future is merely an illusion" (Calaprise 2000, 75), and Kierkegaard's illumination that "the present moment is that ambiguity in which time and eternity touch each other" (1972, 89) speak about the same present. Moreover, we cannot satisfactorily study either Einstein's or Kierkegaard's thesis without also studying the other. The present is the meeting point of nothing if, as Einstein's contention implies, it does not even exist. So it is important to know whether and how it exists if we are to say anything about its relation to eternity. And from the other direction, the denial of the reality of the present comes to very little un-less we have attained a comprehensive idea of what the present is, and that must include acquainting ourselves with those subtle ambiguities Kierkegaard's poetic statement speaks of.

The same goes for other terms that are central to the investigation of time in both traditions. "Experience," to take another example, is repeatedly referred to because experience, for instance of time's flow, provides indispensable data—is perhaps the only source of data—for the investigation. And when thinkers as different and distant as Mellor and Levinas study the experience of time's passage, the object of their study is one and the same, even if the manners of their study (one will focus on the relationship between tensed beliefs and tenseless truth conditions, the other on cycles of fatigue as an inexorable element of the human condition) and the conclusions they arrive at (one denies the reality of time's passage, for the other such passage is constitutive of reality) are worlds apart. Furthermore, as with the term "the present," it could very well be that the findings of the one concerning "experience" are pertinent to the inquiry conducted by the other.

Unfortunately, a two-sided disinterestedness prevails. Continental philosophers seem oblivious to analytic worries concerning the reality of time and tense. And analytic philosophers seem indifferent, not to say dismissive, of continental attempts to penetrate the present's phenomenology and existential significance. But, to repeat, no discussion is adequate that ignores either the physical or the human elements of time.

The question, then, is how these two philosophies of time may be re-related to each other. One perspective, to which there are surely alternatives, sees the analytic inquiry as more basic, in the way that bread is more basic than butter. It conceives the analytic occupation with the reality of time as a scaffold on which phenomenological meditations on time must rest. Butter can be eaten on its own, but that is not how it ought to be consumed. At the same time, just bread is not fulfilling—we need the butter. The aim of this book is to outline this analytic scaffold, and to show that the scaffold, the analytic enterprise, contains within it the seeds of the phenomenological project—that, if the analytic enterprise is carried out far enough, it naturally engenders the phenomenological project. Thus, this book deals primarily (though not exclusively) with the questions that come up in the course of the analytic investigation. But it is driven by the curiosity that later finds its satisfaction in the phenomenological investigation.

The integration of the two traditions is significant in both directions. Through it the analytic investigation gets embedded in a framework the horizons of which far exceed those it has outside it. Thus, settling the analytic question of the reality of time's passage does not bring the philosophical investigation to a close but sets the stage for a multitude of new questions concerning passage. Phenomenology, for its part, earns as conclusions of a systematic inquiry the working hypotheses it otherwise merely stipulates.

I believe this book points to resolutions for some of the central issues that traditionally make up the metaphysics of time. It does so, however, not by offering a metaphysical theory in which answers are given and explanations are expounded, but rather, in the tradition of philosophers such as James and Wittgenstein, by working through these issues to the point at which the intelligibility of the theories generated in response to them begins to falter. A resolution to the original metaphysical questions then follows from the realization that, as the arguments here will show, the questions themselves get their meaning from the very theories that purport to answer them. With the demise of the theories, the intelligibility of the questions is lost as well.

1.2 Tense and Tenselessness

Einstein's claim that there is in reality no distinction between past, present, and future goes to the heart of the metaphysical question about time, which, from its inception in antiquity, focused precisely on this issue. Present-day analytic philosophers writing on time are successors to this tradition. They are concerned with the question of whether our everyday tensed language, a language in which the past, present, and future figure indispensably, is indicative of the structure of temporal facts. When we say that the concert started twenty minutes ago, are we speaking about an event which is past, or is the (tacit) reference to the past merely a feature of the way we speak and think about the event but not of the event itself? Or, if during a skydive Sarah thinks to herself "I'm experiencing zero gravity now!," is she commenting on a present experience, or do experiences, like all events, in themselves lack all tensed properties and are only apprehended by us as though they are past, or present, or future, though they are not? Tense—as ubiquitous in experience, thought, and language as, say, color—gives rise today to questions of the sort that troubled early modern philosophers concerning the so-called *secondary qualities*: does it belong to the things perceived or only to our perceptions of things? Or, more generally, is reality tensed, or does it only appear tensed to us?

This question can be rephrased by means of a distinction that, to an extent, parallels the distinction between primary and secondary qualities, and which will be central to our inquiry—the distinction between *tenseless* and *tensed* relations. Consider the statement "Kennedy was assassinated in 1963." It is customary to distinguish between two items of temporal information that this statement imparts. First, we learn that 1,963 years separate the assassination from another event—the circumcision of Christ, with which the Gregorian calendar begins. More accurately, it tells us that the later event *succeeds* the earlier event by 1,963 years. This kind of temporal relation between events is referred to as a *tenseless relation*. In general, tenseless relations are defined to be relations of succession: we give the tenseless relation between events e_1 and e_2 when we say that e_1 is later than, or earlier than, or simultaneous with e_2 (I will have much to say about the term "tenseless relation" later on, but for now let me introduce it as it is commonly used). Second, assuming we know today's date, the statement that Kennedy was assassinated in 1963 tells us that this event is *past*, and also how long ago from the present it took place. The location of an event with respect to the present is referred to as the *tensed relation* of the event. We give *e*'s tensed property when we say that it happened x years ago, or will happen in y weeks from today, or, in general, by stating that it is past, or present, or future. We will get to know these two types of relations in great detail.

Now we may ask: are tensed relations part of reality, is there a present with respect to which events really stand in a temporal relation, or is it the case that, as was claimed about color at one time (and is still rehearsed by some today), there is no present outside of our apprehension and so nothing for events to have a tensed relation to? Are events truly past, or present, or future, or do tensed relations belong merely to the way we perceive things, and not to the way they really are, where as "real time," "objective time," consists solely of tenseless relations among events?

When these and related questions are probed, *ontological* issues come up. Must it be the case that for the sentence "Galois was killed in a duel" to be true now, Galois has to now be in the domain of existents? Does the fact that a sentence about him is true now entail that he must be counted as in some sense "real" now, even if he does not exist now? If not, what present facts, of which Galois is not a constituent, make a sentence about him true? The emergence of ontological quandaries is a major focus of this book.

Analytic philosophers are, for the most part, divided into two camps: tensed theorists and tenseless theorists.[1] Members of the first group are also known as A-theorists, or presentists; and those of the second group as B-theorists, or eternalists. But, as will become clearer in what follows, the steepest challenge facing both groups is to state their position coherently and defensibly. This explains the multiplicity of titles the views possess. Every so often a new formulation is suggested that is deemed by its authors to constitute a significant improvement over previous versions. The new position is then endowed with a new name so as to distinguish it from its defective predecessors.[2]

Use of the names "presentism" and "eternalism" is becoming more and more widespread. But the authors whose positions we will study prefer the still common names "the tensed view" and "the tenseless view." We will follow suit. These names also better serve discussions that, like the present one, are pervaded by such terms as "tensed facts," "tenseless relations," "tenseless truth conditions," and so on. But, to stress once again, under the headings "the tensed view" and "the tenseless view" I also include versions of presentism and eternalism respectively, and of A-theories and B-theories respectively. Setting aside differences in detail, which in terms of our purposes will be of little consequence, the multiplicity is of names, not of contents.

Tensed theorists contend, to put it roughly, that there is an ontological difference between the present, on the one hand, and the past and the future, on the other. "All and only present things are real" serves as a compressed expression of the view in most of its incarnations. Sometimes the tensed view focuses on time's passage, on how future events are made "real" by becoming present and then lose their ontological superiority as they move into the past. Tenseless theorists reject this ontological hierarchy, asserting instead that all events are "equally real," and that the distinction between past, present, and future pertains to our experience and to the way we think and speak, but not to the things we experience, think, and speak about.

We all mention time's passage occasionally, and without exception we speak and think of events as being either past, present, or future. The tenseless camp's suggestion that events are not thus comes to us as a surprise, which, in the absence of compelling grounds, would be dismissed offhand. But such grounds are found. Chapter 2 presents three independent arguments that support the tenseless view's stance. The first, derived from McTaggart, is logical. It builds on the claim that past, present, and future are incompatible attributes: if x is past then it is not present and not future; if it is present, it is not future and not past, and so on. But every event is, at some point, past, then present, and then future. The argument is meant to persuade us that the supposition that events really possess all three temporal attributes, albeit successively, leads to a logical contradiction, in the light of which we are supposed to withdraw this supposition. The second argument is metaphysical and builds on the claim that real, objective properties of things cannot be perspective dependent. But, so continues the argument, whether an event is past, present, or future depends on the temporal perspective from which it is being considered. So these properties are "subjective," belonging to the way we perceive things, not to how they really are. The third argument is empirical. It is claimed that relativity theory forces on us the tenseless doctrine.

Tensed theorists have the opposite job, that of furnishing the naive platitude that events are either past, present, or future with solid metaphysical foundations. This turns out to be a daunting task, which is made even more difficult by the powerfulness of the tenseless view's attacks on the position. In chapter 3 two very different attempts to stand up to this challenge are discussed. The first consists of simply taking the familiar notion that there is a "Now," which slides down the moments of time, endowing the events and things that occupy the moment it is visiting with reality, and casting this notion into a metaphysical framework. On this version of the view, the "moving Now" is regarded as a metaphysical primitive. The metaphysical theory provides it with a supporting semantic framework, and uses it to explain temporal phenomena. The second tensed position I discuss is subtler, and despite appearing at first to be outlandish, turns out to be the more defensible of the two. According to this second doctrine, the claim that only the present exists must be taken in a stricter sense than is at first attached to it. It must be taken to mean that we cannot say of past and future events that they ever were, or ever will be, real in the way that present things are. More dramatically, we can express the idea by the conjecture that all God's creation consists of is the present moment. Talk of the past and future turns out to be mediated by, and to elliptically pertain to, present materials (more accurate formulations are developed in section 3.2). Defending this view requires a sophisticated semantics, which I borrow from Dummett.

The received view is that one and only one of these doctrines—the tensed view or the tenseless view—is correct. More specifically, two usually unstated and uncontested suppositions underlie the vast amount of literature that the debate between the two camps has produced. First, it is assumed that these two theories are jointly *exhaustive*, leaving no room for a third alternative. Second, it is assumed that the two positions are diametrically *opposed*, each denying what the other affirms. I will reject both suppositions. As for exhaustiveness, to be more accurate, it will emerge that this supposition is both correct and incorrect. It is correct in that there is, indeed, no room for a third metaphysical theory of time. Whatever can and should be achieved by a metaphysical theory is already achieved by the tensed and tenseless doctrines. Plainly, then, no alternative metaphysical theory is found among the pages of this book. The characterization is incorrect in that, as I will explain presently, the philosophy of time is not exhausted by the metaphysical enterprise; only its initial stages are.

Contrary to the second supposition, namely, that the two doctrines are opposed, I will contend that the two theories in fact have a great deal in common. In a nutshell, the two theories share a fundamental and weighty metaphysical assumption, namely, that the difference between past, present, and future concerns the *ontological status* of events and things. More specifically, the assumption is that things and events have an ontological quality to them, and that the philosophical question concerning time is whether this quality is a function of their position in time or is temporally invariant. Tensed theorists claim that the ontological status of things varies with time, that, for example, owing to their temporal locations, the Empire State Building is real in a way that Herod's palace in Jerusalem is not; and the onus on them is to flesh out the ontology so that their claim says more than the trivial and universally accepted platitude that the Empire State Building exists now but did not exist two thousand years ago, while Herod's palace in Jerusalem existed two thousand years ago but does not exist now. Tenseless theorists assert in contrast that the Empire State Building and Herod's palace are on an ontological par, they are "equally real," and their task is to flesh out the ontology so that their view does not get implicated with the obvious falsehood that Herod's palace exists now and the Empire State Building existed two thousand years ago.

My concern is not to decide between these rival alternatives but to study the assumption they share, namely, the idea that there is an *ontology* here waiting to be fleshed out, or, what amounts to the same, the idea that *reality claims*—claims to the effect that events and objects are or are not "real"—are the key to the philosophical understanding of time. I will call this idea *the ontological assumption*. To be clear, note that when X says that events that are not present are "not real," she is making an ontological statement. And when Y says that they are "real," she too is making an ontological statement. Underlying both statements is the presupposition that there is an issue at hand concerning the ontological status of the events in question. Thus, with these very statements, both X and Y are tacitly invoking the ontological assumption.

To thwart misunderstanding: the shared assumption is that if there are real differences between the past, present, and future then they are *onto-logical* differences. My position will be that there are real differences between being past, being present, and being future, but that these differences are not ontological.

This in itself requires clarification, for it is not immediately obvious what ontological differences or differences in "ontological status" exactly are. We know what real, "non-ontological" differences are. There are real differences between electrons and positrons, for example, differences in electric charge. There are real differences between the first-person and the third-person perspectives. And there are real differences between numbers and clouds. None of these would be classified as "ontological." We get closer, perhaps, to differences in "ontological status" when we reflect on the fact that George Bush is real but Santa Claus is not, or when we consider the fact that there are horses but there are no and there never were (and according to one reading of Kripke, there could not have been) unicorns. These examples do not capture the ontological difference that is at the center of the dispute between tenseless and tensed theorists, but they gesture in the direction where such differences are to be sought. As I will discuss in detail later, I am skeptical about the possibility of adequately fleshing out the notion of "ontological differences," at least as it is used in connection with the dispute about time. At this stage, all I want is to emphasize that my position is that, while there are no "ontological" differences between the past, present, and future, far from being "subjective," or "merely mental," the distinction between the past, present and future is as real as a distinction can get. This will set the stance developed in this book apart from that of both tensed theorists and tenseless theorists, whose common working assumption is, to repeat, that if there are real differences between being past, being present, and being future, they are ontological differences.

As I said, much attention will be devoted to this assumption. This seems to me appropriate since, despite its centrality to the metaphysics of time, a study of the ontological assumption is rarely conducted, the reason being, once again, that both sides to the analytic debate take the assumption for granted.

The conclusion of this study will consist in the following claims: that making the ontological assumption is natural, even inevitable, in the context of the philosophical investigation of time, and that, moreover, grappling with its offshoots—the tensed and the tenseless doctrines—is indispensable for making headway in this investigation, but that the ontological assumption and its offshoots cannot be sustained and must ultimately be transcended. Chapter 4 is devoted to a detailed exposition of these claims.

As for the first claim, I locate the origins of the philosophical bewilderment time gives rise to in ordinary, everyday situations and utterances. This is not to say that mundane occasions necessarily arouse bewilderment; but, if such bewilderment does arise, it is often from reflection upon the temporal aspects of ordinary experiences. Among the first observations that come before one's attention when such situations become the subjects of philosophical inspection concerns the causal and perceptual inaccessibility of the past. The past is apprehended as fixed and unalterable. That it is impossible to affect things of the past or to be in any kind of sensual contact with them is the source, I argue, of the suspicion that things of the past (and similar observations pertain to future things) have a different ontological quality from present things, which are perceivable and affectible. That's how, almost from the first step, the ontological assumption enters into the metaphysics of time.

This inaccessibility of the past is, in the beginning at least, phenomenological—it has to do with how we apprehend the past. Now, the gist of phenomenology, as a philosophical method, is to engage in the quite formidable task of describing how things are apprehended by us *before* making any ontological assumptions and discovering, as a by-product of its success in describing what the past is for us, that there are no ontological assumptions that need to be, or indeed that can be, made in this context. Phenomenology preempts ontological issues before they can rear their head, and takes its subsequent achievements as validating this strategy. The claim that the question "Are past things and events real or not?" is not a meaningful one serves as the starting point of the phenomenological inquiry, which later receives retrospective justification from the inquiry's results. That means that phenomenology never grapples with this question directly.

But, as stated above, I believe the analytic preoccupation with this question is not superfluous. To the contrary, whatever insights we attain about time are left hovering without roots over shaky ground as long as the best we can do vis à vis the ontological issue is sidestep it. Accordingly, the strategy in this book is shifted with respect to the phenomenologist strategy. Phenomenology evades the attempts to cast temporal distinctions in ontological terms and jumps ahead to start the investigation from a point that is already beyond these attempts. We, on the other hand, take these attempts head on and work through them to the conclusion that they cannot prevail, that is, to the understanding that time does not concern the ontological standing of events and things. In other words, we reach as a conclusion the point that phenomenology simply assumes at the outset.

Taking on attempts to answer the question "Are past things real or not?" means taking on the tensed and tenseless views, the "No" and "Yes" answers respectively, and working through them. Doing so reveals that the metaphysical doctrines are indispensable to the investigation in two ways. First, the difficulties in which our apprehension of time is initially immersed are exposed, pinpointed, and articulated in the course of developing these theories. As often happens (in mathematics and the sciences, for example), the theories yield the "research problems" they then address. To take an example, the observation that "experience is always present" (for instance, that only present pains are painful), does not yet constitute a thesis that one can sink one's teeth into. Only theories explain this claim (or explain it away) turn it into such. Similarly, claims such as that the past is fixed, or that the future is open, though they correspond to something we are all acquainted with, require development before they can be tackled analytically. The tensed and tenseless doctrines do that service: they constitute structured frameworks within which these claims can be elaborated and made precise. The explanatory doctrine is crucially instrumental in formulating that which gets explained. Prior to the development of the doctrine, all we have are somewhat vaguely stated intuitions. By presuming to resolve our perplexities, the metaphysical theories provide clear coordinates for where our confusion lies.

The second pivotal role the tensed and tenseless theories play has to do with the second claim made above about the ontological assumption, namely, that ultimately this assumption has to be transcended. In arguing for this claim, I begin by discussing reality claims in general, and showing that, as it stands, the above question "Are past things real or not?" lacks any definite meaning. We just do not know what to make of the assertion that, for example, Herod's palace in Jerusalem is real, or of the converse, that it is not real (when, again, these assertions are meant to convey more than the obvious falsehood that Herod's palace in Jerusalem exists now, or its trivially true negation). There is no sense that can be attached to this use of "real" that would lend coherence to such assertions, or to the questions they answer. To the extent that tensed and tenseless theorists just assume some such sense, they are assuming a we-know-not-what.

But, more challengingly, tensed and tenseless theorists can be read not as assuming the meaningfulness of reality claims, but as creating a sense for them, and in particular for the word "real" as it figures in the articulation of their tenets. Such a sense would then retroactively endow with meaning the question "Real or not?," the question their positions are propounded as answers to. Again, the idea is that, in analogy with similar occurrences in science, the theory has a role in fixing the meaning of some of the key terms with which it is articulated, in our case, of the term "real." Of course, for that to happen, the theory has to be successful, and here, in contrast with the scientific case, we cannot appeal to empirical validation to judge its success. Rather, it is its coherence that needs to be evaluated. To do so, I focus on other technical terms introduced by tensed and tenseless theorists, terms such as the "moving Now" on the part of tensed theorists, or "tenseless relations" on the part of tenseless theorists. The critical examination of these terms raises questions concerning their own intelligibility. This in turn renders them unfit for supporting the problematic reality claims in connection with which we meet them. If the terms "tenseless relations" and "moving Now" cannot be used coherently, then no reality claim can be upheld by means of either.

The conclusion in chapter 4 is that tense does not pertain to reality claims: there simply are no ontological distinctions to be drawn along temporal lines. Although the attempt to formulate a theory that constitutes a coherent and defensible answer to the question "Real or not?" is vital to the philosophical investigation of time, in the end, neither the results of this effort nor the question that prompts it can be sustained. The investigation must move beyond them, transcend them. This is not taken as a negative thesis, a mere rebuff of a confusion that could have been avoided to begin with. Rather, it should be thought of as a lifting of a veil, the overcoming of a way of looking at things, a way that is initially natural but not final—the ontological way. To repeat, the ontological assumption facilitates the mapping and analysis of notions that are central to our understanding of time. It underpins the claims that: the present is pointlike; experience is always present; the past is fixed and the future open. It drives certain attempts to flesh out what temporal passage is all about, and aims to provide metaphysical grounds for some of our tense-based biases, such as the contrast between fearing future pains and being relieved about past ones. Transcending the ontological assumption sets these and related issues in a new light that is previously not available. It is in the new treatment of these issues, achieved by the transcendence of the ontological assumption, that the positive nature of the conclusions of chapter 4 becomes manifest. Chapter 5 is devoted to this post-ontological examination.

Two misunderstandings should be cautioned against before we proceed. First, from what has been said thus far it should be evident that I am not about to defend the tensed view (or the tenseless view). Yet, as mentioned, many writers on time hold that we are faced with a forced choice between exactly two options: either we are tenseless theorists, or else we are tensed theorists. According to these philosophers if a position is not a version of the tenseless view then *ipso facto* it is a kind of tensed view. This move is forestalled by the distinction between *real* and *ontological* differences between the past, present, and future. Only the latter difference is used in the tensed claim. As I explained, one can reject this position, and yet hold the former, namely, the claim that the differences between being past, present, or future are real and objective though they do not pertain to the "ontological status" of events and things. It is this option that I explore in the coming chapters, and especially in chapter 5, where I attempt to flesh out real—but not ontological—differences between being past, present, or future.

Second, in what follows, reference will often be made to the vocabulary with which philosophical queries are expressed and treated. In particular, the relationship metaphysical terminology bears to everyday discourse will be examined. The point to stress is that by everyday discourse I will mean *scientific discourse* as well as so-called ordinary language. This needs stressing especially in light of the above statement that no theory is to be propounded in this book. Such a statement may mistakenly be thought of as betraying an antiscientific sentiment. As far as the spirit of this book goes, the contrary is the case. The present work is influenced by science as it is by philosophy, and strives to be sensitive to scientific language and appreciative of its authority, as is reflected in its treatment of relativity theory.

To summarize, here is an overview of the integrative move from the analytic to the phenomenological study of time that this book proposes.

(1) The philosophical inquiry of time is provoked by a reflection on the temporal aspects of ordinary experience, something that could be identified as naive phenomenology. Such reflection draws attention to the perceptual and causal inaccessibility of events and things that are not present.

(2) The perception of an impassable gap separating us from events and things that are not present raises issues concerning their ontological status.

(3) The preliminary formulation of these issues marks the beginning of the systematic inquiry. Methodical phenomenology circumvents these ontological issues and moves directly into a full-fledged phenomenological investigation. The path advocated in the coming chapters, on the other hand, consists in taking on the ontological questions. This analytic effort yields two metaphysical theories: the tensed view and the tenseless view.

(4) Working through these theories leads to the exposure of a common assumption underlying the tensed/tenseless debate, namely, the *ontological assumption*. A study of the ontological assumption's origins highlights its naturalness and its indispensability to these views.

(5) However, critically examining the ontological assumption brings about its demise and demonstrates that neither the tensed nor the tenseless doctrine, both of which are underpinned by it, constitutes a tenable solution to the kinds of ontological problems for which they are proposed.

(6) This conclusion alters how the role of the metaphysical theories is perceived in the investigation. From being thought of as final solutions (between which we have to choose) to perplexities the assumption gives rise to, they come to be regarded as stages in the investigation, specifically, as facilitators of the movement that transcends the ontological assumption.

(7) By now it becomes evident that the theses that make up the metaphysical theories cannot alleviate our puzzlement. Indeed, the contrary is

the case: by endorsing any of them we are replacing, to paraphrase Wittgenstein, an unspecified confusion with a systematic one. But neither can we simply ignore these theses; that would be tantamount to ignoring the unspecified confusions that plague our initial understanding of time. Hence we turn to a reevaluation of the problems that are delineated and addressed by the metaphysical theories, a reevaluation that is conducted from the post-ontological perspective attained through the transcendence of the ontological assumption.

(8) Finally, the circle is closed and the philosophical activity concerning time returns to the phenomenology with which it begins. However, it now engages the phenomenological task without worrying about getting disoriented by the ontological conundrums that naive phenomenology invariably runs into, and that have now been left behind. Thus, to take an example I mention in the concluding chapter, we can approach Husserl's notions of "retention" and "protention" without being weighed down by the metaphysics that accompanies them; we can endorse the insights of phenomenology, but not the "reduction," or "bracketing," in which they are originally shrouded.

Connecting the two traditions in this manner—conducting an analytic analysis of the ontological issue and deriving from it a conceptual groundwork for phenomenology—is the objective of this book. The positive phenomenological work, of which, in the space of the book's final chapter, I give one or two examples, ensues henceforth. And not just this. As I also briefly outline in that chapter, the analytic analysis can serve as a foundation for an attentiveness that in various nonphilosophical contexts has the potential of deepening our understanding of time, and of our being in time. I have in mind situations with a certain moral content to them, or contexts that can be characterized, broadly speaking, as religious.

One last note before we plunge into metaphysical waters. Over the past few decades there have appeared a torrent of papers and books along the pages of which the tensed/tenseless debate rages. In this book I discuss only a sample of this literature. I am trying to focus not on the specifics of the debate, but on the hidden, underlying common grounds shared by most, if not all, proponents of either the tensed or the tenseless view, regardless of differences in detail between individual versions of one of these theories. The representatives I discuss in detail—Mellor, Parfit,

Dummett, Schlesinger—were chosen because the elements I wish to high-light are most conspicuous in their theories. It could be that other rendi-tions of the theories are more powerful or persuasive. But that does not make them more suitable for this book, which is not concerned with taking sides in the debate. I hope that the coming chapters will convince the reader that the claims presented in them really pertain to a core shared by most if not all currently available versions of either the tensed view or the tenseless view.

2 Time's Supposed Illusoriness

Among his many observations on time, Einstein also remarked that "when you are courting a nice girl an hour seems like a second. When you sit on a red-hot cinder a second seems like an hour."[1] "That's relativity," he joked. But of course you don't have to be Einstein to know that "time sometimes flies like a bird, sometimes crawls like a snail," as Turgenev puts the same point (*Fathers and Sons*, chapter 17); you just have to pay attention to ordinary experiences. In the light of such experiences, the claim that time's passage is an illusion, made not by a playful skeptic but as a factual claim, sounds astonishing.

And yet, with a little more reflection, disturbing questions come up: is it really time that passes, or is it rather events that pass through time (what's the bank and what's the river, to invoke an old metaphor)? Does this flow have a rate, and if so, what is it? And is it something that really happens, or, as Einstein's comment could be taken to tacitly suggest, does time's passage belong to our psychology, to how we experience things, and not to how they really are?[2] To put this last worry into other words, do events really change, with time's passage, from being future to being present and then past, or is it merely in our apprehension of them that they seem to possess these tensed locations?

These worries may appear, initially at least, to be quite crude. Yet the claim that time's passage is merely an illusion needs to be taken seriously, for these very worries are the basis for three independent, solid arguments that seem to establish it. The arguments are logical, conceptual, and empirical. They do not aim at merely raising the possibility that time's passage is an illusion, as general skeptical arguments do. They purport to establish that as a matter of logical, conceptual, and empirical fact, time's passage is indeed an illusion. Time's passage and the distinction between the past, present, and future are inextricably linked: somewhat loosely, for time to pass is for future evens to become present and then past. So the conclusion of these arguments can be paraphrased as the claim that the distinction between past, present, and future is not part of reality. The two formulations amount to the same: tense, it is claimed by either formulation, is a mode of thought, speech, and experience, and not an element of reality itself.

2.1   The Logical Argument

The logical argument for the unreality of tense is McTaggart's. It first appears in "The Unreality of Time" (1908)[3] and is rehearsed today by prominent thinkers such as Mellor.[4] McTaggart's argument, which at first blush seems too simple to be good, consists of two fairly plain premises:

1. Past, present, and future are, in McTaggart's language, "incompatible determinants." That is, these temporal categories are mutually exclusive: if an event e is past, then it is not present and it is not future; if it is present then it is not past and it is not future; if it is future then it is not past and it is not present.

2. Each event has all three determinants, that is, each event is past, present, and future. Indeed, it would be absurd to maintain of anything that it is only past, or only present, or only future.

The conclusion that follows is that since nothing in reality can have incompatible determinants, the distinction between past, present, and future is not part of reality. To take an example, the eruption of Vesuvius, which destroyed Pompeii, is past. But either pastness is its only tensed attribute, or else it also has the attributes of presentness and of futurity. Yet these are incompatible determinants. So in reality it has none of these attributes, that is, it is not tensely located at all. That is not to say that this eruption is not in time altogether. It is—it has a date. But it is only in our minds that in addition to occupying a certain moment in time, it is also past, or present, or future.

This ends the argument, but just begins the argumentation. The immediate rejoinder is that the eruption is now past, but it is not now future or present. Rather, it *was* future and *was* present. McTaggart anticipates this rejoinder, and is ready with an answer. Saying of Vesuvius's eruption that it is future at a time t_1, and present at t_2, and past at t_3, is to no avail, for each of these times, t_1, t_2, t_3, is itself past, present, and future. So now we've replaced the one original contradiction with three new ones. Introducing the times at which the event is past, present, and future is like trying to tow a car with three broken-down ones. We can of course introduce new times, a time t_{11} in which t_1 is future, a time t_{12} at which t_1 is present, t_{13} at which it is past, a time t_{21} at which t_2 is future, t_{22} at which t_2 is present, and so on. And this can go on forever. The infinite regress, however, works in favor of McTaggart, for in every new stage, new contradictions are lurking. The regress could have undermined his argument only if at some point it would have led to a contradiction-free moment or event. But it does not. So McTaggart's argument stands.

Dummett rehearses the argument in an illuminating manner. Replacing the assertions "*e* is past," "*e* is present," and "*e* is future," with "*e* is past," "*e* was present," and "*e* was future" amounts to replacing first-order tense-predicates with second-order ones: "*e* is now past," "in the past *e* was present," and "in the past *e* was future." But, Dummett points out, in addition to these three second-order predicates there are six others: "*e* is now present," "*e* will be present," "*e* will be past," "*e* will be future," "*e* is now future" and "*e* was past." And among these nine predicates there are plenty of contradictions. For example, "*e* is now present" contradicts "*e* is now future." The protest that *e* does not have all nine second-order properties at the same time moves the debate one level further up, landing it in third-order predicates such as "*e* will have been past." But this level is occupied by twenty-seven tense-predicates, many pairs of which are mutually contradictory.

The regress can continue indefinitely, but contrary to what McTaggart's critics had hoped to establish, this regress damns his opponents alone. Surveying the entire regress with one glance, we cannot find one level that is contradiction-free. There is not one point throughout the regress to which one who wishes to rescue the tenses from the charge of contradiction can escape. It's not that by going up a level from first-order to second-order predicates we arrive at a set of predicates that is initially clear of any contradiction; the contradiction is already there, waiting for us. And so with all further steps we make down the regress. To employ another simile, proceeding in this manner can be likened to fleeing a blazing tower all of whose flights are already on fire: one flees the top floor only to find that the floor underneath is burning as well, as is the one below it, and so on.

Still, McTaggart's argument usually boils down to a tedious quarrel as to the regress's verdict, each side claiming it damages the other. So, for those weary of regresses, Mellor offers an ingenious regression-less version of the argument. Before presenting his formulation, we need to reconsider what the argument is actually saying. Let's return to the eruption of Vesuvius. According to McTaggart's argument, the condition on which the sentence "The destruction of Pompeii by Vesuvius is an event of the past" is true does not consist of a tensed relation—namely, its being the case that this event *is past*—for if, as the argument concludes, the tenses are not real and in particular there is in reality no such thing as *the past*, then nothing is past. So Tarski's schema "'p' is true if and only if p," which in our case is "'e is past' is true if and only if e is past," does not obtain. Instead, it can be suggested that the sentence "Vesuvius erupted in the past" is true on some other, tenseless, condition, for example, on the condition that it is tokened now, many years after the eruption. In general, on the well-known "token-reflexive"[5] account of tensed statements (which we will return to in greater detail and precision later in the chapter), tokens of past-tense sentences are true if they are tokened later than the event they are about. So, according to this account, a token of "Vesuvius erupted in the past" is true on the condition that it is tokened—written, thought, uttered or read—later than the eruption.

Note, in passing, that the term "token" is used here, and will continue to be used throughout the book, to denote something to which *a specific date can be attached*—an occasion on which someone speaks, prints, writes, reads, or thinks a certain sentence. This use diverges from another standard use of the term, according to which a particular copy, say, of Camus's *The Stranger* contains a particular printed token of the sentence "Mother died yesterday." Here "token" denotes an object that persists through time, whereas for us it will denote rather an event that occurs at a given time. Thus, for us the token will be not the sentence printed in a particular copy of *The Stranger*, but the occasion of someone reading this sentence, or copying it, or of Camus's writing it.

Returning to the tensed and tenseless accounts of the truth of "The destruction of Pompeii by Vesuvius is an event of the past," the two accounts are alike in that for both the relevant linguistic entities are *tokens*, rather than types of sentences. Types of tensed sentences do not have determinate truth-values: "Today is Monday" is true on some occasions and false on other occasions. The same holds of "The destruction of Pompeii by Vesuvius is an event of the past." Some of the tokens of this sentence are true, others are false. But each of these tokens has a single fixed, unchanging truth-value. It cannot be both true and false. Again, this is true on both accounts. The difference between the tensed and tenseless accounts is that in the former truth conditions are nonrelational, whereas in the latter they are relational in the following sense. The tensed truth condition on which a token of "The destruction of Pompeii by Vesuvius is an event of the past" is true is the nonrelational condition that the event in question is past. In specifying this condition no mention is made of the *temporal relationship* between the event and the token whose truth condition this condition is. That is, this relationship does not enter into the condition. In contrast, this relationship is integral to the tenseless truth condition of this sentence: a token of the sentence is true on the condition that the event in question—the destruction of Pompeii by Vesuvius— stands in the temporal relationship of being earlier than the tokening of the sentence.

Mellor's crucial observation is that to insist, as McTaggart's opponents do, that tensed conditions constitute truth conditions for tokens of tensed sentences is to imply that tokens can be both true and false. For, as time flows, tensed conditions change and with them the truth-values of tokens describing these conditions. For example, up to the moment of Vesuvius's eruption, the tensed conditions that obtain are that this event is future, and these conditions establish the falsehood of all tokens of "The destruction of Pompeii by Vesuvius is an event of the past." After the eruption, the tensed conditions that obtain are that this event is past, conditions in light of which all tokens of "Vesuvius erupted in the past" are true. It turns out that if McTaggart is wrong, that is, if the tenses are real and time flows, then each token of "Vesuvius erupted in the past" is both true and false, a blatant contradiction, the contradiction McTaggart uncovered.

Of course, it cannot be objected that these tokens have different truth-values at different times. Tokens, to repeat, have determinate, unchanging, truth-values. The other escape is to correct the account so that those tokens of "Vesuvius erupted in the past" that occur before the eruption are assigned "false" as their truth-value, and those that occur after the eruption are assigned "true" as their truth-value. This move, indeed, fixes the truth-values of tokens and removes the contradiction. But it concedes everything to the tenseless theorist, and is tantamount to endorsing the tenseless, relational token-reflexive account. For, like this account, it relies on the fixed temporal relationship between the event and the token that describes it, that is, if relies on the fact that given a token p that is earlier than the event e, it is *always* the case that p is earlier than e. And likewise for tokens that are later than the event. If we are unwilling to accept the tenseless token-reflexive account, then we are pushed back to the contradictory idea that the truth-value of tokens is given by changing tensed facts.

This is Mellor's version of McTaggart's argument. It is free of those infinite regresses that have made it difficult for McTaggart's supporters to make their case. It may, on the other hand, also lack the elegant simplicity of McTaggart's original formulation. Be that as it may, whether we are looking at McTaggart's original argument, or at Dummett's or Mellor's variations on it, the conclusion is the same: there are no tensed facts, or in McTaggart's words, "nothing is really present, past or future" (Gale 1968, 97). In the next two sections we will examine two other arguments that establish the same conclusion.

2.2 The Metaphysical Argument

As a preparatory exercise for the metaphysical argument against the reality of tense, consider the difference between "Ingres is buried here" and "Ingres is buried in Pére Lachaise." Assuming the first sentence is tokened at the Pére Lachaise cemetery in Paris, both sentences describe, correctly, the same datum, namely, the burial place of the nineteenth-century painter Ingres. The glaring difference between these two descriptions is, however, that the first sentence is true only when tokened in the cemetery, whereas the other is true regardless of where it is tokened. We can say that the first sentence is "perspectival," that its truth-value depends on the perspective from which it is tokened, that it describes how a certain states of affairs appears from a certain point of view—from inside the Paris cemetery. The second sentence, in contrast, exhibits no such dependence. It is given from nowhere, as it were, and is objective, in the sense of being not perspectival.

The argument we are about to consider rests on the assumption that reality has a nonperspectival description, that a complete description of the world can, in principle, be given, one that omits no facts and consists purely of nonperspectival formulations. Dummett (1978, 356) writes:

I can make drawings of a rock from various angles, but if I am asked to say what the real shape of the rock is, I can give a description of it as in three-dimensional space which is independent of the angle from which it is looked at. The description of what is really there, as it really is, must be independent of any point of view. . . . I personally feel very strongly inclined to believe that there must be a complete description of reality; more properly, that of anything which is real, there must be a complete—that is, observer independent—description.

"Ingres is buried in Paris" gives us an idea what "observer-independent" descriptions are. Parfit says that in general to attain such a description we should "imagine a description of our universe as it would have been if life had never developed: a description given from no place within this universe" (1996, 6). This exercise is less intimidating than it sounds. Look at a globe. It shows that Paris is west of Prague, and it shows this geographical fact from no particular viewpoint. A token of "Paris is west of Prague" would constitute a true description, irrespective of any facts about the spatial and temporal location of its tokening. Such a sentence would thus be a part of a complete description of reality, a description that would hold true even in a lifeless universe, a description which, just like Dummett's portrayal of the rock, is of the world "as it really is."

The important claim here is not merely that those things of which there is an observer-independent description are elements of reality as it really is, but that *only* things of which there is an observer-independent description are elements of reality as it really is. Thus, it is not the case that in addition to being west of Prague, Paris also has the property of being *there*, or of being 3,000 miles from *here*. Imagine looking at Europe from a satellite. We'd have no difficulty pointing to various points on the continent which are selected, for example, by their longitude and latitude coordinates. But assume that in addition to locating Paris and Prague, we are asked to point to where *here* is in Europe. The request would make no sense—no place in Europe has the property of being *here*. Or, to be more precise, that a certain location is *here*, or is *there*, is not a further geographical fact. Rather, it belongs to a certain observer's perspective, an accidental observer who happens to see things from an angle that lacks any uniqueness. In this sense, the belief that a given location is here or there is subjective.

The notion of "a complete description of reality" enables Parfit to expound his argument in favor of the tenseless view:

On the tenseless view reality could be fully described in tenseless terms. . . .

. . . [A complete description] says where every object is, and at which times. Could we say, "But one crucial fact has been left out: viz. which of all these places is 'here' "? We could not. In a lifeless universe, the concept "here" would fail to apply. On the tenseless view, the same is true of the concept "now." In a lifeless universe, the concept "now" would not apply. (1996, 3, 6)

Think of a temporal analogue of Europe's map. A line that represents time, along which events are arranged according to their date (something akin to the time coordinate in the diagrams of physicists) can serve as such an analogue. Now, the claim put forth by Parfit is that just as it makes no sense to ask where *here* is on the map of Europe, so it makes no sense to ask where *now* is on this coordinate-line.

Note, however, that the spatial case is not an essential component of Parfit's argument. All the argument rests on is the notion of a complete, a nonperspectival description. The spatial analogy merely serves as an "intuition pump," which we could do without, but which helps pave the way to that viewpoint that is in "no place within this universe." This it does quite effectively:

When we claim that there exist many distant people, such as New Zealanders, we are not claiming that these people exist here. But, though these people do not exist here, they exist, and are real, in the same straightforward way as the people who exist here. Similarly, Tenseless Theorists claim, past and future people exist, and are real, in the same straightforward way as the people who exist now. If we object that these people do not exist, we can only mean that they do not exist now. And that does not give them a lesser kind of reality. It is merely like the claim that distant people do not exist here. (1996, 5)

What Parfit finds objectionable is the idea that the present is in some sense "ontologically privileged," that it is "more real," whereas "the ontological status" of the past and future "is inferior." "It is unclear how we should interpret such claims" (1996, 4, 6), he says. What could this ontological distinction consist in? Such claims single out a certain perspective—that of the present—appointing it, as it were, as a tribunal on ontological matters, on what there is, contrary to the maxim that the only facts concerning reality as it really is are those figuring in a perspective-independent description of that reality. Imagine someone concluding that a certain table is standing on only two legs, just because from the angle he is looking the other two legs are not visible. To conclude that only the present exists because only what is present is (now) visible is to commit the same fallacy.

To be sure, Parfit is not denying that many of the utterances we make daily concerning the tensed locations of events or time's passage, utterances such as "John returned from the States two days ago" or "the president is in a meeting now," are true. We are not wrong in thinking and saying of various events that they are present, for, when they occur, they are indeed present. We are wrong only when we attribute *objectivity* to such thoughts and statements, failing to acknowledge their "perspectival" nature. To acknowledge their perspectival nature is to see that such daily utterances are "theoretically redundant," that they would not figure in a complete description of reality, that they could be replaced by "clearer and otherwise acceptable" (1996, 2, 3) statements, namely, tenseless sentences that are provided by the token-reflexive account.

In sum, Parfit's argument establishes that time's passage, and the distinction between the past, present, and future, would not figure in a complete description of reality. Hence, Parfit concludes, they are "merely part of mental reality," not to be thought of as "features of time itself," but as "merely mind-dependent, or [as] aspects of the way things seem to us" (1996, 7).

2.3 The Empirical Argument

The third argument establishing the unreality of tense is, according to some philosophers, the most compelling, for it seems to enjoy the support of an authority few would dare challenge—physics. It is rare, very rare, that a philosophical problem is settled empirically, by science. Yet, at first blush, this is precisely what seems to have happened in the case of the metaphysics of time. As Putnam (1975a, 204–205) states toward the end of his 1967 paper "Time and Physical Geometry":

I conclude that the problem of the reality and the determinateness of future events is now solved. Moreover, it is solved by physics, and not by philosophy. . . . Indeed, I do not believe that there are any longer any philosophical problems about Time, there is only the physical problem of determining the exact geometry of the four-dimensional continuum that we inhabit.

The solution to the philosophical problems consists, we shall shortly see, in establishing that tense, just like the Ether, has been shown by relativity theory to be nonexistent, that is, not to be part of reality. Davies (1984, 124) puts the claim as follows:

The abandonment of a distinct past, present and future is a profound step, for the temptation to assume that only the present "really exists" is great. . . . The theory of relativity makes nonsense out of such notions. Past, present and future must be equally real, for [even for people living at the same time] one person's past is another's present and another's future.

Putnam's 1967 paper is not the first occasion on which the thesis that relativity theory forces on us the tenseless theory of time has been voiced. As already mentioned, Einstein himself is often quoted as saying that "the distinction between past, present and future is merely an illusion." Nor is Putnam's formulation of the argument the last. New ones are still being put forth, and the debate they spark concerning the ontology of spacetime continues (see, e.g., Dieks 2006). However, the essentials of these new formulations, the essentials that concern us, at any rate, are already found in Putnam's original discussion.

The argument proceeds as follows. First the tensed conception of time is assumed, that is, it is assumed that time flows, and consists of a past, a present, and a future. Then, employing relativity, contradictions are derived, which compel us to abandon the tensed theory. The assumption that time is tensed is fleshed out by means of two theses. The first is that "All and only things that exist now are real" (Putnam 1975a, 198). The second is that, in contrast with the past and present, the future is open, that is, it is *not* the case that "the outcome of future events [is] determined at the present time" (ibid., 201). This thesis is further explained by the contention that at least some future-tense statements "have no truth-value" (ibid.). The contradictions that these theses in conjunction with relativity lead to are taken as proof that, contrary to the first thesis, "All future things are real, and likewise all past things are real, even though they do not now exist" (ibid., 204); and, contrary to the second thesis, all "statements about the future *already* have a definite truth-value" (ibid.), that is, they are already true or already false. By means of these arguments, relativity uproots the key elements of the tensed conception of time and provides solid empirical grounds for espousing the tenseless theory of time. Let's study the details of the arguments.[6]

We begin with the argument against the notion that "All and only things that exist now are real." Let us suppose that what is real for me is real for you and vice versa, at least when you and I occupy the same place at the same time. (Here "real for x" seems to mean what x can truly *say* is real, and the idea is that if one person can truly say that something is real, so can any other person who is in the same place at the same time.) This supposition seems indisputable, certainly in light of relativity theory, which bans the idea of privileged observers. In particular, the theory emphasizes that neither of us enjoys privileged access to ontology, to "what there is."

Next, we bring in the central consequence of relativity theory, namely, that simultaneity is not an absolute (invariant, in relativistic terminology) relationship. Two events, e_1 and e_2, that are simultaneous according to the clock of one observer, α, may be measured to be temporally separated by other observers, β and γ. Moreover, β may measure e_1 to precede e_2 whereas γ will measure e_2 to precede e_1. To take an example, assume that α measures e_1 and e_2 to be simultaneous, and to occur one billion kilometers apart from each other. If β and γ are moving along the line connecting the two events but in opposite directions, each of them moving at roughly 50 percent of the speed of light with respect to α, then the time interval separating e_1 and e_2 according to β's and γ's clocks will be 32 minutes—in β's frame of reference e_1 precedes e_2 by 32 minutes, and it succeeds it by 32 minutes in γ's frame of reference.

Now assume that α, β, and γ cross each other at a given moment, and let us assume that this intersection is event e_1 (shown in figure 2.1). At the moment they meet, the three observers agree that e_1 is a present event that is taking place at the location of their intersection. However, for α, e_2 is also a present event, for it is cotemporal with e_1, whereas for β it is a past event, and for γ it is still future. But now assertion (1) runs into a serious problem. For, according to α, e_2 is present and so is real. And we have

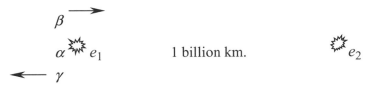

Figure 2.1

assumed that if an event is real for one observer, then it is real for any other observer that is located at the same place and the same time as the first observer. In our case, this means that e_2 is real for β and γ as well, even though it is not present in their "frames." Realizing this compels us to renounce the initial postulate (1), "All (and only) things that exist now are real" and to accept instead (2), "All future things are real, and likewise all past things are real, even though they do not now exist."

Thus, a fairly simple train of thought seems to establish *on empirical grounds* that the present is not "more real" than the past and future. And to renounce the ontological distinction of the present is, for many tenseless theorists, to renounce the notion that there is a real difference between the past, present, and future. This distinction, and with it time's passage—future events becoming present and then receding into the past—are shown by relativity theory to belong to the way *we* experience reality and talk about it, and not to the way reality itself is.

Note that a disagreement between the three observers α, β, and γ about the *time order* of the events is inconsequential. They can agree to disagree on this matter. That is, they can agree that according to α's watch e_2 is simultaneous with e_1, whereas on β's watch it precedes it and on γ's watch it occurs later than it. There is nothing to prevent such an accord, for these differences have no *further* implications. In particular, they do not imply any ontological disagreements; they say nothing about whether or not an event "really exists." Matters are different when it comes to tense. For tense, it is being assumed, has to do with an event's ontological status. Imagine an argument between α and β about the reality of e_2, in which α defends the tenseless tenet (2), insisting that this event is real, just as real as is, say, their arguing at that moment, while β, faithful to (1), is adamant that this event does not "really exist." Here, as Putnam puts it, they "cannot both be right" (1975a, 202)—either this event is real or it is not. So we are left with no other option but to forsake one of these claims, and relativity tells us that it is β's tensed position that must give in.

To discuss how relativity theory undermines the second tensed thesis, namely, that the future is open, let us assume that event e_2 is the closing of the polls in some intergalactic elections. Event e_1 continues to be the intersection of α, β, and γ. Let us assume also that at the instance the polls are closed, the outcome of the elections is announced throughout the galaxy by means of a powerful light pulse, red if Mr. x is elected, green if Ms. y is elected.

As before, e_1 and e_2 are cotemporal according to α, but when e_1 occurs, e_2 is past for β and yet future for γ. This means that at the moment of their intersection, the elections are over for α and β, and their results fixed, while for γ the race is still open, with 32 minutes remaining before the outcome is decided. Under these circumstances, the sentence "The light pulse is, or will be red" is *already* true or *already* false for α and for β, for whom the elections are past and over. But, according to the second thesis of the tensed conception of time, namely, that future tense descriptive sentences lack a definite truth-value, for γ the very same token of the sentence "The light pulse is, or will be red" lacks a truth-value.

This seems unacceptable; α, β, and γ share the same epistemic circumstances, occupying, at the moment in question, the same location. How can one and the same token have a truth-value for α and β but lack one for γ? Thus, relativity theory obliges us to recognize that, *as a matter of empirical fact*, every descriptive sentence, including those describing future events, already has a definite truth-value. In other words, if for α and for β the elections are already decided, then they must also be decided for γ who is right next to α and β at that moment. Here, again, the initial disagreement as to whether the elections' results are already determined is a consequence of the tensed insistence that the closing of the ballots is *past* for two of the observers but *future* for the third. It is the notion that the future is open, in contrast with the fixed past, that creates the difficulty. Removing this notion reinforces the above argument to the effect that future events are just as "real" as past and present ones.

2.4   The Relationship Between the Three Arguments

It is quite unusual in philosophy to have three independent and powerful arguments for the same thesis. The claim that time's passage is an illusion, that in relation to time our experience is sharply unlike what we experience, seems to enjoy this good fortune. Matters are not that simple, however. Roughly, the complexity arises from the fact that it is impossible to separate the thesis that time's passage is an illusion from the argument that supports it. In other words, the content of the claim that time's passage is an illusion, the way it is to be understood, depends on how it is argued for. Thus, the three arguments presented above cannot be taken simply as establishing the same conclusion, since (as will be discussed in greater detail in chapter 4) the conclusion of each derives its meaning from the argument itself.

The dependence of the thesis on the argument bears both an advantage and a disadvantage for the tenseless view. The disadvantage is this: if the argument is vital for giving the tenseless thesis its meaning, for breathing life into it, then, contrary to how tenseless writers routinely express themselves, their thesis is not self-explanatory. Tenseless thinkers write as though we all understand the possibility that time does not really flow, and their task is to persuade us that this thesis is correct. But if we cannot so much as comprehend the tenseless thesis without the far from trivial arguments that support it, their task is graver: it is to convince us of their theory's intelligibility.

On the other hand, opponents of the tenseless view face a more difficult task as well. They cannot merely attack the idea that time's passage is an illusion; they cannot, that is, merely point to the undeniable and impressive discrepancies between this thesis and our experience, language, and thought. They must contend with the details of the arguments as well, for these arguments endow the thesis with meanings that may override our ordinary concepts.

The thesis that there are triangles whose angles add up to more than 180 degrees, or that events that are simultaneous according to one observer are not simultaneous according to another observer, would be rejected as preposterous if presented on their own, without the theories from which they are derived. In light of these theories, however, which constitute arguments for these theses, the discrepancies between such theses and the way we (continue to) ordinarily think about triangles and simultaneity no longer figure as telling considerations against them. Rather, they become challenges that our comprehension must meet by adjusting our notions to the theses.

The same goes for the tenseless thesis. If one of the arguments supporting it turns out to be viable, then the tenseless thesis becomes something which our understanding of time must strive to accommodate. The only way to nullify this challenge is to develop rebuttals of the arguments that defend the thesis. And since there are three independent arguments, three separate rebuttals are required. Moreover, if a fourth argument comes along, it too will need to be treated separately. Finally, even if all known arguments fail to do so, the possibility of a future argument vindicating the intelligibility of the denial of time's passage cannot be ruled out, although, prior to the actual appearance of such an argument, this idea is in a dubious position, similar to that of non-Euclidean triangles prior to the discovery of non-Euclidean geometry.

2.5 Tense in a Tenseless World

The tenseless theory consists of an argument establishing that there are no tensed facts. But that's only one part of the theory, for, if indeed there are no tensed facts, then all the facts that appear to be tensed must be accounted for tenselessly. Such tenseless explanations of the many manifestations of tense in language, experience, and thought make up another, no less essential, component of the tenseless theory. Let us mention some of these manifestations.

First among them, perhaps, is the sense that time flows, a sense we express by common locutions such as "this last year flew by so fast!," or "I thought it would never end," or "two weeks have already gone by and you haven't called the plumber yet." A no less conspicuous manifestation of tense consists of what Mellor calls the "presence of experience": the fact that "Whoever I am, and whenever I believe my experience to be present, that now-belief will be true" (1998, 44). We live in the present, in the sense that only present experiences are actually experienced. Past and future ones are, somehow, in the shadows, inactive, inert. To use Mellor's words again, "Being present seems to be essential to any experience, i.e., essential to its being an experience" (ibid., 40). A theory according to which "experiences, like other events, are in themselves neither past, present nor future" (ibid., 45) must explain why we nonetheless inescapably believe our experiences to be present.

Alongside the presence of experience we should cite again what was referred to back in section 1.2 as the perceptual inaccessibility of the past, by which we mean that things that are past cannot be seen, heard, smelled, and so on. We cannot see or hear Benjamin Franklin, nor can we now enjoy yesterday's sunset, or the coffee we drank for breakfast five hours ago. To be more accurate, we cannot see Benjamin Franklin directly, though we can see him in paintings. We can see Marilyn Monroe in films and photographs, as we can yesterday's sunset, but not "live," "in person." As for yesterday's coffee, it is no longer accessible in any way or form. The contrast between seeing in person and seeing, for example, on TV, hearing live and hearing through a recording, helps capture the sense in which the past is inaccessible. As much as I'd like to hear Maria Callas or see the launching of *Apollo 11*, I cannot: Callas's singing and the rocket's launch belong to the past. Now all I can hear is a recording of Maria Callas and all I can see is a film of the launch. The future is also inaccessible, though more definitely: no TVs or recordings can provide images and sounds from the future. That we can only perceive the *here* and the *now* is another blatant constraint that tense puts on our experiences.[7]

(But we have to note here a great difference between *here* and *now*. Things of the past and future, that is, things that are not present, are inaccessible in a way that things that are not here are not: we can travel in space and make perceptual contact with many things that are not here. But we cannot travel in time. I will not argue for this claim. But from claims I will establish later it will follow that we cannot think of experiences that are future as also being present and/or past. This will entail the incoherence of the idea of time-travel. Hence, although the perceptual inaccessibility of things that are not temporally present can serve as the basis for a metaphysics that ontologically distinguishes things that are temporally present from those that are not, the perceptual inaccessibility of things that are not spatially present does not lead to a spatially tensed metaphysics.)

Another, related, manner in which tense exhibits itself has to do with the difference between remembering, experiencing, and anticipating. Anticipating what it will be like to see Ingres's *La Grande Odalisque* for the first time was an experience qualitatively different from actually seeing it, and these two experiences are experientially distinct from remembering that first time. Looking at *La Grande Odalisque* now, for the second time, is yet another type of experience, as is imagining what it will be like to see it again in the future. These experiential expressions of tense are sometimes alluded to in the literature in the form of a query: why is it that we only remember the past and anticipate the future, and never vice versa? This query becomes even more pressing if it is denied that anything is really past, or present, or future.

Then there is the manner in which our attitudes toward our own experiences display biases to tense. These biases were brought to the fore in Prior's (1959) paper "Thank Goodness That's Over." We are all familiar with the growing dread that accompanies the approach of a future painful experience, as well as with the relief that usually ensues once the experience is past and over. In many cases the tensed location of an experience, it being future, present, or past, markedly affects our attitude toward it. If we live in a tenseless world, we need to explain why tense seems to have such effects.

We next come to change. Take as examples a banana that turns from green to yellow as it ripens, or a car that goes from one city to another. Now, it can be pointed out that in both cases, as in all other instances of change, the object that undergoes the change has different properties at different times: the banana is yellow at t_0 and green at t_1, and the car is in Boston at t_2 and in New York at t_3. But these facts alone seem to leave out another element that is essential to change, namely, time's passage. Merely having different properties at different times appears, superficially at least, to be not unlike having different properties at different spatial locations. And a banana that is yellow at one end and green at the other does not embody change. Time, and only time, is the dimension of change, and the reason, it seems, is that time flows—it is as time passes that the banana changes its colors and the car its location. Granted that, initially, that is how we perceive change, it is incumbent upon tenseless theorists, who deny time's passage, to account tenselessly for change, and to do so in a way that will register the element we customarily associate with time's passage in a way that will preserve the asymmetry between time and space.

We close this partial list of manifestations of tense with the asymmetries and directionality we know time to have. The future, so we speak and behave, is open, the past fixed. We can deliberate as to whom we're going to vote for in the next elections. But our vote in the previous elections is fixed and no longer changeable. We can be careful with what we will say, but we cannot take back things we should not have said. We know with certainty that the sun rose this morning, but we can speculate about the odds that it will go nova in ten hours, and thus never rise again. These contrasts between the past and the future are related to the *direction* of time's passage. Time's passage moves us away from the previous elections and toward the next elections. We grow old as time passes, not young, and cups fall and break, but scattered pieces of glass do not spontaneously gather together to form a cup. But if nothing is really past or present or future, then the momentous contrast between the future's openness and the past's fixity becomes an illusion (not to say a delusion) that needs to be accounted for, as does the obstinately irreversible direction of time's passage.

Different thinkers provide different details as to how to meet the challenge of contending tenselessly with these pervasive manifestations of tense. The differences are not that significant. Relying on Mellor's version of the theory, let me outline the basic strategy. (In chapter 5 I will elaborate on some of the points.) The tenseless account of tense relies on the distinction between the facts of reality and our *beliefs* concerning these facts. Once this line is drawn, the aim is to confine tense to the mental and conceive it as a feature of our beliefs, and not of reality. The device that achieves the elimination of tense from tenseless accounts of reality is the aforementioned token-reflexive account of meaning. As we already briefly saw (sec. 2.1), according to this semantic theory, tensed propositions get their meaning and truth value from tense-less truth conditions:

for every tensed proposition "P" about any event *e* any token of "P" is true if and only if it is as much earlier or later than *e* as "P" says the present is than *e*. (Mellor 1998, 31)

Thus, "It will rain tomorrow" is true if and only if it is tokened roughly twelve to twenty-four hours before it rains. "James returned from Paris a month ago" is true if and only if one month separates James's return and the tokening of this token. And "The Mars probe is now in orbit" is true if and only if the Mars probe is in orbit at the time this token is tokened.

The availability of tensed truths and tensed beliefs that are grounded in tenseless conditions facilitates tenseless explanations for the manifestations of tense listed above. We will discuss some of them later on (in chapter 5), but let us just get a taste of how these explanations go. Take for example the uneasiness experienced as a disagreeable experience approaches, and the relief felt once the experience becomes, with time's passage, a thing of the past. The tenseless theorist denies of course that the experience, or anything else, is future and denies that time passes. But he need not deny that that's how we believe things to be. And, it is enough that one *believes* a disagreeable experience is approaching and then *believes* that with time's passage it becomes past, for one to first experience uneasiness and then relief. The horrid experience need not itself be future and need not approach as time passes. All the tenseless theorist needs to do is provide tenseless facts that generate and justify the belief that it is future and that time passes. The token-reflexive account points to such facts. According to this account, the sentence "next week's visit to the dentist will not be a pleasant one" is given meaning and truth by the tenseless fact that it is tokened seven days before the visit to the dentist (as well as, of course, by the fact that the visit is unpleasant). Hence, with recourse to nothing but this tenseless fact, one arrives at a warranted tensed belief that a week from today one will suffer an unpleasant experience.

And the sense that with time's passage the experience is getting closer is likewise accounted for by tenseless facts, facts that induce changes in one's tensed beliefs. Thus, the accumulation of beliefs produces, among other things, a sense of time's passage. This sense is further shaped and supported by tenseless facts about causation, specifically, by the fact that causes always precede their effects (as Mellor establishes in his theory of causation [cf. Mellor 1995]). I shall not discuss further details until later. I simply want to stress that tenseless theorists have the means—theories of causation and meaning—with which tenselessly to explicate the all-encompassing labor performed by tense in our belief system.

This, however, does not yet explain *why* our experience of reality, and our language, should be thoroughly tensed, even though reality is tenseless. That we know the tenseless mechanism behind our tensed beliefs does not tell us why there must be such a mechanism. According to Mellor, the reason is evolutionary. As we shall see later (section 4.3), the possession of tensed beliefs is vital for the success of our actions. In particular, we would not survive without the ability to perform certain actions at given times. The ability to do that relies entirely on the possession of tensed beliefs— you would not be able to take your medication at 9:00 PM, unless you knew that the time *now* was, say, 8:45 PM. Thanks to evolutionary processes we are endowed with mechanisms that, on the basis of tenseless sensory inputs, produce the required tensed beliefs. But, to repeat, the content and justification of these beliefs are fully accounted for in terms of tenseless facts.

We thus close this chapter by remarking that, although our picture of reality is dramatically altered by the tenseless view, our experience of reality is left untouched, as are our everyday thoughts and language. Given this, the theory's apparent gross incongruity with our pretheoretical acquaintance with time and tense should not be held as an obstacle to its endorsement. In fact, with powerful arguments in its favor, and effective explanations that square it with the impressive manifestations of tense in experience and language, the theory seems hard to resist.

3 Time's Supposed Concreteness

The claim that time's passage is an illusion is prima facie unacceptable. An unacceptable claim needs to be backed by substantial argumentation—such as the arguments surveyed in the previous chapter—in order to break through the resistance it encounters from our intuitions, from what we think our experience tells us. Indeed, the natural stance is that time passes, making future events present and present events past. Most philosophers defending tense add that there is an ontological distinction between the present on the one hand, and the past and the future on the other.[1] Enjoying the convenience of regarding tense as a central feature of time itself, tensed theorists do not need to labor so hard, as do their tenseless counterparts, to account for the pervasiveness of tense in experience and language. On the other hand, they do need to invest much effort in repelling the assault tenseless theorists mount against tense.

However, it is not our aim to settle the tenseless/tensed debate, but rather to get to know the tacit metaphysical presuppositions sustaining these views. Thus, this chapter will not concentrate on the tensed rebuttals of the tenseless arguments, but will focus instead on presenting the manners in which the natural, familiar, tensed stance on time is developed into a mature metaphysical doctrine.

In section 2.4 of the previous chapter it was suggested that the contents of the tenseless theories of time are shaped by the arguments sustaining it. The connection between an argument and the view it serves is even more marked in the case of the tensed view. We shall consider two arguments and see that they lead to quite distinct renditions of the tensed view of time. One argument builds on the pervasiveness of tense in our daily discourse, experience, and thought, and specifically on what it conceives as a "Now" that moves through time. The resulting theory is supposed to be, from among all metaphysical theories of time, the closest to our everyday conceptions. The other argument arises from a form of verificationism. I shall call the view of time emerging from this theory of meaning a "solipsism of the present moment."

3.1 The "Moving Now"

As just stated, the tensed theory we now turn to consists in an attempt to cast everyday notions and commonsense sensibility into a metaphysical framework, to equip familiar temporal conceptions with a metaphysical basis and endow them with philosophical respectability. Its hallmarks are the notion that the present is ontologically privileged, and what Schlesinger, on whose texts we base the presentation of this doctrine, describes as "movement through time" (1980, 23):

According to a view deeply ingrained in all of us, the NOW is something that moves relative to the series of points that constitute time. Temporal points from the future, together with the events that occur at those points, keep approaching the NOW and after momentarily coinciding with it they recede further and further into the past. The NOW is, of course, not conceived as some sort of object but rather as the point in time in which any individual who is temporally extended is alive, real, or Exists with a capital E. . . .

A typical event, on this view, to begin with is in the distant future; then it becomes situated in the less distant future; it keeps approaching us until it becomes an event occurring in the present. As soon as this happens the event loses its presentness and acquires the property of being in the near past. The degree of its pastness continually increases.

In the same vein Broad states that "at any moment a certain short segment of the series (of one's experiences) is marked out from all the rest by the quality of presentedness. . . . change has to be postulated [as] the steady movement of the quality of presentedness along the series in the direction from earlier to later" (Gale 1968, 138).[2] The special status of the present is proclaimed by Reichenbach (1957, 20) as well: "even when no human being is alive any longer, there is a 'now'; the 'present state of the planetary system' is then just as much a specification as 'the state of the planetary system at the time of the birth of Christ.'" Back to Schlesinger, speaking of the rival tenseless view, he writes (1980, 33) that "it impoverishes time greatly because it renders all moments equal, as every single moment is equally simultaneous with all the tokens that are uttered at that moment. But all moments in time are by no means equal; there is always a privileged moment. . . . there is one particular point that is real and alive, while every other point exists only in one's memory or in one's anticipation."

What we have in these quotations is not exactly an argument establishing the existence of a "moving Now," but rather descriptions of it. But it seems that the description is taken to constitute an argument, whose force comes from the assumption that anyone familiar with ordinary experience and language will immediately recognize the "moving Now" as an integral, irreducible, and irremovable component of what we experience and speak about. Perhaps this argument can be spelled out as follows. Let us assume that in the description and justification of many of our dispositions we invariably invoke the "moving Now." The examples we will turn to momentarily are supposed to establish that we do. Let us also assume that we are rational, and rational in many of our reactions, attitudes, and dispositions. That is, our descriptions faithfully capture reality and our judgments are sound. Then, insofar as beliefs about the tensed properties of events are constitutive of our rational judgments and dispositions, our conception of reality, and specifically of the tensed aspects of reality, must include these tensed properties. To sum up:

1. We are rational.

2. Our rational judgments, dispositions, and beliefs concern the tensed properties of events.

3. Hence, the tensed properties of events must be included in our conception of reality.

We have already encountered a case, familiar to each and every one of us, in which time's passage, rather than the illusion that time flows, seems to figure *indispensably*—pain. Prior's exclamation of relief, "Thank goodness that's over!," poses a challenge to the tenseless theorist because it certainly seems that pain can only be understood in tensed terms. Pain is painful when, and only when, it is *present*. Pains of the past and the future are not painful. Moreover, future pains are a source of concern in a way that past pains are not. That's why a pain's becoming past and over brings relief. The tenseless description of pain leaves all of this out. The tenseless fact that, say, at t_1 the pain is over cannot be the fact that brings relief, for this fact—that at t_1 the pain is over—is an unchangeable fact, which obtains at all times, and in particular already at t_0, prior to the time of the pain. Yet no relief is felt then. Or, as Prior (1959, 17) puts it:

"Thank goodness that's over!" certainly doesn't mean the same as, e.g., "Thank goodness the date of the conclusion of that thing is Friday, June 15, 1954," even if it be said then. (Nor, for that matter, does it mean "Thank goodness the conclusion of that thing is contemporaneous with this utterance." Why should anyone thank goodness for that?)

What we are glad about is the pain's *passing away*. This is such a fundamental feature of experience that it would appear that any metaphysical theory that strives to cohere with our experience of reality must include time's passage in its depiction of reality.[3]

Schlesinger describes another state of affairs for the understanding of which time's passage is vital. Ivan Denisovitch is sentenced to fifteen years in the Siberian Gulag. A week after his arrival, he is "naturally profoundly distressed at the thought that he has to endure fifteen years of inhuman hardship before regaining his freedom" (1982, 510). But from a tenseless viewpoint his condition at that moment is not really different from his condition a week before his release—his time in the Gulag has two ends, two doors in time, as it were, an earlier one and a later one, and a week after his incarceration begins he is removed from one end the same amount of time as he is removed from the other a week before his release.

The fact that even tenseless time may have direction is immaterial here, says Schlesinger. The tenseless facts involved in this situation, like all tenseless facts, are permanent, unchanging facts, which, in this case, are known to Denisovitch. And, from a tenseless viewpoint, these are the *only* facts. So, from a tenseless viewpoint, there are no facts that would justify Denisovitch's preference for proximity to one end of his incarceration over the other. A week after his arrival at the Gulag he should be in the same state of mind as the one he finds himself in a week before his release. It should be mentioned in passing that some tenseless theorists bite the bullet, and admit that a difference in Denisovitch's attitudes would indeed be irrational. We shall return to these philosophers later (section 5.5).

But let's consider this train of reasoning from a different perspective. A week after his arrival at the Gulag Denisovitch is anguished—fifteen years have yet to go by before he is free again. A week before his release he is jubilant—fifteen years have already passed and in a week's time he will be free. Assume also that in between, as time passes, his despair diminishes and his spirits gradually lift. Now, imagine that in the Gulag he meets a tenseless philosopher, who persuades him that time does not really flow. After reflection Denisovitch concludes that there is no basis for his experiencing these shifts in his sentiments, which in his mind are directly linked to how time's passage is bringing his release closer. But then his friend explains that, although there are no tensed facts and time does not flow, there are tensed beliefs, in virtue of which one is not only justified but in fact compelled to continue thinking and experiencing time's passage exactly as one has hitherto. Upon receiving this clarification Denisovitch is truly confused. He is convinced time does not flow, but he is told he should continue believing that it does. He feels like a desert traveler who has just learned that the oasis he is seeing is a fata morgana, but who is also told he should nevertheless continue believing it is real. This he cannot do. He cannot fool himself into believing something he knows is not the case, even if the illusion is an extremely convincing one. "Either time really flows, which would account for my varying sentiments, or else it does not, in which case these sentiments are unwarranted," he thinks to himself.

The upshot of this is, again, that a theory that strives to cohere with basic, irremovable features of experience cannot deny time's passage. Imagine that several years into his sentence Denisovitch is asked where he'd like to be: one week away from freedom as he was upon his arrival, or one week from freedom as he'll be before his release. Tenselessly thinking he should find himself in the predicament of Buridan's ass, and not know what to answer. If on the other hand it is rational for him to prefer the second option, and if in describing this preference and defending it he invariably invokes the fact that time passes, it would be irrational of him to nevertheless hold that time does not pass. Rationality has to have its pick: either it sides with the tenseless indifference to the above choice, or else it must insist on the reality of time's passage.

As a final example: "suppose a person P says on 1 January 1982, which is his fiftieth birthday, 'How I wish I was ten years younger,' and explicitly denies that what he means is that he wishes that he had been born ten years later so that in 1982 he would be only forty years old. No, he does not wish to change the date of his birth and is fully satisfied to be fifty years old in 1982. What he would like is that the NOW should shift back to 1972" (Schlesinger 1982, 512). Here again, Schlesinger observes, there is no plausible way of rephrasing the wish to be ten years younger in tenseless terms while retaining the *sense* of this wish, for the wish just is to be back in 1972.

Someone might retort and point out that, to be accurate, what P wishes is not exactly that it now be 1972, but that everything be as it was in '72. A world just like the world of 1972 would satisfy P, irrespective of what year it is. So what P is asking for, in effect, is that, for example, 2 January 1982 be identical in all respects to 2 January 1972. But consider the fact that making P's wish come true in this manner would require that as the date changes to 2 January 1982, "infinitely many events occur that were not supposed to happen in the natural sequence of occurrences, none of which can be accounted for. . . . According to [the tensed view] however there is only one event which would need explanation: the sudden shift of the NOW from 1982 to 1972" (Schlesinger 1982, 514). Thus, on the tenseless theory, the only way to make sense of P's wish is by introducing a sharp break in the world's natural evolution. But that is not what P is asking for. Once again, the sense of mundane and familiar notions is inextricable from the notion of time's passage.

The metaphysical picture emerging from such considerations is one in which a moving NOW runs along the moments of time, successively conferring upon each moment m a "unique privileged status" (Schlesinger 1991, 428). This metaphysics regards the present as "distinct from every other temporal position, for while the future is yet to be born and the past is rapidly fading, the present is palpably real. This characteristic . . . is a transient feature of the moment; m grows bright, and comes to life for an instant, after which its presence or immediacy is passed on to the next moment" (ibid.). To repeat, this picture derives its attractiveness from its coherence with experience and language. However, the style of depictions such as the one just quoted, which are supposed to capture those aspects of time that correspond to our experience and language, may obscure the fact that we are dealing here with a systematic *metaphysical* doctrine. To remind ourselves of this fact, let us explore some of the details of this doctrine, details that can help highlight its metaphysical character.

In the paper just quoted, "E PUR SI MOUVE," Schlesinger suggests the following scheme. Reality consists of a set of possible worlds, such that "'presentness' keeps changing from one world to the next" (1991, 430). In each of these possible worlds the NOW occupies a certain segment of the time line. Each world "is in a privileged state of enjoying actuality" during the time interval which in that world is marked by presentness. In world W_n, for example, presentness occupies the brief period of time m_n, spanning from t_i, say, to t_j. In this world, moments following m_n are future, and those preceding it are past. Only m_n is "real and alive"; moments of the past and the future, on the other hand, are not "palpably real." World W_n *is* followed by world W_{n+1} in which moment m_{n+1} enjoys presentness. W_{n+1} is actual during this period of time. And so on.

For this scheme to be useful, the sense in which W_n *is* followed by world W_{n+1} must be *different* from the sense in which events follow each other within each world. Succession within a given world is fleshed out ordinarily, in terms of events being earlier or later than one another. But this temporal ordering does not order worlds. Succession between worlds, on the other hand, is given in terms of the location of the "now" in each of them. W_n is "followed" by W_{n+1} because the "now" is located in W_{n+1} at m_{n+1}, a moment which is later than m_n, the moment which the "now" occupies in W_n. Strictly speaking, then, W_{n+1} is not later than W_n. Rather it "succeeds" it in the series of possible worlds, which is generated according to the location of presentness in each of them.

By means of this conception of the present Schlesinger defends the tensed view from the objections raised against it by tenseless theorists. Among other things, he provides an analysis of the notion of "becoming" that fleshes out its ontological content; he explains how tensed theorists can coherently contend with the otherwise embarrassing question of the rate of time's passage; and how they can circumvent McTaggart's argument (essentially, by cashing in on the fact that an event turns out to be past, present, and future in distinct worlds, rather than in one and the same world).

This sketch of Schlesinger's scheme is, of course, too brief to do it justice (we'll return to it in section 4.6). But it suffices to give us an idea of how time's passage can be cast into a systematic *theory*. It shows that, its initial affinity with ordinary language and experience notwithstanding, in its full-blown form, the "moving Now" view is formulated with a far from ordinary vocabulary, and brings to its support archetypically metaphysical machinery such as the "many worlds" apparatus. This fact about the tensed theory is just as apparent in the second version of it, which is the subject of the next section.

3.2   Solipsism of the Present Moment

The tensed doctrine we turn to now is quite intricate. For reasons that will emerge shortly, it may be called "a solipsism of the present moment." I choose to describe it as an offshoot of Dummett's antirealism. That is by no means meant to imply that Dummett would defend, or even have sympathy for, a solipsism of the present moment. He does not express any such sympathy in his recent book, *Truth and the Past* (2003). And the famous chapters of *Truth and Other Enigmas*, in which Dummett develops the themes of his antirealism and on which this section is based, do not contain a theory about time. Moreover, it is not clear how committed he is to the claims he explores there (in *Truth and the Past* he calls "The Reality of the Past," the chapter of *Truth and Other Enigmas* on which I rely most heavily, "an experiment"). So the present section may very well be contested as an exegesis of Dummett's philosophy.

Still, if only for the sake of our discussion, I will argue that Dummett's verificationist antirealism entails an identification of the realm of facts with the world as it is *now*, at present. Put bluntly, the world just is the world as it is now. This, we will see, is tantamount to epistemologically and metaphysically privileging the present. On the basis of this consequence I will suggest that Dummett's analysis of truth invites the elicitation of a tensed conception of time, a conception which, I believe, is both shaped by and in turn underpins his views on truth. Since Dummett's antirealism constitutes a fertile and solid ground for the development and defense of this "solipsism of the present moment," we shall start with a brief overview of this territory.

As Ruth is looking through the windows of the terminal and sees John's airplane roll down the runway, she thinks to herself and then solemnly remarks to Jane, who is at her side, "John's plane is taking off now." Let us call this token of Ruth's present-tense sentence, tokened at 6:00 PM on May 5, 1996, "*A*." Dummett describes two accounts of the truth and meaning of *A*, the realist account and the antirealist account. For the realist, our understanding of [a] statement (and therefore its possession of a meaning) just consists in our knowing what has to be the case for it to be true. The condition for the truth of a statement is not, in general, a condition which we are capable of recognizing as obtaining whenever it obtains, or even one for which we have an effective procedure for determining whether it obtains or not. (1978, 358)

The antirealist, on the other hand, maintains that

the meanings of statements are given to us, not in terms of the conditions under which these statements are true or false, conceived of as conditions which obtain or do not obtain independently of our knowledge or capacity for knowledge, but in terms of the conditions which we recognize as establishing the truth or falsity of statements. (Ibid., 358–359)

Disagreements between the realist and the antirealist are about what truth consists in, and not in general about the actual truth-values of given sentences. When Ruth tokens A, she is tokening a true sentence according to both accounts. For the realist, the condition for A's truth is simply that John's airplane is taking off at that time. A would have been true even if Ruth had not been capable of recognizing that this condition obtains. Its obtaining, regardless of its being recognized, would have sufficed. For the antirealist, on the other hand, A is true in virtue of Ruth's *recognizing*, or at least her being able to recognize, the condition that establishes A's truth, namely, on her being able to recognize the taking off of John's plane.

As mentioned a moment ago, when realists and antirealists agree that a given sentence possesses a truth-value, they do not disagree as to what its truth-value is—it does not happen that a sentence will be true on the realist view and false on the antirealist view.[4] However, the difference in their conception of what truth consists in *does* entail a possible disagreement as to whether a certain sentence does or does not possess a truth-value. As Dummett explains, since, on the realist view, "this condition [the condition for the truth of a statement] is taken to be one which either does or does not obtain independently of our knowledge, it follows that every statement is either true or false, likewise independently of our knowledge" (1978, 358). According to the antirealist account, however, some descriptive sentences—those for which no conditions obtain that can be recognized as establishing their truth or their falsehood—lack a truth-value.

It is now May 5, 2006, ten years after that sad day, and no trace of John's departure exists. All airline documents have long been discarded, John is dead, and Ruth, as well as everyone else, does not remember the event—

there is absolutely no evidence as to whether on May 5, 1996, at 6:00 PM, John took off on an airplane or not. According to the realist the sentence "Ten years ago today John's plane took off"—we shall designate it as "*B*"—has a definite truth-value: it is true by virtue of the same condition which established *A*'s truth at the time, namely, that John's plane took off on that day. Thus, on the realist view, *B* is true whether Ruth or anyone else can recognize this condition as establishing the truth of *B* or not. No one is in a position to find out whether on a given patch of Jupiter's surface there is a stone exactly 3.14 kilograms in mass, but we think that the assertion that such a stone exists is either true or false. The realist regards *B* as having the same status.

In light of this, the realist can insist that a "truth-value link" correlates the truth-values of *A* and *B*, and in general of sentences that describe the same situations or events. The situations or events, which may be recognized on some occasions and be utterly unrecognizable on other occasions, constitute this link. For the realist, this is nothing but a basic consistency demand: tokens describing the same things must agree in truth-value.

For the antirealist the situation is different. A token of *B*, produced on May 5, 2005, is true only if there are at that time conditions that can be recognized as establishing its truth, for example, if a boarding pass is found, or an entry in Ruth's diary that tells of John's departure, or even simply a vivid memory in Ruth's mind. But there are no such traces. So for the antirealist, *B* is not true. Nor is it false—no conditions that establish its falsity are recognizable. Rather, it lacks a truth-value. It appears, then, that the antirealist is not committed to the truth-value link: *A* and *B* describe the same event, but *A* is true and *B* is not, for it lacks a truth-value.

The disagreement between the realist and the antirealist comes out in connection with a past-tense sentence, a sentence describing a past event. I wish now to suggest that this is a consequence of the manner in which Dummett's antirealist position is informed by his sensibility concerning time. The following passage from Dummett's paper will serve as the basis for explicating this conjecture, and will guide us through the rest of the discussion. In this passage the antirealist's position is distinguished from a misformulation of it that is difficult to avoid but must be guarded against. Because of its importance, I quote it in its entirety:

No matter what maneuvers he attempts, the antirealist will be unable to avoid inconsistency in recognizing the existence of the truth-value link if he formulates his contention as being that a past-tense statement, made at any given time, is true at that time only if there is at that time a situation justifying the assertion of the statement. Rather, he must state his general thesis by saying that a statement in the past tense is (or was, or will be) true just in case there is *now* or will subsequently be a situation whose existence we can *now* acknowledge as justifying the ascription to that statement of the value true. Thus, a statement in the past tense, made a year hence, will be true just in case there is either *now* a situation which we can recognize as obtaining and which we *now* regard as justifying the statement that the past tense statement will be true when uttered a year hence; or else there will be, at some future time, a situation which we can then recognize as obtaining, and whose occurrence at that future time, we *now* regard as entailing the correctness of the statement that the past tense statement will be true when uttered a year hence. Likewise, a past-tense statement made a year ago was true then just in case there is *now* a situation which we can *now* recognize as obtaining and as justifying the assertion that that past-tense statement was, when made, true. The thesis thus relates the truth or falsity of past-tense statements, whenever made, not to the evidence available at the time of utterance, but to the evidence that is *now*, or may later become, available for ascribing to those statements the property of being true when they are uttered. (Dummett 1978, 368, my emphasis)

I have italicized the word "now," which appears in this passage eight times, because understanding the antirealist position precisely consists in understanding how the present figures in it. Clearly, according to this passage, the present has a unique epistemological role that separates it from the past and the future: it is present situations or states of affairs, and them *alone*, that may constitute evidence for the truth or falsity of past-tense statements. Dummett's formulation, to be accurate, also mentions that a subsequent, that is, future situation may be that which justifies the ascription of the value "true" to a past-tense statement. But he emphasizes that the future situations he has in mind are those whose existence we can *now* acknowledge as justifying the ascription of truth (rather than falsehood) to the given statement. Thus, in such cases as well, the truth-value of the past-tense statement is attached to present conditions—to those conditions in virtue of which we can *now* regard a future situation as justifying the ascription of the value true to the given statement.[5]

According to the above passage, then, an analysis of meaning and truth turns on the uniqueness of the present. The unique reality of the present cannot, therefore, be regarded as merely a feature of language, for it belongs to the background that is presupposed by the possibility of language. To repeat, what Dummett emphasizes in this passage is that his view is not that the meaning and truth-values of sentences uttered now are related to present conditions, whereas, e.g., the meaning and truth-values of yesterday's utterances are related to yesterday's conditions. As the last sentence in the quotation states, the truth (or falsity) as well as the meaning of *any* statement, whenever made, is related to evidence that is available *now*, not at the time it is made. We shall return to the unpacking of this difficult claim in a moment.

It should by now be abundantly clear how the antirealism being considered here is intertwined with the issues in the philosophy of time that are of concern to us. But let us make this connection more explicit by spelling out the relationship between the tenseless view and the realist conception of truth, and between the tensed view and the antirealist conception of truth.

The tenseless theory of time consists in the assertion that "there is in reality no difference between the past, present, and future" (Mellor 1981, 58). An important way of fleshing out the difference denied by the tenseless theorist is in terms of the truth conditions of sentences: "in reality" there is no difference between the past, present, and future in that truth conditions are always tenseless conditions, conditions that are not past, present, or future. Any event, situation, state of affairs, or object in the history of the world, regardless of its temporal location—regardless of whether we count it as past, present, or future—is, or can be, that which establishes the truth and meaning of some sentence. To take an example, a token of "His play was first staged eleven years ago" is true on the tenseless condition that eleven years separate that premiere from the tokening of "His play was first staged eleven years ago." This is a permanent, unchanging condition. In specifying it, nothing is said about whether the two events—the premiere, and the tokening of the sentence—are past, present, or future. To repeat, on the tenseless view there are no temporal constraints on truth conditions, which may be of any temporal location and may include conditions which we speak and think of as past and future, though they are unchanging.

Dummett, in contrast, identifies truth conditions with *present* conditions. In our example, the condition on which a token of "His play was first staged eleven years ago" is true is a present condition. Since the premiere, being a past event, is *not* a present event, it cannot count among the conditions on which the token is true. Thus, on Dummett's view, there *is* a difference between the past, present, and future, the difference being that only present situations, events, or states of affairs are eligible to figure as evidence for the truth or falsity of sentences. This comes very close to affirming precisely the ontological differences between the past, present, and future that the tenseless theorist denies.

To see this, let us diverge for a moment from Dummett's terminology and associate those situations, events, things that establish the truth of sentences with what is "real." I mean to call this evidence for the truth of sentences "real" only in a loose sense, in the sense that those elements in virtue of which a descriptive sentence is true are parts of reality—are, in fact, exactly the parts of reality the sentence pertains to. Appealing to this association we can say that on Dummett's view—in which the present is distinguished from the past and the future in that only present conditions are truth conditions—only present objects, events, states of affairs, are "real." Thus, Dummett's antirealism can be regarded as his own rendition of what some philosophers of time regard as a basic intuition, namely, that "only the present is real." Support for this hypothesis can be found in his assertion that "we cannot frame any description of the world as it would appear to one who was not in time, but we can only describe it as it *is*, i.e., as it *is now*" (1978, 369, my italics). In this assertion, *being* is explicitly identified with *being now*.

The pivotal position of the present should not be taken to entail a total repudiation of the past and the future. We can speak of past and future events, remember past ones, anticipate future ones, and so on. We can also speak of and experience time's passage. We may observe, for example, that much time has passed since our last visit to Paris. And in doing so we may be making a correct observation (if indeed much time has elapsed since we last visited Paris). But, when we speak of past and future events, the meanings and truth-values of our statements are given by strictly present conditions. Any talk of the past and the future that is not understood as obtaining its meaning from the present and *the present alone* is, according to Dummett's view, unintelligible. The uniqueness of present conditions can be underscored by the following (by now familiar) asymmetry: the statement that in the past conditions obtained that at the time constituted a sentence's truth conditions gets *its* meaning and truth from present conditions. But the statement that present conditions constitute a sentence's truth conditions gets its meaning and truth from present conditions as well, and not from past ones.

As already stated, our purpose is to obtain a useful perspective of the space jointly defined by the tenseless and tensed views, and not so much to enter into the details of the exchange between them. I do, however, wish to consider one "tenseless" objection to Dummett's position, for doing so will enhance our understanding of a subtle and crucial point in this complex doctrine. It pertains to the aforementioned "truth-value link."

Consider a tenseless description of John's departure: "May 5, 1996, 6:00 PM—John's plane is taking off." Let us call this sentence T. If Jane asks Ruth a week before John's departure when his flight is scheduled to leave, Ruth may use a token T_1 of T as a response. She can also produce a second token T_2 of it at the time of his departure, say, as a note she enters into her diary as she sees the plane taking off. And, though it would be grammatically awkward, she could token a third token, T_3, ten years later, reminiscing on the events of that day. Evidently, all tokens of T have the same truth-value, regardless of when they are tokened. There is a *systematic* link between their truth-values, based on the fact that they report the same event. This link does not hold only between "tenseless" sentences. The tenseless formulation of the link, in which dates are used rather than tenses, merely illustrates it more vividly. But consistency requires that the link hold also between tensed descriptions of that event, that they too must agree in truth-value. If this is not apparently evident, consider the following reasoning. If T_2 is true, then A, "John's plane is taking off now," tokened on the same occasion as T_2, is also true; and if T_3 is true, then B, "John's plane took off ten years ago," tokened on an occasion similar to the one in which T_3 could have been truthfully tokened, must also be true. Thus, the truth-value link between T_2 and T_3 induces a truth-value link between A and B.

Yet, says the objection, a violation of the link is exactly what the antirealist's account entails. According to this account, the present-tense token of A that Ruth produces as she sees the plane roll down the runway is true, for conditions which she recognizes as establishing its truth obtain at the time of its tokening. But ten years later, with no evidence available to establish its truth, a token of B, a past-tense sentence which reports the exact same occurrence, lacks a truth-value and is thus not true. This, it is claimed, is a flagrant violation of the link, and a sheer contradiction. As Dummett puts it on behalf of his opponent: "an antirealist interpretation of past-tense sentences appears incompatible with acknowledging a systematic link between truth-values of differently tensed sentences uttered at different times" (1978, 363).

Dummett agrees that this incompatibility cannot be part of any coherent position. According to him, the insistence on a systematic link between truth-values of sentences that report the same thing is not one over which the antirealist can negotiate. This becomes evident when the relationship between the meanings of *A* and *B* is considered. It is not that *A* and *B* must mean the same thing. Even if they describe the same events, statements made at different times do not always have the same meaning. For instance, *A*, "John's plane is taking off now," can cause Ruth to rush to the terminal windows to see John's plane take off. *B*, "John's plane took off ten years ago," cannot be used to cause her to do so. And since, in one formulation or another, everyone agrees that meaning is not extricable from use, we cannot regard *A* and *B* as sharing the exact same meaning.

Yet, they do speak of the same event, and so their meanings are not unrelated either. They are systematically linked, and to state the necessary agreement between their truth-values just *is* to specify at least one essential component of this link. Moreover, Dummett (1978, 363) observes that "it is from an understanding of the truth-value link . . . that we derive a grasp of what it is for a statement in the past tense, whenever made, for example one made now, to be true." If this is indeed the case, then, for example, *B*'s meaning is inextricable from the link between its truth-value and *A*'s. Think of how a child learns the use of the past tense. She learns the meaning of "Grandma was here yesterday, remember?" from associating this token with the token of "here's Grandma!" uttered yesterday upon Grandma's arrival. This learning process relies, of course, on the two tokens being true (or false) together, namely, on their being connected by the truth-value link. Thus, if *B* is to retain its meaning, the link cannot be renounced. In light of this, it is not disapprovingly that Dummett rehearses the realist's characterization of the truth-value link as "a fundamental feature of our understanding of tensed statements" (1978, 363–364), as something without which our language cannot even be conceived.

The task the antirealist faces, therefore, is to show that her theory respects the truth-value link, and recognizes its indispensable role in language. There is a real challenge to be met here, because her position certainly does allow that two tensed sentences, *A* and *B*, for example, that correctly describe the same event from different temporal perspectives, and thus appear as though they ought to be connected by the link, in fact do not share the same truth-value.

Dummett, however, has a reply ready, which brings to light the essence of his position. To study it, let us restate more accurately the contradiction that has been supposedly uncovered in Dummett's position. It is 6:00 PM, May 5, 1996, we are standing with Ruth in the terminal, watching John's airplane take off. The antirealist agrees with the following assertions Ruth makes on this occasion:

(1)   Whatever will be the case in ten years' time, if I then tell someone "John's plane took off ten years ago," my statement will be true.

(2)   If ten years from now there will be no evidence whatsoever that John's plane took off today at 6:00 PM, then the statement made then "John's plane took off ten years ago" will lack a truth-value (and so will not be true).

These two sentences appear to contradict each other quite explicitly: one says the token of "John's plane took off ten years ago" produced ten years hence will be true and the other says that that very token will not be true. This contradiction seems to directly result from a breach of the truth-value link: to respect the link means to recognize that only (1) can be true.

The antirealist's rebuttal of this accusation turns, as we shall now see, on the recognition that, in effect, *two notions of truth* are employed above, one in sentence (1) and another in sentence (2). The objection results from a failure to take note of this. Let me quote a passage which alludes to the difference between these notions of truth:

We can thus always say quite generally that a statement is true only if there is something in virtue of which it is true. But to say that we are in time is to say that the world changes; and, as it changes, so the range of even unrestricted quantifiers changes, so that that over which I quantify now when I say "There is something in virtue of which . . . ," is not the same as that over which I shall be quantifying when I use the same expression in a year's time. (Dummett 1978, 373)

Let us begin explicating this passage with a simple example. If I say today "The sun will rise tomorrow," this sentence is true in virtue of facts that obtain today, and therefore, *not* in virtue of the conditions in virtue of which the sentence "The sun has risen this morning" will be true tomorrow. Indeed, today I am warranted in asserting that the sun will rise tomorrow by past experience, valid induction, laws of planetary motion, and so on. These materials make for a different type of warrant than the one to be furnished tomorrow by the veridical perception I shall experience then. Similarly, I cannot, now that today's sunset is over, attach to the exclamation "What a beautiful sunset!" the meaning it had when I uttered it three hours ago, as I was enjoying the sunset. Truth and meaning do not depend on how things were back then, but are related to conditions I can recognize *now*, for example, my memories, or a photograph I took of the colored skies. I can describe the conditions that obtained three hours ago, the conditions to which the meaning and truth of that earlier exclamation were attached, and even state that at that time, those were the conditions to which the meaning and truth of the statement were attached. But, since "we are in time [and] the world changes," I cannot now treat them as the truth conditions to which any of my present utterances are attached.

Still, simply claiming that the meaning and truth of sentences uttered three hours ago were attached to conditions that obtained three hours ago, and more generally, the suggestion that with time's passage what we count as truth makers changes, seem to tacitly imply that not all truth conditions consist of present conditions. But, this consequence is at odds with the contention that truth conditions are *always* present conditions. This tension has to be defused if the antirealist's position is to be a viable one. And it *is* defused, once it is acknowledged that it is *always* from the *present* vantage point that the observation that conditions that are not present were, or will be, truth conditions, is made. The assertion that that over which even unrestricted quantifiers range now is not that over which they will range ten years' hence, is *not* meant to override, and is not in conflict with, the basic premise that truth and meaning of *all* statements are related *only* to present conditions. Rather, it too is to be interpreted in light of, and in subordination to, this basic premise. When, in the passage quoted above, Dummett speaks about what the phrase "That in virtue of which . . ." will cover tomorrow, the meaning and truth of *this statement itself* are related to the present.

In general, all statements without exception, including those in which future conditions that will furnish future meanings and truth-values, or past conditions that furnished past meanings and truth-values, are alluded to, including, that is, all sentences making up the present discussion, are attached to conditions obtaining *now*. Speaking of the meaning and truth-value of past and future tokens, and doing so in relation to past and future conditions, does not threaten the hegemony of the present, but constitutes a further instance of it, for the meaning and truth of whatever is being said in this "metadiscussion" are *themselves* attached to present conditions.

We can now remove the semblance of contradiction that (1) and (2) initially create, by observing that the notion of truth is attached in (1) to conditions different from those it is attached to in (2). In (1) the notion of truth is attached to present conditions, that is, the taking off of John's airplane, and it is used to say that the sentence "John's plane took off ten years ago" will be true in ten year's time. The notion of truth that figures in (2), on the other hand, is associated with conditions that will obtain then, ten years from now, and is used to say that the sentence "John's plane took off ten years ago" uttered ten years' hence might then lack a truth-value. To put it in other words, in (1) truth is associated with what is covered by the expression "That in virtue of which . . ." as it is used *now*, while in (2) truth is associated with what will be covered by the same expression *ten years hence*. We can say that the notion "truth" comes to be connected to a temporal index: "truth$_1$" is truth which is associated with what is covered by the expression "That in virtue of which . . ." as it is used *now*; "truth$_2$" is truth which is associated with what will be covered by the expression "That in virtue of which . . ." *ten years hence*. And the crucial point is that the distinction between truth$_1$ and truth$_2$ *itself* is made in the present: the sentence stating it is true$_1$. That is how all this fits with the antirealist's contention that only *present* conditions can be truth conditions.

Distinguishing between these two uses of the notion of truth, so that both can be employed without contradiction, is exactly what the two sentences (1) and (2), within which "John's plane took off ten years ago" is enclosed, do. The mistake is to think that we can tear a token of the past-tense sentence "John's plane took off ten years ago" out of (1) and (2), and consider it on its own. If we imagine we can do so, we lose sight of the fact that in (1) the enclosed sentence is related to truth$_1$ whereas in (2) it is related to truth$_2$, and so we fall into the false impression that asserting that it is true in one case and asserting that it lacks a truth-value in the other results in a contradiction.

Imagining the enclosed sentence is accessible on its own, says Dummett, is tantamount to attempting to "stand in thought outside the whole temporal process and describe the world from a point which has no temporal position at all" (1978, 369), that is, from nowhere. It is only from such an unthinkable standpoint that it may appear as though a future token of "John's plane took off ten years ago" can be produced now. The truth is that all we have access to is a present replica of this token, enclosed within sentences such as (1) and (2), which tell us what it is a replica of.

It is worth restating one more time the claim which is the key to a proper understanding of the antirealist's position. It is that the above distinction between the two notions of truth is itself made in the *present*, that is, that (1) and (2), both of which are tokened in the present, are true owing to *present* conditions that are recognized as establishing their truth. Sentence (1) is true for obviously present reasons: we see John's plane accelerating on the runway, we recognize the conditions that establish the truth of "John is taking off," and (using the same notion of truth) therefore also of a future token of "John's plane took off ten years ago." Sentence (2) is true for likewise *present* reasons, namely: time flows, the world changes, and, as (2) tells us, since the word "true" that appears in it is attached to conditions that will obtain in ten years' time and are not now accessible, we cannot now say what we will say then when we produce a token of "John's plane took off ten years ago," we cannot now attach to these marks and noises the meaning we shall attach to them then, and we cannot now say what the truth-value of the token will be. In other words, (2) simply states that conditions change with time and mentions the possibility that, therefore, in the future we will not be able to say of a token of "John's plane took off ten years ago," tokened then, that it is true. And, although (2) is about future conditions, the meaning and truth of (2) *itself*, as of any sentence, are attached to present conditions. In sum, the truth of both (1) and (2) is grounded in *present* conditions, but the notions of truth figuring in their respective articulations are not the same, which is why they do not contradict each other.

We thus learn that Dummett's rejoinder involves reinterpreting the sense of the truth-value link. For the realist, the link consists in a systematic connection between the truth-values of a sentence tokened in the present ("John's plane is taking off") and a sentence tokened in the future ("John's plane took off"). According to Dummett, on the other hand, the link holds between sentences that are tokened in the *present*. "John's airplane is taking off" has to be consistent not with a future utterance of "John's airplane took off," but rather with a present token of "In the future, 'John's airplane took off' will be true," that is, with (1). And it is consistent with (2) as well, which merely states that the future token is indeed *future*, and thus cannot now be tokened, and *ipso facto* cannot now be recognized as true.

I believe Dummett's rejoinder is an effective one. To see its strength, recall McTaggart's argument. Its gist was that *"e is past," "e is present,"* and *"e is future"* predicate mutually incompatible properties to *e*, and that the tensed theorist is committed to the truth of all three. This move is blocked by Dummett. Everyone agrees that *at present* only one of these statements is true while the other two are false. In essence, on Dummett's view, as it has just been reconstructed, there is no access to other, nonpresent tokens that could create a contradiction. If, for example, *"e is present"* is true, then the only tokens of *"e is past"* that are available are false. To generate a contradiction we need a true token of *"e is past,"* namely, one attached to truth conditions that are future and thus are not present. But on Dummett's view, there are no such conditions. Only present conditions—events, objects, relations, states of affairs—are the sort of thing in virtue of which a statement, *any* statement, can be true or false. The sentence "Tomorrow '*e* is past' will be true" is itself true, but its form only demonstrates Dummett's point—that we have no access to a future token of *"e is past,"* only to a replica of it that is embedded in a sentence that is tokened at present. And without such access, a contradiction cannot be formulated.

Now recall one of the standard attempts to circumvent the contradiction McTaggart claimed was entailed by the tensed view. It consisted in pointing out that, if *"e is present"* is true then *"e is past"* and *"e is future"* are, contrary to McTaggart's claim, false. Rather, *"e will be past"* and *"e was future"* are true. This response may bear superficial resemblance to Dummett's rejoinder. The two, however, should not be confused. Indeed it is Dummett's own rendition of McTaggart's argument that shows the futility of replacing simple tenses such as ". . . is past" with complex ones such as ". . . will be past" and ". . . was future" (see section 2.1). The chief difference between Dummett's antirealism and the standard maneuver is that the latter *does* allow for future and past conditions to function *at present* as truth conditions. Thus, on the conception of tense attacked by McTaggart and Dummett, *"e was future"* is true on a past condition that obtained *then*, when *e* was future. Similarly, "*e* will be past" is true on a future condition that will obtain *then*, when *e* will be past. However, there are many other past and future tensed conditions, for example, *e* will be future, and *e* was past. The point Dummett makes in defense of McTaggart is that if we allow these past and future conditions to figure as truth conditions then the result is that, indeed, the sentences attached to them, including "*e* will be future" and "*e* was past," are all true. Hence the contradictions.[6]

This completes the survey of the tensed position I'm attributing to Dummett. Time's passage, which changes that over which unrestricted quantifiers range over, is given in it a central place, and the present is shown to be ontologically privileged in the sense I've tried to explain above. However, this doctrine does not at all recognize a "moving Now." The "moving Now" belongs to a viewpoint that absorbs in one glance all of time and "sees," as it were, the "Now" run along the many moments time is made up of. This wide perspective allows one to "perceive," among other things, past and future tokens of sentences. Dummett, in contrast, looks at time from inside this sequence of moments, and confines us to the present, making past and future thoughts and utterances utterly inaccessible. By so doing, Dummett undermines the possibility, or rather, shows we never were in a position to so much as conceive the possibility of bringing sentences that are true at different times into contradiction with each other.

By way of ending this discussion of Dummett, I wish to make a conjecture about the motivations driving his philosophy. Dummett's antirealism can be seen as the outcome of bringing together two thoughts. First, that *truth* conditions are *verification* conditions, that is, that being a *truth* condition means being recognized as such, in principle at least. Second, that verifications always happen in the present, that is, that *verification* conditions are restricted to, and in fact identifiable with, *present* conditions. I wish to suggest that the second thesis is more fundamental in Dummett's scheme of things, and to hypothesize that his theory of meaning is inspired by and in turn lends support to his conception of time. To see the reasoning driving this speculation, one has to think of the *present* as the domain of the tangible, the existent, the experientiable—in short, the "real," of that to which the meaning and truth of descriptive sentences are attached. In other words, one has to get into the frame of mind that is determined by the salient intuitions driving the tensed view. One way to turn these intuitions into a solid metaphysical position would be to introduce the term "verification conditions" and then identify verification conditions, on the one hand, with *truth* conditions, thus obtaining the antirealist's thesis, and on the other, with *present* conditions. Together, the two identities yield the identification of present conditions with truth conditions—the tensed thesis discussed in this section. Presented in this manner, the antirealist's thesis comes to be seen as a product of the effort of defending a tensed metaphysics.

Before closing this chapter, it should be noted that there are other attempts to formulate a viable tensed position. The most noteworthy to have emerged recently is that of Craig (2000), which differs from both versions of the view we've discussed. It does not collapse the past and the future onto the present and so is not a solipsism of the present moment; and it does not stipulate the existence of an entity such as the "moving Now." Nevertheless Craig champions "ontological tense," an offspring of the ontological assumption, protecting it from the kind of objections other versions of the tensed view are vulnerable to by asserting that "talk of time's flow is metaphorical for objective temporal becoming" (2000, 257). So we have objective temporal becoming, which ontologically privileges the present, but it is shielded behind metaphors and so is not exposed to attacks as is, say, Schlesinger's "moving Now." As I mentioned in chapter 1, though positions such as Craig's may be more refined and defensible than the doctrines we have been studying, they are less interesting from our perspective because the nature and centrality of the ontological assumption are not as readily discernible from them. Hence Craig's view does not receive here the detailed attention that, in other contexts, it deserves.

Let me use the occasion, however, to register dissatisfaction with the popular suggestion that talk of time's flow is metaphorical. When Smith tells us that too much time has passed since he last saw his daughter, is he speaking metaphorically? Only in a very loose sense, in the sense in which almost all talk is metaphorical. To say that Smith is killing time fishing is metaphorical. But to say he is passing his days golfing, or that so and so many years have passed since the last eruption of Vesuvius, is to relate certain facts in the most literal fashion possible.[7] More on time's passage later (section 5.4).

4   Tense Beyond Ontology

We are now acquainted with the two theories that have monopolized the discussion in the metaphysics of time from antiquity up to the present. Each of them strikes some essential chord in our philosophical sensibility—the tenseless theory highlights the intractable, ineffable intangibility of time's passage; the tensed theory, its deep, irremovable undeniability. Hence, each protects a vital element in our conception of time. Yet the two theories negate one another, and thus cannot be held together. So the question becomes the surrender of which of the two would be the least costly for our understanding of time.

Arguments making a case for some version or other of one of the two theories occupy much of the literature in the metaphysics of time. A third school strives to find some midway between them, to formulate an intermediary that takes some elements from each theory and rejects others. We, however, will proceed down a different course. Rather than choose and defend one of them, we will look at the two theories as together forming a useful structure, one that does not answer our philosophical quests, but which takes us an important part of the way toward the answers. The two theories can be likened to two tilted pillars leaning against each other, pushing in opposite directions, thereby sustaining each other: they stand or fall together. As stated in chapter 1, rather than finding a resting place within this structure (which, we will see, is not really an option), our aim is to climb on top of it and thus reach beyond it. In this chapter, we will adapt the metaphysical structure for this purpose.

Doing this involves working not on the theories, but on ourselves. What we need to do is reorient ourselves with respect to these theories, an act through which two things will happen. First, we will stop viewing the theories as providing solutions and explanations concerning time, and instead come to think of them as mapping where in our conception of time those thorny points that call for explanations are located and what is their nature. In fact, we will see that without the theories, we cannot so much as formulate the time-related issues that require philosophical treatment. Second, our reorientation will involve coming to see that both metaphysical theories of time are not tenable. More strongly, the conclusion will be that we don't really know how to understand either theory.

That the philosophical queries concerning time do not so much as make sense apart from the theories that purport to resolve them, and that these theories are untenable, means that the queries too are untenable. That is, the realization we attain at the end of the analysis is that we have not framed well-defined questions. By coming to this realization, a systematic dissolution of the traditional philosophical questions concerning time is brought about. That marks progress. But more important, in the course of doing so, we achieve a host of insights concerning time and tense that would never be arrived at without the analysis of the metaphysical queries. It will take two chapters to complete this move. First, in this chapter, we will work on arguments establishing that the theories are not tenable. In the next chapter we will focus on the dissolution of the particular queries that make up much of the metaphysics of time and the extraction of a new understanding of tense.

The reappraisal of the philosophical role of the metaphysical theories of time is a vital axis supporting the present work. Accomplishing this task relies to a great extent on the awakening of an awareness to the existence of diverse vocabularies that figure in the philosophical inquiry. In the next section we will seek and strive to become attentive to the presence of a technical vocabulary that emerges alongside our more familiar, ordinary one, and to the way the two vocabularies blend into each other. It is this specialized vocabulary, developed in the course of the metaphysical enterprise, which enables the framing of seemingly well-defined questions concerning time (as will be discussed in the next chapter). But it is also this specialized vocabulary that entails that the metaphysical theories are not tenable, as we will see starting with section 4.2.

4.1 The Emergence of Ontology

It is not self-evident that the metaphysical inquiry must be conducted by means of a technical, and more specifically, an ontological, terminology.

The origins of this terminology should be traced, then. They are to be found in the beginnings of the inquiry, which are rooted in a philosophical inquisitiveness prompted by ordinary experience. We have absolutely no difficulty understanding Jack when he tells us that it's been two years since he last visited France. Nor are we perplexed by his solemn remark that that visit now lies in that "bucket of ashes," as Carl Sandburg calls the past, having been carried there by "time's passage." And yet, this remark may easily—one does not have to be a philosopher for this to happen— invite a swarm of questions which suddenly engulf one in a mist of uncertainty: Does the past indeed consist of "ashes"? Is nothing more left? Is there no way in which what is past nonetheless remains *real*? How can we access it, even in our memories, if there is in reality nothing to access? What exactly is this "passage," on the invisible wings of which events are carried to the past? Is it time that passes, taking present events into the irretrievable past, or is it we that move into the future, leaving those past events behind? And at what rate is the distance between us and those past events growing?

These are preliminary, naive, and somewhat amorphous questions. But they are nevertheless disturbing, *philosophically* disturbing. I said one does not have to be a philosopher in order to raise them. Still, they certainly do express a distinctly philosophical interest. Suppose someone proceeds to address them. As they stand, it would be difficult to attach a definite sense to them. They need to be made more precise, the terms appearing in them need to be clarified, metaphors should be replaced with definitions. This explicative challenge already invites the introduction of new terms. And we know from the survey of the metaphysical theories presented in the previous chapters that the terms figuring in the discussion are ontological. Tensed theorists focus on the ontological superiority of the present; tenseless theorists on ontological equality that holds among all events. Our first task is to inquire why it is that ontology provides the terms for the philosophical analysis of time and tense.

The everyday situations and experiences with which our curiosity may first be ignited are not immediately apprehended as involving ontological issues. Jack is not making a reality claim when he reports that two years have elapsed since he last tasted a real croissant. His nostalgia seems to be prompted not by that last croissant's "unreality," but by its inaccessibility: Jack cannot now see, taste, or smell it. Here the analogy with space that tenseless theorists invoke can be useful: we are prone to missing distant places and people, not because they do not exist, but because they are not accessible. Other examples underscore the fact that, initially, the issue is not one of ontology, but of accessibility. Most of us overeat occasionally, and regret it. We regret it, not because this act becomes "unreal," but because there is no way this action can be undone.

In general, we are all occasionally hit over the head with the brute (and at times brutal) fact that what's done is done, the past cannot be changed. We can't, for example, mend a chair we promised to fix if it was consumed by a fire yesterday. Nor, evidently, can we see it: perception manifests the same tensed properties as actions, and, specifically, past events are not accessible to perception. "The meteorite shower is over, there is nothing to see anymore," or "You can't see the photographs because they too were destroyed in the fire" are perfectly good *explanations* of why certain things cannot be seen: they are no longer present, they are past. Phenomenologically speaking, being past entails being inaccessible to action or perception. The apprehension that our past actions, and in general past objects and events, are utterly out of reach may become so vivid that, in certain moments, we can actually come to doubt whether they ever existed at all.

There are many ways for things to become past: objects may *burn, be eaten, be demolished, eroded* and so on. Movies, meteorite showers, and events in general simply *end*. The point to stress, however, is that sentences in which one of these verbs is employed for the sake of reporting that an event or an object has become past do not explicitly express any ontological distinctions, and in particular say nothing about the "ontological status" of past things in comparison with that of present things. They do not even hint that there is such an issue. It is a truism that a chair that was burnt no longer exists. But this truism is not expressed by any *reality claims* and therefore does not constitute a point of contention between tenseless and tensed theorists. Both would agree that burnt photos cannot be seen because, in contrast with lost photos, which also cannot be seen, burnt ones no longer exist. Both would agree that it is one thing not to be able to enjoy a Vermeer from the Gardner museum because it has been stolen, and another thing not to be able to enjoy it because a vandal has demolished it. We think of the difference as consisting precisely in that in the latter case, but not in the former, the picture no longer exists to be seen. Still, to repeat, such daily references to past things as nonexistent *do not* yet express that concerning which the philosophical debate develops.

It is only once attention is turned toward philosophical interests, and questions are posed that are explicitly philosophically minded, that the language of mundane utterances does provoke the formulation of *reality claims*. For example, to the question "Why can't we see the fireworks?" the answer "because we missed them, they are now past and over" is a perfectly good and ordinary one. But the further question, "Why cannot things that are past and over be seen?" already expresses a curiosity that goes beyond the ordinary, and is likely to invoke an answer that begins to breach the boundaries of the ordinary as well. For example, it may be replied that past things are not perceptually and causally accessible because they do not exist and are therefore "not real." Such an explanation may very well make up the (first approximation to an) answer.

It is plain to see that this response comprises two parts—the assertion that past things do not exist, which still belongs to everyday language and is not contentious; and the added clause, that they are "not real," which is already a *reality claim*. Thus, setting out to probe more deeply something's becoming past invites an analysis of the ordinary locution "*x* no longer exists" that is no longer ordinary: "*x* no longer exists" comes to mean that *x* is no longer "part of reality." With this tenet having been reached, we are well on our way toward a tensed metaphysics. But we have also opened the door to the opposing metaphysics, the tenseless one which will insist that something may not exist now and yet be "part of reality," or, to use Parfit's formulation, be "equally real" as things that do exist now.

The important point to note is that the quest for a better understanding of the inaccessibility of past things introduces a novel interest in the nature of tense, a *philosophical* interest. Furthermore, engaging this interest and bringing matters under philosophical scrutiny involves redescribing them by means of fresh terms that do not figure in the original depiction of the phenomenon in question. And as we just saw, the phenomenological inaccessibility of the past makes *ontology* the natural choice for a provider of the new terms with which tense is depicted.[1] Thus, our philosophical query comes to be centered on, for example, the tensed contention that only objects enjoying the "quality of presentness" are "real and alive." Tenseless theorists contest this contention, and maintain that a burnt chair is, admittedly, perceptually and causally out of reach but is nevertheless "just as real" as the chairs now around us, only removed in time, and therefore inaccessible.

The philosophical enterprise, then, like many theoretical endeavors, solicits, and is carried out by means of a *new vocabulary*. It concerns questions such as whether things existing now enjoy some kind of "ontological privilege" that past things, like dinosaurs, do not enjoy, or whether conversely dinosaurs "are, in the tenseless sense of 'are,' just as real" (Parfit 1996, 4) as present-day animals. In elaborating the theses prompted by such questions other new terms show up, such as the term "tenseless relations," which is pivotal for the tenseless view, and which we will look at closely later in the chapter.

The need for a specialized language in which the point of contention is expressed highlights the observations made a few paragraphs ago: although the phenomenology of tense sets the philosophical investigation on an ontological track, in itself it does not contain the ontological distinctions the investigation focuses on as it advances. We speak of dinosaurs as no longer existing, and in this we already pave the way to an ontological analysis. But in itself, this assertion, about which there is universal agreement, does not yet express that over which the metaphysical discussion evolves. It is only with the advent of a unique philosophical vocabulary, consisting of terms such as "ontological privilege" and phrases such as "all events are equally real," that the subject of the philosophical analysis can be stated. In other words, the ontological content of the study of time surfaces only with the appearance of the inquiry's special words and terms.

To recap, the emergence of an ontologically centered philosophical analysis of time has the following structure:

1. Ordinary experience is marked by the perceptual and causal inaccessibility of past and future things.

2. The language that goes along with this experience consists of assertions that do not constitute reality claims and do not express the kind of ontological distinctions that figure prominently in the metaphysics of time.

3. Yet, when a philosophical agenda is set, this initial phenomenology dictates that the theses that are propounded as explanations, and which become the subjects of the philosophical analysis of tense, will be framed in ontological terms.

4. These new terms constitute an addition to our vocabulary. They are not to be found in the words and grammatical forms that originally capture the distinction between the past, present, and future.

The appearance of a new vocabulary may be hard to notice because it consists, initially, at least, of terms and phrases that may seem ordinary. Thus, at first blush, the statement that "only the present exists" may sound like nothing but an innocuous generalization based on ordinary observations one frequently hears, such as: "most of the photos no longer exist but some, which were saved from the fire, do." But then this very statement can be appropriated by the metaphysical enterprise and transformed into a *metaphysical* thesis, as becomes evident when we encounter it in the midst of a metaphysical theory. There we find it along side statements such as "the NOW runs along the moments of time, successively conferring upon each moment *m* a unique privileged status," or as the negation of "Past, present, and future events are equally real," locutions that belong to anything but ordinary discourse. Together with terms such as "tenseless relations" and "the NOW," the phrase "only the present exists" becomes part of the specialized jargon in which the philosophical inquiry is conducted.

We observed that certain philosophically minded questions can surface naively—anyone can wonder, and many people who are not philosophers do occasionally wonder, whether the past really consists of "ashes," or how it is that time's passage has the many powers it allegedly has—of healing,[2] comforting,[3] teaching,[4] and more. Next we observed that taking a further step in the direction of elaborating these prephilosophical reflections lands us on metaphysical turf, and involves casting the reflections in ontological terms. With these terms, preliminary questions that are *par excellence* philosophical can be posed: Are past and future events real? Are there in reality a past, a present, and a future? Does time flow, or is time's passage an illusion? Once these questions are explicitly formulated, the philosophical inquiry has been launched.

We can now see how this inquiry necessarily leads to the forced choice described back in section 1.3. We spoke there about the "ontological assumption," the assumption that tense pertains to the ontological status of things, and that therefore the proper philosophical analysis of tense is to be done in terms of reality claims, claims to the effect that events and things are or are not "real." We have just traced the evolution of the philosophical inquiry from the initial phenomenological observations with which it begins to the emergence of the ontological assumption and the ontological debate. Once the ontological issue comes to the fore and the question "Is the present ontologically distinguished with respect to the past and the present?" takes center stage, the analytic effort will concentrate on formulating and defending the "Yes" and "No" answers to this question. It will culminate with the development of mature metaphysical doctrines—the tensed and tenseless theories. The ontological vocabulary narrows the choice to a tenseless "No" in response to the question "Is the present ontologically special and does time really flow?," and a tensed "Yes."

I close this section by rehearsing the promise made at the opening of the chapter and that will be fulfilled in the next chapter—the promise for a dissolution of the philosophical questions concerning time. These problems must be well formulated before they can be tackled. The metaphysical theories enable doing just that. They do so in two ways: first, by directing the inquiry to hitherto unnoticed difficulties. The onus on tenseless theorists to account for the ubiquitous experiential manifestations of tense stimulates an effort to map these manifestations. That's how we come to confront, among other things, the presence of experience, the sensitivity of our attitudes to tense, the intrinsic pastness of the remembered, and the futurity of the anticipated. Tensed theorists for their part face the obligation of defending time's passage from tenseless attacks, and so are forced to deal with specific issues: to give sense to the ontological claims they make in connection with time's passage, to respond to questions relating to the rate of time's passage, and so on.

Second, the metaphysical theories contribute the technical terms with which the problems can be accurately framed and detailed. The specialized vocabulary we have been focusing on figures in the formulation of the different challenges each camp faces. For example, the claim that the present is pointlike is driven by arguments among whose premises figures the present's alleged "ontological superiority." The same goes for the problem of the presence of experience. Initially this problem is stated quite ordinarily: "Whoever I am, and whenever I believe my experience to be present, that now-belief will be true" (Mellor 1998, 44). But, as we will see in section 5.2, this characterization of the problem is not adequate, and the more refined description of the presence of experience employs the special terms taken from the theories. To take a final example, the introduction of the noun phrase "the moving Now," which functions as the *name* of the element of transience, invites the inquiry into the ontological quality of this element, and into the rate of its passage.

In short, the development of full-blown doctrines generates well-specified challenges, as well as a specialized terminology, which facilitates their formulation. Thus, philosophical difficulties are made definite by means of the same vocabulary that serves the theories developed in order to address these difficulties.

More generally, the metaphysical theories are a response to the perplexity that afflicts us once we direct our philosophical curiosity to the temporal aspects of experience; but, more important for our purposes, it is through these theories *alone* that our best attempt to clearly express and specify our original disquiet is made: the specialized vocabulary figuring in these theories is also the vocabulary that serves in articulating the agenda for the philosophical inquiry. Ordinary language, by which, it should be stressed again, I mean both daily and *scientific* language, lacks the vocabulary with which the time-related challenges for metaphysics could be posed. In this respect the metaphysical game turns out to be circular: it emerges that the metaphysics of time is not only a means for settling questions generated by those early bafflements, it is also the ground that breathes life into these questions.

4.2   Incoherence of Joint Uses of "Real"

Back in section 1.3 I claimed that these two supposedly conflicting and incompatible theories—the tenseless and the tensed theories—have much in common. They share what we have been referring to as the ontological assumption. The two theories diverge simply about whether certain events and things—those that are counted by us as past and future—are real or not. Tenseless theorists say they are; they are as real as those counted by us as present. Tensed theorists say they are not: only what is present is real. But that the issue is one of deciding whether they are real or not is something both sides to the debate take for granted.

We now turn to study this joint premise. It is taken for granted by both sides, but we have been calling it an *assumption*, precisely because it is far from evident that a commitment to reality claims is what tense is all about. In fact, as we will see in this section, this assumption is not tenable. Since it sustains both theories, in light of its demise, neither theory can be upheld. Realizing this does not mean abandoning the theories, but rather locating them elsewhere in the larger scheme of our philosophical investigation. Ultimately, they have a role in dissolving our philosophical perplexity, and in carrying us beyond it—the role outlined at the opening of this chapter. And recall that the thrust that advances the inquiry beyond the metaphysical enterprise is generated by the demonstration of the theories' inadequacy. So we need both the theories and the arguments against them, arguments that will target the intelligibility of the common assumption underlying them.

We will establish the theories' inadequacy in this and the following sections. But note that even prior to the systematic arguments to be presented, endorsing either the tensed or the tenseless view requires accommodating oneself to some enduring uneasiness. This is most evident in the case of the tenseless view. It seems next to impossible to conceive of reality as tenseless. Tenseless theorists admit that tense is an indispensable and ineliminable mode of thinking, speaking, and experiencing. So, in a sense, it is not even a genuine option for us to conceive of the world as tenseless— whatever theoretical convictions we adopt, we are bound to continue experiencing reality, and thinking and speaking of it, as tensed. One cannot therefore comfortably settle into the belief that it is not tensed, to a belief, that is, which conflicts with all of one's experiences, thoughts and utterances. Similarly, accepting the tensed theory cannot come without some reluctance, certainly in view of the vigorous assault mounted against the theory's conceptual foundations by tenseless theorists. These counterarguments highlight the perhaps insurmountable difficulties that face an attempt to flesh out in acceptable, consistent, and coherent terms what exactly the present's "ontological superiority" is supposed to come to.

No doubt, given how perplexing time is, a theory that promises conceptual clarity will be attractive, even if it is not perfect. But the theories available to us provoke resistance at a relatively basic level. Though they purport to explain the temporal aspects of experience, they seem in fact to distort this experience. Indeed, as we will now see, these theories clash with deeply grounded ways of speaking and thinking.

Our targets are located within the theories' specialized vocabulary. Hitherto we have pointed to special terms that belong to only one of the two theories, terms such as "tenseless relations" or "the moving Now." But the more interesting specialized vocabulary is shared. In particular, we need to focus on the word "real" as it figures in the fundamental tenets of both views, for instance, in the tenseless assertion that all events, past, present, and future, are "equally real," and in the tensed claim that only the present is "real." These are strange uses of the word, uses to which it is more difficult to attach a definite sense then may at first be assumed. To see this, we will study in a moment some features of its "normal," that is, ordinary, familiar uses.

Questions may be, and frequently are, raised concerning the appropriateness of studying a word's ordinary uses in the context of a specialized, metaphysical investigation. Indeed, such studies are often dismissed as trivial, inconsequential, and so on. I shall not deal with worries of this sort because, as Austin (1979, 92) remarks, "It is not sure importance is important: truth is." Moreover, in the context of the metaphysics of time, disinterest in ordinary usage would be particularly out of place. The metaphysics of time does not begin with what physics has to say about time (though it is, and ought to be, attentive to what physics has to say; see section 5.7). Nor is it launched by theological meditations, or with the idiosyncratic ideas of a certain philosopher (though, again, these may become significant later on). It is a fact about the metaphysics of time that it does not at first take interest in what comes up in these "higher" contexts. Rather, as has been amply stressed hitherto, and as a quick survey of the literature from Aristotle to contemporary texts shows, the examples it initially attends to are taken from daily discourse, sentences such as those one hears over the news: "The space shuttle is now in orbit," "The president has ended a three-day visit to France." It is with respect to such mundane, tensed utterances that we ask: what is the correct metaphysical picture and the correct theory of meaning for them? Is it the tenseless view with its attendant token-reflexive account of meaning? Or is it the tensed theory, which insists on tensed conditions as truth conditions for such utterances?

That the metaphysics of time is preoccupied with everyday utterances is something tensed theorists do not deny. After all, ordinary discourse inspires their theory and is the kernel around which it is constructed. But it is no less acknowledged by tenseless theorists. Smart opens his paper in defense of the tenseless view with an observation about daily experience, namely, that "certainly we *feel* that time flows" (1980, 3). Mellor builds his tenseless theory around ordinary sentences such as "Jim races tomorrow" and puts forth arguments demonstrating their indispensability and irreducibility. Parfit's discussion as well aims at providing a new understanding of what we mean when we say, for example, "The first atom bomb is exploding now" (1996, 1). Indeed, it is this preoccupation with daily discourse that prompts Parfit to remind us that "the disagreement between these views is not about our language, but about the nature of time" (1996, 1). Evidently, then, common usage is not something that can be dismissed. Of course, the vocabulary of an investigation, any investigation, cannot be restricted at its beginning to common usage. But nor can it afford to simply ignore it.

Let us, then, consider the word "real," which figures prominently in the articulation of the tenets of both the tenseless and the tensed theories. An illuminating discussion of this key word is found in part VII of Austin's *Sense and Sensibilia*. The first point Austin makes about the word "real" is that it is

an absolutely normal word, with nothing new fangled or technical or highly specialized about it. It is, that is to say, already firmly established in, and very frequently used in, the ordinary language we all use every day. Thus in this sense it's a word which has a fixed meaning, and so can't, any more than can any other word which is firmly established, be fooled with ad lib. . . . Certainly, when we have discovered how a word is in fact used, that may not be the end of the matter; there is certainly no reason why, in general, things should be left exactly as we find them. . . . But still, it is advisable to always bear in mind that . . . before indulging in any tampering on our own account, we need to find out what it is that we have to deal with; and that tampering with words . . . is always liable to have unforeseen repercussions. (1962, 62–63)

Now, although Austin cautions that we "can't just 'assign' any meaning whatever" to the word "real," he also warns against seeking a sharp definition of the word, one that would fix in advance all its uses:

The other immensely important point to grasp is that "real" is *not* a normal word at all, but highly exceptional; exceptional in this respect that, unlike "yellow" or "horse" or "walk," it does not have one single, specifiable, always-the-same *meaning*. (Even Aristotle saw through this idea.) (Ibid. 64)

This observation should not be mistakenly taken to suggest that "real"

[has] a large number of meanings—it is not ambiguous, even "systematically." (Ibid.)

Nor does its being not normal make it "metaphysical":

and reflect that many philosophers, failing to detect any ordinary quality common to real ducks, real cream, real progress, have decided that Reality must be an *a priori* concept apprehended by reason alone. (Ibid.)

Being not normal does not mean that "real" is ambiguous or metaphysical, but simply that it does not lend itself to being boxed within a fixed set of definitions. To sum up, on the one hand, "real" already has firmly established uses and cannot be reinterpreted so as to assume just any meaning tailored for it; and on the other, its meaning, or meanings, cannot be captured by definitions or rules in accordance with which it ought to be used. However, although its meaning cannot be exhausted by definition, some "salient features of the use of 'real'" can nevertheless be sketched. Of the four features Austin outlines, I will mention two.

First, Austin remarks that "real" is what he calls a "substantive hungry" word. To explain this, he asks us to compare the following pair of sentences:

These diamonds are real

These are real diamonds

with their grammatical look-alikes:

These diamonds are pink

These are pink diamonds.

The point of this comparison is this:

> Whereas we can *just* say of something "This is pink," we can't *just* say of something "This is real." And it is not very difficult to see why. We can perfectly well say of something that it is pink without knowing, without any reference to, what it *is*. But not so with "real." For one and the same object may be both a real *x* and not a real *y*; an object looking rather like a duck may be a real decoy duck (not just a toy) but not a real duck. When it isn't a real duck but a hallucination, it may still be a real hallucination—as opposed, for instance, to a passing quirk of a vivid imagination. That is, we must have an answer to the question "A real *what*?," if the question "Real or not?" is to have a definite sense, to get any foothold. And perhaps we should mention here another point—that the question "Real or not?" does not always come up, can't always be raised. We *do* raise this question only when, to speak rather roughly, suspicion assails us—in some way or other things may be not what they seem; and we *can* raise this question only if there *is* a way, or ways, in which things can be not what they seem. What alternative is there to being a "real" after-image? (Ibid. 69)

So the first significant feature of the uses of the word "real" is that they require an answer to the question "A real *what*?," if the question "Real or not?" is to have a definite sense.

The second part of the above quotation leads to the second feature I wish to highlight, which is stated explicitly here:

A definite sense attaches to the assertion that something is real, a real such-and-such, only in the light of a specific way in which it might be, or might have been, *not* real. "A real duck" differs from the simple "a duck" only in that it is used to exclude various ways of being not a real duck—a dummy, a toy, a picture, a decoy, &c.; and moreover I don't know *just* how to take the assertion that it's a real duck unless I know *just* what, on that particular occasion, the speaker has in mind to exclude. . . . the function of "real" is not to contribute positively to the characterization of anything, but to exclude possible ways of being *not* real. (Ibid. 70)

Some more examples underscore the role of the word "real" as one of excluding possibilities:

pictures are genuine as opposed to *fake*, silk is natural as opposed to *artificial*, ammunition is live as opposed to *dummy*, and so on. (Ibid. 71)

The upshot of all this is that:

we make a distinction between "a real *x*" and "not a real *x*" only if there is a way of telling the difference between what is a real *x* and what is not. A distinction which we are not in fact able to draw is—to put it politely—not worth making. (Ibid. 77)

Placed against Austin's observations, it is not hard to appreciate that the uses made of the word "real" (and its derivatives, such as "really," "in reality," etc.) in the course of articulating the tenets of the metaphysical theories of time suffer from significant faults. Let us take as a first example Parfit's assertion that "past and future people exist, and are real, in the same straightforward way as the people who exist now." What could this reality claim come to? When we are told that past people are just as real as present ones, that in fact "all events are, in the timeless sense of 'are,' equally real," what could this mean? Past events and people are supposed to be "real" as opposed to what? To being decoys? Fakes? Fictions? Well, we are told that they are just as real as present ones. But for this to be helpful we need to know what is meant by the assertion that present people are "real." That they are "real" just as past people are evidently won't do. What is necessary is a specification of a form of being *not real* that is excluded by the assertion that present people are "real." But, again, none of the familiar ways of being not real is relevant here. Parfit is not reassuring us that past and present people are real rather than made of wax, or fictitious.

Perhaps Parfit is merely out to reject the tensed contention that "only what exists now is real." Perhaps all he is saying is that all things are real in the way past things are thought not to be by tensed theorists. But the tensed assertion "only what exists now is real" fails to manifest either of the above features of the uses of "real": we are not told a real *what* is at issue, nor what is the specific way this thing may be *not real* that is being excluded by the tensed tenet. In other words, we have not been convinced that we understand the tensed use of "real." So Parfit's assertion cannot be rescued by being interpreted as the negation of the tensed tenet.[5]

The same goes for Mellor's thesis that "there is in reality no difference between past, present, and future." This assertion brings out a further difficulty: at first, it is not even clear the reality of what exactly is being queried—of past events and objects, of "the Past" itself, or of the distinction between past, present, and future? A real *what* is at issue here? In one sense, the tenseless view pertains to past things—as *past* things, it denies their reality: if "nothing in reality is past, present or future" (Mellor 1998, 47), and if the French Revolution *is* a past event (in the ordinary rather than in the tenseless sense), then there is no French Revolution. Yet, in another way, the tenseless thesis pertains to an event's "pastness": it is not the reality of the event itself that is being denied, but of what we initially think of as one of its temporal attributes. Of course the French Revolution is real; only its pastness isn't. In yet a third way, it is the past, present, and future as such, as objective and distinct temporal realms that are independent of any events that may belong to them, whose reality is at issue.

Tenseless theorists take it for granted that their formulations express the second of these options, failing to mention this inner duplicity that is hidden in the way they standardly frame their basic tenets. They seem to take the affirmation that past and future events and objects are "just as real" as present ones to be tantamount to the denial that there really are a past, a present, and a future. But that should strike us as odd. It is not as though the affirmation is a simple negation of the denial. After all, the two assertions have different subjects—one affirms the reality of past and future *things*, whereas the other denies the reality of pastness and futureness as *qualities*. So why think of the two contentions as equivalent?

It might be thought that tenseless theorists ignore this ambiguity because the two assertions are thought to be tightly implicated in each other: denying an event's pastness is regarded as identical to asserting its reality and vice versa. But this alleged connection does not hold. A denial of the pastness of the French Revolution is by no means synonymous with an affirmation of its reality. Firstly, because it could be that this event is not past or present but future, or that there is no such event altogether. Second, tenseless theorists deny its presentness and futurity as well, and these denials are certainly not taken by anyone to imply the event's reality. In light of such remarks, tenseless theorists might accept that they are in fact making two claims: that the French Revolution is real, and that the quality of pastness is not real. Be that as it may, their failure to explicitly make the distinction is, I believe, indicative of the insensitivity with which they employ the word "real."

And at any rate, Austin-type remarks apply to both tenseless claims. What could the affirmation of the reality of the French Revolution come to? It is a "real" Revolution—as opposed to what? A fictional one? A mock revolution? A botched revolution? Evidently nothing of the sort is relevant in the present context. Nor does it help to say it is "real" in the way that present events are, for, as before, we are bewildered by the assertion that present events are "real." And the claim that the quality of "pastness" is not real is even more perplexing: is "pastness" a fake quality? A decoy? All of this is in addition to the obscurity emanating from the duplicity that lurks behind tenets such as "there is in reality no difference between past, present and future," a duplicity concerning *what* exactly the theory asserts to possess or to lack "reality."

Hence, Parfit's and Mellor's supposedly innocuous use of reality claims in formulating the basic tenets of the tenseless view proves to be, when subject to the kind of criticism suggested by Austin's analysis of such claims, problematic, irreparably so. Other formulations of the tenseless view are plagued by troubles of the same type, because making such reality claims just is what makes these formulations into versions of the tenseless theory.

Turning to the tensed view, as already noted above, similar deviations in the uses of the word "real" are just as characteristic of its various formulations, all of which rely on the same problematic terminology. More briefly, let us look at a few representative examples. Broad belongs to those tensed theorists for whom the past is as real as the present, in contrast with the future, which is not: he "accepts the reality of the present and the past, but holds that the future is simply nothing at all" (1923, 66). Schlesinger,

we recall, denounces the tenseless view for insisting that "there are no privileged moments in time and events do not momentarily become more real
as they are embraced by the Now." According to his view, "the NOW is
. . . the point in time in which any individual who is temporally extended
is alive, real, or Exists with a capital E" (1980, 23). Dummett is not as
explicit as Broad and Schlesinger in distinguishing the present in terms of
its advantaged reality, but, as we saw, the claims he makes can, with no
significant distortions, be paraphrased in this language. In particular, it was
suggested (see 3.2 above) that Dummett's insistence that only present conditions can count as truth conditions expresses an ontological distinction
of the present—that is how the dictum "only what exists now is real" gets
fleshed out in his system.

I suppose it is clear enough that the questions "real as opposed to what?,"
and "the reality of what exactly is at issue?," are just as embarrassing for
tensed theorists as they are for tenseless theorists. "Only the present is real"
implies that the past and the future are not. But by claiming that the past
and the future are not real, tensed theorists do not mean that they are
decoy; nor do they mean that the present is real because it is not fake. So
what do they mean? And if *what* they are speaking of are events, rather
than pastness, presentness, and futurity as such, if their claim is that only
present events and things are real, then what ways of being not real do
they think they are excluding with this claim? They cannot fare any better
than their tenseless counterparts when confronted with these questions.

Let me mention again that, nowadays, arguments of the type just
rehearsed are often brushed aside as "unscientific." The notion that the
philosopher may learn from the language of "the man on the street" that
her own words are perhaps unintelligible seems preposterous. How could
mere observations about ordinary linguistic practices, which is what one
finds in Austin's remarks, be preferred over a "semantic theory" for the
word "real" of the kind offered in the theories of the philosopher (and
which Austin himself states is *not* what his remarks constitute)? In the end,
are we not "after the truth of the matter, rather than what most people
would say"?[6]

Well, can anyone have access to some "truth of the matter" that lies over
and above what people say? Certainly not, especially if by "what people
say" we include, in addition to the rich and varied verbal transactions that
fill our everyday, also what mathematicians, physicists, and scientists in

general say. As already stressed, it is our ordinary, everyday utterances that first ignite our philosophical curiosity and provide it with its notions. It's also these utterances that constitute the subject of the metaphysician's investigation. It is therefore advisable to heed to Austin's advice (voiced before the hostility toward this kind of "unscientific" philosophy climbed to the levels it has attained in some quarters of today's philosophical world) and "not dismiss as beneath contempt such humble but familiar expressions as 'not real cream'; this may save us from saying, for example, or seeming to say that what is not real cream must be a fleeting product of our cerebral processing" (1962, 64).[7] The words of "the man on the street" are just as much a part of our philosophical inquiry as are the inquiry's specialized terms; and carelessness in employing them, just as bound to result in confusion.

A worthier objection to considerations such as Austin's does not contest the importance of obtaining acquaintance with ordinary usage of words, but points out that often progress in a given field is made by means of a specialized vocabulary that is developed in the course of research, and in particular through novel meanings that are assigned to familiar terms. In the sciences we encounter such developments quite regularly. "Simultaneity" is a famous example. Here is a term whose meaning was deeply reshaped, a word that has acquired new uses, in the course of the evolution of a theory. Or, to take another familiar example, the word "triangle" came to refer, in the context of non-Euclidean geometry, to entities that were literally unthinkable prior to the appearance of this new theory of geometry. In general, the at times unexpected novelties that come with new discoveries are often described by means of existing words, which, in the context of the new theory, are endowed with new uses and meanings. Refusing to acknowledge this is a form of reactionaryism which turns its back on discovery and progress. Indeed, one charge that is often leveled against so-called ordinary language philosophy is that it is reactionary in exactly this way, that it fails to accommodate changes that the meanings of words undergo as our knowledge and understanding advance. That language is already in place ("It [the language-game] is there—like our lives" [Wittgenstein 1969, §559]) may be taken to mean (mistakenly, of course) that words already have fixed meanings, and that any novelty that comes along must do so only within the constraints set by these already established, inflexible meanings.

If we do not want to be guilty of this error, we must allow the possibility that the tenets of the metaphysical theories of time can only be read in relation to them. Defenders of either the tenseless or the tensed theories will be registering a valid complaint if they insist that it is wrong to analyze their tenets as if the words they are stated in are simply those familiar from other mundane uses. The use they are put to in the context of the theory, they will stress, is not mundane, but *theoretical*. Imagine someone rejecting the assertion that simultaneity cannot be relative to a frame of reference because no ordinary uses of this term reflect such relativity. Such a reaction would be a gross example of the antiscientific dogmatism just alluded to. But then, is not the branding of the uses made of the word "real" in the context of theories of time as "devious," without heeding to the manner in which the word obtains its meaning *from* the theory, just another instance of the same type of error? Let the *theory* give the word "real" the sense it needs to have for it to convey the truth about time, just as relativity theory gives the word "simultaneity" the meaning it needs to have so that the truth about space and time can be articulated.

Thus, for example, it may be claimed that Mellor's view is sustained by the token-reflexive account of tense, an account that enables him to flesh out a distinction between "tenseless relations" and "tensed relations." With this distinction in place, he can explain, for example, the assertion that "nothing in reality is past, present or future" by giving a theory of meaning in which truth conditions are always tenseless conditions. He would thus be employing the token-reflexive account of meaning for the sake of establishing a special use of the word "real," a use required for expressing the theory's account of temporal reality. Likewise, the statement that "only what is present is real" can be viewed as stemming from, and gaining intelligibility from, Dummett's antirealist theory of meaning.

To repeat, it may be argued that the basic tenets of each version of either theory do not stand alone, but are sustained by the arguments put forth in defense of the theory in question. In the context of these arguments certain uses of words that otherwise are not permissible become endowed with a sense. Specifically, the claim is that, indeed, the word "real" is used irregularly in articulating the theories' tenets, but that these special uses are sanctioned by the theories themselves. This is a serious claim, and the coming sections are devoted to it.

Before that, another line of objection should be addressed. Even if Austin's remarks are not dismissed as unimportant, they may be claimed to be simply wrong. In particular, they may be seen as instantiating the fallacious "contrast theory of meaning," as Gellner, one of the bitterest enemies of "linguistic philosophy," called it (Gellner 1959, 40–44). According to this unfortunate "theory" any term must have both a possible example and a possible counterexample for it to be meaningful. More particularly, the theory claims that factual statements are meaningful only if their negation is also meaningful. Or, to put it differently, factual assertions are meaningful only if they exclude some possibility—the possibility expressed by the negation. It is alleged that Austin is invoking this theory when he insists that asserting that x is real is meaningful only against ways in which it can be asserted that x is not real.

But surely many assertions are meaningful that blatantly violate this demand. Thus, we all know that $2 + 2 = 4$, and yet we would not know what to make of the idea that there is a counterexample to this truth. Nor would we know how to answer someone who wanted to know what possibility is being excluded by the assertion that all bachelors are unmarried, and yet we understand this claim. There are, goes the objection, too many counterexamples to the "contrast theory of meaning" for it to be a viable doctrine, and in particular to constitute a valid constraint on uses of "real."

Objections of this type entirely miss Austin's point. Austin, like other linguistic philosophers, never aimed at general theories of meaning, or at universal theses that tell us something about the meanings of words independently of the way these words are used.[8] To the contrary, he saw the program of conjuring up general theories of meaning as misguided, and would thus be the first to denounce the idea of a "contrast theory of meaning." Rather, he specialized in the more modest, probably more challenging and certainly more fruitful project of describing and highlighting "salient features" of the uses of key words, and of stressing the sensitivities of meanings to contexts. In particular, he obtained valuable insights from studying "salient features" of the uses of "real," a word that figures centrally in the articulation of many philosophical theses, not only about time, and a thorough acquaintance with which is therefore of great philosophical importance. In the case of *this* specific word, Austin's observations are both valid and indispensable, and cannot be undermined by being wrongfully subsumed under the umbrella of the "contrast theory of meaning."

4.3 The Myth of Tenseless Relations

We all know that the American Revolution preceded the French Revolution. We supposedly all know, or are at least ready to admit once it is explained to us, that this fact constitutes a *tenseless relation* between the two events. Indeed, tenseless theorists take it for granted that there are such tenseless relations. Their quarrel with tensed theorists concerns the question of whether in reality the *only* type of temporal relations are tenseless relations, or whether there are, in addition, also tensed relations. The point of contention concerns the exclusivity of tenseless relations, not their existence. I wish in this section to nevertheless raise a question about their existence. I will, in fact, challenge the coherence of the notion of "tenseless relations." It is important to undermine this notion not only because it is as prevalent as it is misleading, but even more so because as long as it stands, the arguments of the previous section against the abuses of the word "real" are not complete. For, as mentioned at the end of that section, theories can be employed for the sake of giving words new uses and meanings.

Specifically, it may be claimed that the tenseless view is sustained by the straightforward distinction between tenseless and tensed sentences, a distinction that can be articulated without resorting to the word "real": tenseless sentences state tenseless relations, namely, relations of precedence, succession, and simultaneity; tensed sentences state tensed relations, namely, the location of events in relation to the present, as occurring now, or as having occurred, or as expected to occur in the future. Once this distinction is in place, the tenseless view can be stated as saying that there are only tenseless relations. We can then go on and explain how such relations provide truth conditions for tensed beliefs and utterances—we do so by means of the token-reflexive account—and thus rid ourselves altogether of the need to resort to tensed relations. The by now familiar formulations of the tenseless theory—can now be put forth: that "nothing in reality is past or present or future"; that "all events, past, present and future, are equally real," and so on. These claims are not to be read on their own, but only in the context of the token-reflexive theory of meaning. It is this theory that gives the above uses of the word "real" and its derivatives the sense they have in the statements of the tenets of the tenseless view. Seen in this light, the tenseless view does not merely prove that time's passage is an illusion, it also endows this assertion with meaning. Therefore, if the claim of the previous section, namely, that the uses of "real" in formulating the theory are unacceptable, is to be sustained, it must be shown that these uses are not legitimized by the theory itself, a task we turn to now.

We start by repeating the observation that the term "tenseless relations" is a novel theoretical term, which appears in our vocabulary only once we venture into a philosophical investigation. The question that it immediately provokes is whether it is supposed to *replace* existing vocabulary or to *augment* it. Science offers examples of both cases. "Oxygen" supposedly replaced "phlogiston," relativistic "simultaneity" replaced classical "simultaneity" (at least in those situations that exhibit measurable relativistic behavior), whereas "neutrino," "weak electromagnetism," and "black holes" supplement existing vocabularies.

Now, if the question "Does the new term *x* replace or supplement terms of the existing vocabulary?" is not a problematic one in the sciences, matters are markedly more complicated in the case of the term "tenseless relations." The reason is that to the question "Does the term 'tenseless relations' replace existing vocabulary?" there is no clear-cut "Yes" or "No" answer, but one composed of both; and the two components of the answer cannot be reconciled with each other.

First, note that "tenseless relations" is not an addition to our pool of terms, at least not in the manner that "neutrino" is. Unlike "neutrino" and other terms that are added in the course of scientific research, it does not designate a new phenomenon, and it is not prompted by and does not go along with new, hitherto unknown observations, with new empirical data. It is not a new type of temporal relation that has been discovered in the course of research. This suggests the term "tenseless relations" is supposed to replace existing terminology and facilitate a more accurate, more correct description of familiar phenomena. Perhaps that's why thinkers working on the metaphysics of time during the first half of the twentieth century, tenseless theorists such as Russell, Ayer, Goodman, and Quine, were united in regarding the term "tenseless relations," not as an addition, but as a replacement, as belonging to a theory whose terms would, ideally, replace those elements of ordinary language that were deemed to be defective—or even as belonging to an "ideal language" that would, in principle, replace ordinary language altogether. Thus, early versions of the tenseless view were *reductive*, consisting of attempts to eliminate tense, in principle at least, from language and thought. Various "translation manuals" of tensed sentences into tenseless ones that were taken to mean the same were suggested for that purpose. For example, in *The Structure of Appearance*, Goodman (1951, 295) writes:

The "past," "present," and "future" name no times. Rather the "is past at," the "is present at" and the "is future at" are tenseless two-place predicates that may respectively be translated by the tenseless predicates "is earlier than," "is at," and "is later than."

On this suggestion, "Kennedy's assassination is now past," means the same as "Kennedy's assassination is earlier than the utterance of this sentence (or the tokening of this thought)."

There seems to be much sense in the eliminative/reductive approach. If the world is tenseless, why shouldn't language be tenseless as well? After all, we desire and expect language to fit reality, and ordinarily we also assume that it does. We ordinarily think of language as capturing things as they are, most of the time, at least. Why should it radically and persistently diverge from reality in connection with time? In science, the notion that language faithfully corresponds to reality is well established. We replace "phlogiston" with "oxygen" and add "neutrino" to our vocabulary because science gives us grounds for believing there are such things as oxygen and neutrinos whereas there is no such thing as phlogiston. Similarly, if there are no such things as tensed relations, if, that is, the world consists of purely tenseless relations, an ideal language should likewise be purely tenseless.

We say "an ideal language" because we may accept that, for reasons of convenience, language may locally diverge from the way things are. We say, for example, that the sun "rises" and "sets," although it would be more accurate to speak in this connection of the Earth's rotation around a fixed sun. The point is that, in principle at least, language *should be able* to provide faithful descriptions of the states of affairs we wish to depict. This is not a marginal demand. It is not merely something to aspire to. From a certain perspective, it is imperative that language be able to do so: a reality that cannot, even in principle, be captured in language cannot be captured in thought either, and so could not be the subject of any theory. I believe this is the real reason why thinkers like Russell, Quine, and Goodman insisted on "translation manuals" that reduced tensed utterances to tenseless ones, thereby facilitating a language tailored for reality.

Let us remark, in passing, that the friendly term "translation manuals" is somewhat misleading, misleading in the way that calling prison a "correctional institution" is. A translation usually *imports* a thought *into* a language which we command, thus enabling us to understand something we do not. The above "translation manuals," in contrast, were conjured up in order to translate something, namely, tense, away, to *export* it *out* of any language we might possess. Their function was not to introduce us to a foreign language, but to make a metaphysical picture palatable, despite its blunt conflict with the native tongue we already understand and depend on. They were not designed to enrich language, but to correct it, cleanse it, as it were, from its ubiquitous tenses.

However, despite the stock and effort invested in these "translation manuals," further work soon proved their inadequacy as means for tenselessly handling tense. A clear presentation of the failure of these manuals is given, somewhat ironically, by Mellor, who, in the course of his defense of the tenseless view, establishes that tensed sentences *cannot* be replaced by tenseless ones. This contention breaks down into two claims: that no tenseless sentence can constitute a translation for a tensed sentence; and that tensed sentences are indispensable. The second thesis is needed to answer those who might hope that, even if tensed sentences are irreducible, they can nevertheless be done away with altogether.

The first step toward realizing the impossibility of translating tensed sentences into tenseless ones is noting that tokens of tensed sentences do not have the same truth conditions as any tenseless sentence that is a candidate to be their translation. Consider a token of the tensed sentence "The lecture is beginning now." Let us call this token T. It is true if and only if it is tokened—uttered, read, thought—(more or less) at the moment the lecture is beginning. This tenseless condition, consisting of the temporal relation between the beginning of the lecture and the tokening of T, is, according to tenseless theorists, the condition on which T is true and to which T's meaning is related. If any tenseless sentence can serve as a translation of T, that is, can have the same meaning it has, it is the sentence that describes this tenseless condition, namely, something like "The tokening of T, and the beginning of the lecture are cotemporal; they occur at the same time." Let us call a token of this sentence S. Now, whereas the truth of T depends on when it is tokened, S is true (or false) regardless of when it is tokened. The date of the tokening, the token's location in time, is part of the state of affairs on which T would be true. But this fact, the token's location in time, is immaterial when it comes to S's truth. So the two tokens do not have the same truth conditions, and as Mellor (1981, 74) says, "two sentences can hardly mean the same if, as here, they are true in quite different circumstances."

It might be instructive to repeat this argument without appealing to the somewhat controversial association of meanings with truth conditions. If you wonder when the lecture is about to begin, T, but not S, can provide you with the information you need. If in response to the question "When does the lecture begin?" you are given a token of S, namely, "The token-ing of T, 'The lecture is beginning now,' and the beginning of the lecture are cotemporal," you will still not know when to show up: the response does not say anything about which tokening of T it is referring to. Say the response is the simpler "The lecture is beginning at the same time in which you are hearing this sentence." You might still be unsure, for it might not be clear which sentence the word "this" in the response refers to (imagine the response is given to you by a foreigner whom you suspect has not yet mastered verb conjugation and might be using the present tense but is in fact talking about a sentence you heard an hour ago). Of course, the context may be one that makes it unequivocally clear that the phrase refers to the sentence being uttered *now*, but in that case the response is in effect tensed. Perhaps the tenseless response is simply: "The lecture is beginning at 6:00 PM." Again, this cannot serve as a substitute for T, for it is useless unless you know what the time is *now*, that is, unless you employ it in conjunction with explicitly tensed information.

The point is that "no sentence could possibly mean the same as another if, as here, it cannot be used at all as the other one standardly is" (Mellor 1981, 75). Suppose John needs to take a medication at 1:00 o'clock in the afternoon. If a reliable source—his wristwatch, the radio, and so forth— provides him with a token of the tensed sentence "It is now 1:00 o'clock in the afternoon," he will be able to take his medication on time. Other-wise, he can only try to guess the right moment. Obviously, if all he is pro-vided with is a token of a tenseless sentence of the kind we have considered as a possible translation, he will not know when to take his medication—

tenseless sentences say that at 1:00 o'clock in the afternoon it is 1:00 o'clock, but not whether it is 1:00 o'clock *now*, which is what John needs to know. Since no tenseless sentence can be used for the same end as "It is now 1:00 PM," no tenseless sentence can translate it. In general, tensed sentences have daily uses that cannot be fulfilled by any tenseless sentences. Thus, no matter how loosely the relation between use and meaning is construed, in light of such examples, we must conclude with Mellor that tensed sentences cannot be matched with tenseless sentences that have the same meaning.

This also shows that tensed sentences are indispensable—to act successfully we must have tensed beliefs. To take his medication on time, John needs to know what time it is now, that is, have a tensed belief of the form "It is now. . . ." Insofar as we act in the world, the success of our actions depends in part on our possession of such tensed beliefs. Mellor's arguments to this effect seem fairly straightforward and incontestable. That is why attempts to formulate and defend the tenseless view by demonstrating the reducibility and/or eliminability, in principle, at least, of tensed sentences were doomed from the outset.[9]

For our present purposes, the consequence we need is that "tenseless relations" does not replace any existing vocabulary. Our language and thought are inevitably and thoroughly tensed. But the question of "replacement" is not thereby settled. For, as noted above, "tenseless relations" is not an addition to our vocabulary either; it does not augment it in the way that, say, "neutrino" does, denoting a new phenomenon, object, or property. Rather, it denotes facts we already know how to refer to.

Indeed, the specialized language of metaphysics is distinctly *unlike* that of science, precisely in that it neither replaces nor supplements existing vocabulary. But then, if we do not find the term "tenseless relations" alongside our familiar terms, and not instead of some of them, where do we find it? The answer is that its appearances are confined to contexts involving *philosophical explanations*. Here the term *can* be said to replace other terms. For, if prior to the appearance of the tenseless theory tensed truths are accounted for by tensed relations, in the new theory tensed sentences are given their meaning and truth-values by purely tenseless relations. Thus, in the explanations of tensed phenomena and beliefs that are offered by the tenseless theory, which, of course, shuns tensed relations or tensed facts, the terms "tensed relations" and "tensed facts" are replaced by "tenseless relations." In Mellor's words, tensed facts are "traded in" (1998, 23) for tensed truths, which are grounded in purely tenseless relations and nothing else.

So far, so good. But, reverting again to one of the above analogies, let us note our peculiar situation: we're like someone who, having discovered that combustion does not involve phlogiston but rather a substance she dubs "oxygen," renounces phlogistic chemistry, but is nevertheless unable to cease speaking of combustion in phlogistic-chemistry terms. Whenever she speaks and thinks of combustion (in our case, of time) it is always in phlogistic (tensed) terms. This awkwardness is not a mere curiosity. It is indicative of the flaws that will ultimately compel us to denounce the tenseless theory as untenable. We start uncovering these flaws with a closer look at the above "trade-in" of facts for truths ("facts" will be used freely, to denote whatever enters into the specification of truth conditions, and will thus include actual as well as possible, and even impossible facts; the important facts for us will consist of various kinds of temporal relations).

The "trade-in," we already know, is executed by means of the token-reflexive account: the condition to which the meaning and truth of "it is now t" are attached is not that it is now t, but that the sentence is tokened at t. The *belief* that it is now t is retained, and continues to be expressed by the true sentence "it is now t," but the *fact* that it is now t is discarded. It *can* be discarded, because it is no longer needed. The only function it fulfilled—constituting a truth maker for the sentence "it is now t"—is now satisfied by the tenseless fact that the sentence is tokened at t. In terms of truth conditions, we no longer need the tensed condition that it is now t because the truth-value and meaning of the *belief* that it is now t can be given by the tenseless condition that the belief is formed at t.

Plainly, the idea that tensed relations can be rendered redundant by replacing them with tensed truths turns on the distinction between facts and truths. Now, there is a perfectly innocent and ordinary sense in which events are distinct from the sentences with which we think and speak about them. When in court the witness testifies "I was at home when he was murdered," no difficulty arises in distinguishing this statement from the state of affairs it is about, which is not part of language at all. Like-wise, we can distinguish between chemical facts and the truths of chem-istry, between the fact that water consists of H_2O molecules and the true sentence "Water consists of H$_2$O molecules"; or between the fact that Kennedy was assassinated in 1963 and the sentence "Kennedy was assassinated in 1963." These are instances of an ordinary distinction between facts and truths.

But in none of these cases does a question of a "trade-in" come up. We cannot, and do not wish to, enact a "trade-in" between these facts and the true sentences that state them. This is precisely the reason we call the distinction between facts and truths in such cases "ordinary." We ordinarily recognize facts, and the sentences with which we refer to and/or describe them; and in our conception and dealings with the world we have use of, and want to preserve, both the facts and the sentences. If a "trade-in" *is* at issue, then we are no longer on ordinary grounds. The purpose of a trade-in is to bring about the realization that some things we thought were facts are not, to reclassify some items that were held to be facts as beliefs. Paraphrasing Mellor, the point of the trade-in is replacing something where it belongs—in our heads.[10] Obviously for such a trade-in to accomplish its purpose the items being traded must correspond to "reality" on the one hand, and to "what goes on inside our heads" on the other. And these latter terms, used in this way, are no longer ordinary but are the products of a philosophical position which is wedded to weighty metaphysical assumptions. So the dichotomy Mellor invokes is not the innocuous distinction between "facts" and "truths" it at first appears to be.

Mellor needs to provide a justification for treating tense separately, for "metaphysicalizing" the tensed-fact/tensed-truth dichotomy and setting it apart from other, ordinary instances of the fact/truth distinction. He has to say why tensed relations can be "traded in" and eliminated by the invocation of this distinction, whereas no one would dream of trading in chemical, historical, or, for that matter, tenseless facts, in this way. Why are tensed relations done away with and all other facts left unharmed? The reason he seems to give is, as stated above, that, contrary to these other cases, tensed relations are dispensable: tenseless relations can do their job and constitute truth conditions for tensed sentences. Not that tenseless sentences can replace tensed sentences—as we saw above they do not have the same meaning. But tenseless sentences describe tenseless conditions on which tensed sentences are true and to which their meanings are related. In Mellor's words, the fact that tenseless sentences cannot replace any tensed sentences does not stop those [tenseless sentences] giving their meanings [the meanings of tensed sentences]. To know that . . . for any B-time t "It is now t" is true at t and only at t, is to know just what those sentences mean. Given just this knowledge, we can produce and understand tokens of these A-sentences anywhere and at any time, and distinguish them from tokens of any other A-sentences whose different [truth conditions] we also know. (1998, 62)

(The B-time of an event is the date on which it occurs. Thus, by giving the B-times of events we show how much earlier or later than each other they are, that is, we give the "tenseless relations" between them. A-times of events tell us where with respect to the present events are located, that is, they give their "tensed relations." A-sentences report A-times.)[11]

Let us take stock of what we have so far. Tenseless beliefs do not replace tensed beliefs, and tenseless truths do not replace tensed truths. But the term "tenseless relations" does eliminate and replace the term "tensed relations" in the context of philosophical explanations, for, according to the tenseless view, there are no tensed relations. Tensed truths are retained, tensed relations are discarded. The elimination is carried out by means of the token-reflexive account, which substitutes tenseless relations for tensed ones in accounting for the meaning and truth of tensed sentences. Finally, tenseless sentences, which describe the relevant tenseless facts, "give" tensed sentences their meaning and truth-value. Let us proceed.

There is, according to the above exposition, a clear asymmetry between tensed sentences and tenseless sentences. Both are *given* their meaning and truth-value through truth conditions, but truth conditions are given *only* by tenseless sentences. How are truth conditions "given" by tenseless sentences? It seems, simply by being described by them. By describing them, a sentence "giving" truth conditions can inform a listener of the conditions on which a given sentence is true (or false). Supposedly, anyone that understands a sentence that "gives" truth conditions can understand the sentence the meaning of which is "given" by these truth conditions, and conversely, to understand a sentence is to understand the sentence that "gives" its truth conditions. If this is so, then the asymmetry between tenseless sentences that also "give" truth conditions, and tensed sentences that only "get" them, is crucial.

To see this, let's turn to the example from the passage quoted above, and let "S" denote a hypothetical token of "It is now t." A token of the tenseless sentence "TL," "'S' is tokened at t," "gives" the tenseless conditions on which "*S*" is true: "It is now *t*" is true if, and only if, it is tokened at *t*, that is, "*S*" is true if, and only if *TL*. What are the truth conditions of a token of "*TL*"? It too is true if and only if "*S*" is tokened at *t*: "*TL*" is true if and only if *TL*. Thus both "*S*" and "*TL*" are true if and only if *TL*. In Mellor's jargon, "*TL*" "gives" its own truth conditions, as well as those of "*S*."

We now ask: do "*S*" and "*TL*" have the same truth conditions? Yes and no. Yes, in that "*TL*" describes the tenseless condition to which the truth-value and meaning of *both* "*S*" and "*TL*" are attached. No, because "*TL*" makes reference to the time at which "*S*" is tokened, but not to the time of the tokening of "*TL*" itself. So although "*TL*" describes the tenseless condition to which the meanings of both sentences are attached, this condition stands in different relations to each—it includes the time of tokening of one but not of the other. These temporal relations figure in the truth condition of each token, and since they are different in each case, "*S*" and "*TL*" do not, in this respect, have the same truth conditions. This difference manifests itself in that whereas "*S*" is true if and only if it is tokened at *t*, a token of "*TL*," if true, is true regardless of when it is tokened. That is why "*S*" and "*TL*" do not have the same meaning.

Meaning is related to understanding, and this difference in meaning induces a difference in what understanding consists in in each case. Understanding consists, in part, in possessing the ability to use a sentence correctly, and in particular, in being able to specify the conditions on which it can be tokened truthfully, in being able to give its truth conditions. These, on Mellor's view, are always tenseless conditions. In the case of tenseless sentences, they themselves describe their own truth conditions. For example, as noted, "*TL*" gives its own truth conditions—"*TL*" is true if and only if *TL*. And to understand "*TL*" is to know that if true, it is true regardless of when it is uttered. For tensed sentences the situation is different. They do not give truth conditions, and in particular do not give their own truth conditions. Their truth conditions are given rather by token-reflexive tenseless sentences. Since these latter tenseless sentences contain the information concerning when the tensed sentences can be uttered truthfully, understanding a tensed sentence "*S*" requires, on this picture, (at least tacit) knowledge of the form "'*S*' is true if and only if *TL*."

Let us, then, imagine a speaker, Helen, who has the ability to make her tacit knowledge explicit, and let us consider a sentence in Helen's idiolect, say, "It is raining now." Her understanding of this sentence consists in part in knowing when it can be tokened truthfully. How can she make this knowledge explicit? She cannot invoke Tarski's "convention T" and give the requisite specification by stating that it can be tokened truthfully if and only if it is raining now, for this does not describe the sentence's tenseless truth conditions. On Mellor's picture, a proper specification of the conditions under which it can be truthfully uttered would be: "'It is raining now' is true if and only if it is tokened at a time at which it is raining." And Helen would have to use this tenseless sentence if she wished to make her understanding of "It is raining now" explicit. The tenseless sentence "gives" (i.e., describes) the truth condition, which "gives" the meaning of "It is raining now." When fleshed out, this is what the idea that tensed sentences are "given" their meaning by tenseless sentences that describe their truth conditions comes to: grasping the meaning of a tensed sentence presupposes the ability to think the tenseless thought (or at least to have the tenseless tacit belief) that describes its truth conditions.

This fits in well with the picture Mellor is working with. For Mellor, directly experiencing tenseless relations, for example, perceiving the thunder succeed the lightening, is an integral part of the mechanism by which we come to understand tenseless sentences. We directly perceive precedence, that is, tenseless relations, and through these experiences we directly acquire an understanding of the sentences that describe the relations experienced—what is experienced is what is described. When a tenseless sentence says that things are thus and so, the meaning and truth of what it says are fixed by things *being* thus and so. There is no gap: the tenseless relations that *TL* describes *are* the conditions on which it is true and to which its meaning is attached. In contrast, when a tensed sentence says that things are thus and so, it is *not* their being thus and so that establishes its meaning and truth, for it speaks of tensed relations, of which there are none. Here there is a gap between what the sentence says and the conditions that give it meaning. And we need to hook up with what gives it meaning before we can understand what it says. Thus, the gap needs to be filled in, mediated, by beliefs about the conditions that endow the tensed sentence with its meaning, that is, by the beliefs that would be expressed, if made explicit, by the tenseless sentences that give these conditions.

Adapting one of Wittgenstein's mechanical images for our purposes may help illustrate the point. Tenseless and tensed sentences can be likened to teeth of gearwheels that share the same axis, rotating together. Only the teeth of the tenseless wheel, however, mesh with how things are, with reality. The teeth of the tensed wheel are not designed to do so; there is nothing in reality they can latch on to. They get motion (meaning and truth) by virtue of their wheel's being on the same axis with the tenseless wheel, which is rotated, through the perfect, gapless fit that exists between its teeth and reality. Because the meanings of tenseless, but not of tensed sentences, attach "directly" to the conditions that endow sentences with meaning, tenseless conditions cannot be "traded in" for truths, whereas tensed conditions can and ought to be.

The upshot of all this is that, although tensed sentences cannot be reduced, or translated, into tenseless sentences, they are nonetheless parasitic on beliefs expressed by tenseless sentences, and this, we saw, entails that an understanding of tensed sentences presupposes an ability to have tenseless beliefs, beliefs which, were they made explicit, would be expressed by tenseless sentences. It is this difference between tensed sentences and tenseless ones that enables Mellor to treat the fact/truth distinction as "ordinary" in the tenseless case, and as "metaphysical" in the tensed case. Thus, "trading in" tensed relations for tensed truths while retaining tenseless relations is facilitated for Mellor by a theory of understanding that, in the above manner, imposes a hierarchy that distinguishes tenseless from tensed sentences.

However, this system (which, to be sure, only concerns Mellor's claim that tensed relations are redundant, not his argument against their reality), is quite evidently question begging: tensed relations are assumed to be inferior, not to play any role in our understanding, and on the basis of this assumption are then gotten rid of. The claim that, in the case of tense, the fact/truth dichotomy is not the ordinary one, is justified by the claim that tensed relations are dispensable; but we now see that the demonstration of their dispensability, via the token-reflexive account, assumes that tensed relations play no role in our understanding. This is blatantly circular.

Even if this circularity is somehow tolerated, the above analysis of our understanding is untenable. Indeed, from within the tenseless picture it is natural enough—something has to carry, as it were, the meaning from conditions that are tenseless to a sentence that is tensed, a task that only tenseless thoughts (or tacit tenseless beliefs) can fulfill. But, whichever way we understand notions like "tacit knowledge" or "tacit belief," this much is clear: if we do have the tacit knowledge that a tenseless state of affairs (the one "given" by "*TL*") is the truth condition for "*S*," then it must be the case that we *could* grasp, for example, the tenseless sentence "*TL*," "'*S*' is tokened at *t*," prior to and independently of our understanding "*S*," "It is now *t*." And this cannot be the case. The reason goes back to the ineliminability and indispensability of tense.

Consider again the sentence "Kennedy was assassinated in 1963." To understand it—for such a sentence to transmit knowledge—one must know what "1963" refers to. It is not enough to know that these numerals indicate a counting that starts at a certain chosen point in time, that 1,963 years separate between that point of origin and the assassination. This tenseless fact is a useless fact to anyone who does not know when the point of origin is with respect to the *present*. Attributing an understanding of a certain symbol to someone—a word, a number, a sentence—requires, at the very least, that that person be able to use it for various elementary, modest ends, and most ordinary uses of dates are tied up with knowing the *present* date. Even if to the question "When were you born?" John correctly answers "1960," he cannot be regarded as someone who understands that he was born in 1960 if he does not know how to answer the question: "How old are you?" or if he thinks that 1960 is in the future. If I do not understand that my appointment with the dentist that is scheduled for March 3 is to take place next week, seven days from *today*, then I do not really understand the use of a calendar.

There are cases in which we happen not to know the present date, or are mistaken about it, and fail to act successfully. Of course, if my calendar indicates that my dentist appointment is scheduled for the third, and I show up on the fourth by mistake, that does not mean that I do not understand the use of a calendar. Nor does it tell against one's mastery of language if from being told, upon arriving in some foreign country, that the date of a festival which is held there once every hundred years is 45454 according to the local count, one fails to learn whether one will live to witness it or not. It may take the newcomer some time to figure out what the present year is according to the local calendar. But if one *never* knows the present date, then one can never use information about the dates of events to act successfully, and there is no license to attribute to such a person an understanding of sentences that fix the dates of events. It is true that, as Mellor says, anyone who knows that "It is now t" is true during and only during t knows what "It is now . . ." means. But only someone who already knows what "It is now . . ." means can know that "It is now t" is true during and only during t. In general, an understanding of a sentence of the form "B occurs at t_1" depends on understanding sentences of the form "It is now t_2."

Thus, it cannot be that being able to think tenseless thoughts facilitates understanding tensed sentences, for it presupposes it. The processes of acquiring tenseless concepts and tensed concepts go hand in hand; they are inseparable. Moreover—and this is the real point I'm driving at—tenseless and tensed concepts are not even notionally separable. Rather, they are fused with each other, with no sharp line, or even a fuzzy border, dividing them. Tensed concepts figure in every occasion that tenseless ones do, and vice versa. Mastery of the uses and senses of so-called tenseless sentences is both a prerequisite and a consequence of mastering the use of tensed sentences, and vice versa. We are taught what "It is now . . ." means when we are told, for example, "It is now raining, and what you are hearing now is the sound of thunder." And we learn what "e occurs at t" means by being told, for example, "Your birthday is in May, and it is on the same date every year," or "Thunder comes after lightning." But we need to have some grasp of temporal succession to understand sentences about the present; and vice versa, we need to have some mastery of tense to understand succession. To understand the tensed sentence "What you are hearing now is the sound of thunder" we need to know that the explanation refers to the sound that is simultaneous, or cotemporal, with it. And we are made to understand the succession report "Thunder comes after lightning" on occasions in which we can associate these words with sounds and sights that are experienced *now*.

If this is correct, that means that we never encounter purely tenseless relations. All factual utterances are always infused with tense, which, again, is exactly what Mellor's arguments for the ineliminability of tense purported to show. And of course, if we never encounter purely tenseless relations, we cannot just help ourselves to the notion of "tenseless relations," not even for theoretical purposes.

The problem with the token-reflexive account is that, contrary to the supposition of those who rely on it, the sentences and relations employed in handling tensed relations are *not* themselves purely tenseless. It is true that "Today's date is February 15, 2007" can be explained by saying that the date of the tokening of this sentence is February 15, 2007. But that is only because the context makes it clear that the phrase "this sentence" refers to the sentence tokened *now*. Before the "tenseless" formulation is "tense-ized" by the context, it cannot do anything by way of clarifying the original sentence. Simply employing auxiliary pointing devices, such as replacing "this" with "this very" ("The tokening of this very sentence is February 15, 2007"), using italics ("The tokening of *this very sentence* is February 15, 2007"), and so forth, will not help. Unless the context makes it clear that the sentence in question is the one tokened *now*, it will remain undecided which sentence is being referred to by the phrase "*this very sentence*." It is not entirely inconceivable that to the question "Which sentence exactly do you have in mind?" someone will answer "The one she spoke during last year's meeting." True, it is unlikely, but then neither is it very likely that today's date be stated by means of the phrase "the date this very sentence is uttered on is so and so," rather than by the ordinary "today's date is so and so."

Again, the following exchange could certainly be a segment of the explanation one gets from the guide at the Kennedy Memorial Library: "On the date of the utterance of *this very sentence* begins the most important period of Kennedy's presidency." "Which sentence do you mean?" asks a visitor, who was distracted for a moment and did not hear the sentence. The guide repeats the famous: "Ich bin ein Berliner."

In sum, to the extent that token-reflexive formulations can explain tensed sentences, that is because *the context makes them tensed themselves*. So, even though the token-reflexive account seems to flesh out in tenseless terms what a tensed sentence says, its ability to do so depends on the context providing the tensed information conveyed by the tensed sentence. Thus, again, understanding a tenseless explanation turns on already possessing tensed language.

In ordinary language this mix manifests itself in the presence of tense in sentences describing relations of succession, precedence, and simultaneity, relations that tenseless theorists regard as quintessentially "tenseless." To return to the example with which we opened this section, we said that the American Revolution preced*ed* the French Revolution, and later mentioned that Kennedy *was* assassinat*ed* in 1963, or that it is raining at the time in which this very sentence *is being uttered*. Tense figures even in seemingly tenseless chronologies of the form:

1712—J.-J. Rousseau is born in Geneva.

1742—Rousseau moves to Paris.

1750—Rousseau's "First Discourse" wins the contest of the Academy of Dijon.

Though it is repressed here, as explained a few paragraphs back, tense does come into play in the use of signs such as "1712."

We thus conclude that any attempt to isolate purely tenseless relations, described by purely tenseless sentences, without recourse to and independently of any terms that are (perhaps only tacitly) tensed, cannot succeed. The meanings of temporal concepts, the process of acquiring temporal notions and of mastering their use, just do not exhibit any discernible elements, any distinctions, to which the terms "tenseless" and "tensed" can be made to correspond.[12] With tense thus not eliminable from language, the notion of "tenseless relations" remains empty. There is not one fact we can point to as truly tenseless. It is not that in addition to occurring in 1963, Kennedy's assassination is also past. That it occurred in 1963 cannot be separated, not even notionally, from the fact that it is past, insofar as our understanding is concerned. And to speak about that which is beyond our understanding is to speak of we-know-not-what.

This is a discovery well worth reaching. It runs in the face of one of the basic assumptions thinkers about time, tensed as well as tenseless, take for granted: that for events to be related tenselessly simply means for them to be before or after or cotemporal with one another. Such relations, we are told, are easily recognized: their conspicuous hallmark is that sentences describing them are true, if true, regardless of when they are tokened. Indeed, "The year of Kennedy's assassination is 1963" is supposedly always true, for, supposedly, there is nothing tensed about this sentence. Supposedly, the "is" in it is "purely tenseless." But I have argued that the term "1963" is not. So, once again, no sentence is "purely tenseless."[13]

Earlier in this section we discussed Mellor's arguments against the previous, reductive and eliminative, versions of the tenseless theory. We then turned to a detailed study of Mellor's own use of the token-reflexive account. What this study revealed is that Mellor's theory of meaning, which portrays the meaning and our understanding of tensed sentences as parasitic on tenseless ones, is, in the end, guilty of the same faults he finds in the work of his predecessors. Purportedly, his theory is nonreductive, and allows that tense cannot be eliminated from language. However, it eliminates tense from our metaphysical accounts, substituting tenseless relations for tensed relations. Plainly, this move can be effective only if the notion "tenseless relations" is not empty. But, we just saw that, if tense is not eliminable from language, the notion *is* empty. Thus, relying on this notion is a roundabout way of pointing to a tenseless language, a language from which tense has been eliminated—only such a language can contain purely tenseless sentences, sentences that describe purely tenseless relations.[14]

The main goal of this section was to answer the question: can the tenseless theory of time constitute a context that gives sense to the irregular uses of "real" that appear in the formulation of its tenets? That the answer to this question is negative must by now be clear. The tenseless theory of time dispenses of tensed relations by means of the token-reflexive theory of meaning, which, in turn, assumes the existence of tenseless relations. With the demise of the notion of tenseless relations, we are left without the theoretical setup from which, we speculated, the divergent uses of "real" might have derived their sense. The term "tenseless relations" proves, upon inspection, to be radically unlike scientific novel terms such as "oxygen" and "neutrino." The latter occur in theories that offer, among other things, new observations and predictions. "Tenseless relations" is, in contrast, a latent term, whose existence is confined to a theory it is supposed to sustain, but which itself is sustained by nothing. As such, it cannot be relied on to support novel uses of old words.

This conclusion will prove fruitful when, in the next chapter, we turn to study the main conceptual puzzles time gives rise to.

4.4 Delusions of Illusions

Alongside and closely related to the idea of "tenseless relations" resides another, no less popular myth: the myth that tense is an illusion. This myth needs to be dispelled as well. We already quoted Einstein's assertion that "the distinction between past, present and future is merely a stubbornly persistent illusion." Without doubt, this stamp of approval from such a supreme authority contributed to the entrenchment of the myth.

What is rarely mentioned is that this sentence appears, not in one of Einstein's scientific or philosophical works, but in a letter of condolence he sent the widow of an acquaintance, hoping to lift her spirits by suggesting that, in a manner of speaking, past things and persons are not really past.[15] This fact does not prove, of course, that Einstein did not truly believe that tense was an illusion. But it raises a question about what he really took his words to mean. At any rate, as we shall now see, the thesis that tense and time's passage are an illusion is unfounded.

The problem with the notion that tense is an illusion is not so much how to believe it as how to understand it. But, like the unworkability of "tenseless relations," the difficulties are not apparent. To uncover them, we need to examine more closely what kind of illusion tense is alleged to be. In the previous section we surveyed arguments establishing the inescapability of tense as a mode of experience, language, and thought. Our cognition, we saw, is inevitably and indispensably tensed: if we think about it, we cannot help recognizing that events have tensed temporal locations, that they are past, present, or future. John is contemplating the setting of the sun. He might not be paying attention to when, in tensed terms, it is happening. But if he is, then he cannot help thinking that the sun is setting *now*. According to the tenseless view, however, there are no tensed facts, "nothing in reality is past, present, or future" (Mellor 1998, 47), and in particular the setting of the sun is not past, present, or future. So John is not, and cannot be regarded as perceiving a tensely located event: how can one perceive tensely located events if there are no such things?

That is not to say that perception is infallible; it is only to insist that one cannot perceive, and cannot be taken to perceive, what is not there to be perceived. One might think one is perceiving a pink elephant, but if there is no pink elephant in the vicinity then that person is making a mistake, or hallucinating, or the like. Looking up at the night sky, John is thrilled by the sight of a shooting star—he is sure he is seeing a speck of dust burning as it enters the Earth's atmosphere. Unbeknownst to him, however, the object that he sees burning through the atmosphere is not a speck of dust but an old Soviet satellite spiraling down to oblivion. Can he still be regarded as someone who has perceived a speck of dust? No. He thought he saw one, and perhaps he still does, but he is wrong. In the same manner, according to tenseless theorists, if John thinks of the setting of the sun as a tensed event then he is wrong. Of course, he is not to be blamed: tenses are "a way we have of locating events in time; a compelling way, indeed, *which we could not do without*, but not the way things are in reality"(Mellor 1998, 15, my italics).

By the lights of the tenseless view, then, our position in the world is such that we cannot help perceiving events as tensely located though they are not—if he attends to its tensed attributes, John will inevitably come to believe that the sunset he is enjoying is a present event, though it is not. That is the right description of John's state. Or more precisely, of the prephilosophical John. For (like Ivan Denisovitch—see above), if John has studied the tenseless view, and has been persuaded by the arguments, then he surely no longer thinks of the events he perceives as present events, for he now *knows* that they are not. Previously, he thought of the sunset as occurring *now*. Now he no longer thinks it does, only that that is how matters *appear* to him.

But now a serious problem arises. Can it still be maintained that tense is an inescapable mode of John's perception? I think not. Tense was a mode of his perception not in that he perceived tensely located events; for that to be the case the events he perceived would have *to be* tensely located, which presumably they are not. Rather, tense was a mode of his perception in that he *mistakenly thought* of the events he perceived as being tensely located. Once he no longer thinks of them as such, tense ceases to be a mode of his thinking in the one and only sense in which it was.

Think of memory. Ruth recollects the day Kennedy was assassinated—the horrifying pictures on TV, the shock. That event is now long past, or at least that is how she thinks of it. But she is wrong; she is not remembering a past event, for events are not past (or present or future), she just remembers them *as* past. However, once she becomes convinced that there are no tensed facts, then she no longer thinks of the event as past—she now knows it is not. "Though I inevitably remember things as past," she thinks to herself, "I know that it is only in my thoughts that that is how they appear to be, while in reality, which my thoughts are about, they are not. If 'pastness' belongs to anything, it is to my memories, not to what I remember. So it is not accurate to say that tense is inescapable, for when I remember that horrid day, I no longer think of *it* as past."

Experience produces tensed beliefs. For example, an announcement over the station's loudspeakers can produce in the commuters' minds tokens of

"The train is leaving in two minutes." We saw that these beliefs are indispensable for successful action. Stripped of tensed content, descriptions such as "The train leaves at 2:04 PM" become empty. If one does not know what time it is *now*, this bit of "tenseless" information is useless, one will miss the train. But if, having been won over by the tenseless view, one knows that events are not tensely located, one cannot have beliefs about their tensed locations. One might unknowingly have wrong beliefs, but one cannot have beliefs that one knows are wrong. For example, one cannot both believe there are no tensed facts and also that "The train is leaving in two minutes" describes a fact about the tensed location of an event. So an adherent of the tenseless view cannot have beliefs about the tensed locations of events. At most, she will have second-order beliefs about some of her beliefs, namely, that they are tensed. That is exactly what studying the tenseless view is designed to bring about. It is supposed to alter our understanding of the nature of time, and the alteration consists precisely in our ceasing to regard events as tensely located, that is, in the elimination of our beliefs about the tensed location of events.

This, however, is not a position we can readily accept, for it clashes with a claim we have rehearsed more than enough, namely, that tense is inescapable in that we cannot help conceiving *events and objects themselves* as tensely located. Tense is not a skin that philosophical wiggling can shed from our experiences and beliefs. Quite the contrary, the assertion that tense is an inescapable mode of perceiving and thinking about events and objects describes a feature of our cognition which philosophical inquiry presupposes. To use an analogy mentioned by Mellor, some philosophers claim objects are colorless, but not one of them can help seeing the sky as blue (if it is daytime, that is, and there are no clouds, eclipses, sunglasses, etc.). No amount of theorizing can establish that we do not perceive objects *themselves* as colored, for speaking of objects as colored is part of the language and conceptual stock that makes theorizing about colors possible in the first place.

Similarly, we *do* experience and think of events *themselves* as tensely located. We think and speak of events we remember as themselves past. It's not my memory of the Hale-Bopp comet that I think of as past—I do the remembering in the present! It's the event of its passing near Earth that I inevitably and inescapably think of as past. It's not my hearing the clock-tower's bell chime that I think of as present; it's the chiming itself that is occurring now. And I think of my upcoming trip to Ireland as future, but not the state of anticipation I am in with respect to this trip, which obtains already in the present. In short, we cannot help conceiving of events as tensed any more than we can help seeing the sky as blue.

The acknowledgment that events are inescapably spoken of, thought of, and experienced as *themselves* tensely located cannot be squared with the tenseless dictum that reality is not tensed, a dictum that entails that tense is not an inescapable feature of reality—the philosophically enlightened John *knows* the sunset is not a tensely located event. To put it more strongly, the tenseless view is in a way self-refuting. For, there is a sense in which the claim that we inevitably cognize reality as tensed is not just an observation about our cognition, but is presupposed by the tenseless view. The fact that we apprehend reality as tensed is what makes the claim that reality is not tensed a meaningful one. The claim that space is tenseless is nothing more than an empty truism—no one writes books defending the tenseless view of space because we have no notion of what it would be for space to be tensed.[16] If the tenseless view of time is more than an empty truism, that is because time for us is patently tensed. But then the tense-less view presupposes what it denies: that tense is inescapable. It presup-poses it in that it takes its tenets to be more than hollow platitudes. And it denies it because, as we just saw, the distinction between "mental tensed time" and "actual tenseless time" is a gateway to actual tenseless time. In short, the tenseless view turns out to be an instrument by which we escape that which, *ex hypothesi*, is inescapable.

Here the tenseless theorist is likely to protest that the above argument misses a very simple point. According to her, before we study the tenseless view we do not distinguish between believing that things actually have a tensed location and thinking that that is only how things appear to us. We regard tensed beliefs as beliefs about the tensed locations of things, and we suppose that we experience, think, and speak of events as tensely located because they really are. The tenseless view changes our under-standing, and gets us to realize that things only *appear* to be tensely located. But then, says the tenseless theorist, the tenseless view, far from being in conflict with the assertion that tense is an inescapable mode of thought and speech, is all the more committed to it.

Furthermore, endorsing the view requires not renouncing tensed beliefs, only realizing that these concern the appearance of things rather than the way things really are. So the criticism made above, it might be complained, with its charge that the tenseless view divests us of our tensed beliefs, is misguided. All that tenseless theorists are claiming is that conceptual analysis teaches us that tenses cannot be real, that events are not really past, present, or future. Admittedly, we perceive events as though they are tensely located, and "we must think and speak as if there were [tensed facts]" (Mellor 1981, 78). But this is nothing but the way the inescapable, global illusion of tense manifests itself. Realizing this, we see that philosophical analysis is not a means of actually experiencing the tenseless reality that is beyond this illusion, only of inferring that *there is* such a reality.

It is like with other illusions, the rejoinder continues. On very hot sunny days roads look wet at a distance. And even if we know they are not, still, we cannot help seeing them as though they were spotted with puddles. But there is no mystery here. We know the road is dry, and can explain why it appears wet, by describing the effect the heat emitted from the road's surface has on the refraction index of the air right above the road, as a result of which light rays coming from the sun curve, and it appears as though the sun is reflected from a puddle. That is how illusions work—things appear different from the way they really are, and they continue to appear different even after we learn the truth of the matter. Of two lines of equal length, embedded in a certain geometrical configuration (the Müller-Lyer diagram, reproduced in figure 4.1), one looks longer than the other, and they continue to appear unequal in length even after it is verified that they are not. This fact does not make us suspect that perhaps their lengths are unequal after all; rather, it compels us to explain why they *appear* to be unequal.

Similarly with tense. Events do not have a tensed location, but they *appear* to be tensed, and they continue to appear tensed even when we discover, in this case through conceptual analysis, that they are not. This claim, insists the tenseless theorist, is entirely innocuous. Philosophizing does not open impossible channels of cognition, but it can modify and

Figure 4.1

correct our understanding of the mechanism and reality underlying our cognition. That is its purpose.

The reason this attempt to salvage the claim that tense is an illusion fails is that there is the following crucial difference between the case of tense and the case of ordinary illusions: in the case of ordinary illusions we can specify, and in fact attain, conditions under which our perception is veridical. It is only by reference to the way a truly wet road looks under veridical conditions that talk of a road *appearing* to be wet makes sense. Similarly, it is only owing to the fact that there are circumstances under which we can ascertain that the two lines in the Müller-Lyer diagram are equal in length, circumstances that equip us with the notion "equal in length," that we can so much as describe the diagram as a misleading *illusion*, as a situation in which the lines *appear* unequal though they are not. More generally, the word "illusion" designates a contrast between the way something looks under one set of circumstances, and the way it looks under different conditions, for example, between the way a patch of asphalt appears at a distance on a hot day, and the way it looks when observed from close by; or between the way two lines of equal length look when they are flanked by certain auxiliary lines, and the way they look outside of this configuration. Applications of the notion "illusion" make tacit use of two veridical perceptions: we invoke both (a memory of) a perception of a wet road and a perception of a dry road to describe both how the road looks—it looks wet, and how it really is—it is dry.

The hypothesis that experience, thought, and language may be systematically misleading is not new. However, veridical cases were always invoked in the course of raising it. Descartes assumed we knew what dreaming is when he put forth the possibility that what we take to be our waking experiences are in fact dreams. His hypothesis would have been patently unintelligible otherwise. Ayer had to presuppose that we have all seen genuinely bent sticks to so much as suggest that a straight stick immersed in a glass of water looks bent, that is, that the perception of a stick in water is, as he put it, "delusive."[17] These cases, as do cases involving illusions, evolve around a distinction between the way things appear and the way they are, a distinction that relies on the accessibility, in principle at least, of the way things really are—without such access the distinction could not be drawn, and the cases could not be described. Access to the way things really are is facilitated by veridical perceptions. Hence, someone who never enjoys veridical perceptions cannot be a victim of illusion either. The upshot of this is that the word "illusion" evokes (tacitly) conditions other than those that actually obtain when one is subject to the illusion, conditions in which one's perceptions are veridical.

But what could such conditions possibly be in the case of tense? The problem is that with tense we have no clue, we *cannot* have a clue, as to what conditions could be, other than those that obtain while one is subject to the illusion. Here we cannot draw the distinction between the way things *appear* under certain circumstances and the way they really are, because we cannot so much as conceive circumstances under which they would appear different from the way they *always* do, circumstances in which the illusion were somehow neutralized. In fact, the claim that tense is an illusion together with the claim that tense is inescapable tell us precisely that we cannot, under any circumstances, have access to veridical perceptions. But, as before, this conclusion is self-refuting: conceiving veridical perceptions as unattainable in principle nullifies the logical condition presupposed by any talk of illusion. Nontensed reality is the only source of terms required for describing how things are, a description that is a necessary backdrop against which how things appear can be labeled "an illusion." But if tense is an inescapable illusion, we never access this nontensed reality, and so are stripped of the condition that must obtain if we are to call tense "an illusion." So if tense is an inescapable illusion, we have no means for saying that it is.

Tenseless theorists help themselves to both ends of the stick: they acknowledge, and even insist, that tense is an inescapable mode of thought and experience, which veils tenseless reality from our cognition, and at the same time, they offer a theory that reveals the tenseless truth behind the veil. This cannot work. If tense is truly inescapable, then there is no way we can remove ourselves from our heads and take our inevitably tensed minds for a stroll in the forever hidden tenseless fields of reality. And if, on the other hand, we can understand that reality is tenseless, then tense is no longer inescapable. Either way, tense cannot be thought of as an illusion.

4.5   The Collapse of Dummett's Solipsism

We move on to the tensed theory. Here too we find that, owing to flaws in its internal structure, the theory cannot be relied on for providing meaning to the anomalous uses made of the word "real" in stating its tenets. We will first discuss Dummett's antirealism. We saw in section 3.2 that according to Dummett only present events and objects can figure in the truth conditions that determine the meanings and truth-values of all statements, including statements about future and past events and things. And we saw that this insistence secures the consistency of his view. However, as we shall now see, this manner of privileging the present, namely, tying the truth conditions of *all* statements to the present, makes *the very activity of uttering a statement*—indeed, the very activity of thinking—unintelligible.

Assume that in exactly nine month's time there will occur a solar eclipse. Then the sentence "In nine month's time there will occur a solar eclipse" is now true. "A statement is true only if there is something in virtue of which it is true," and in this case, on the view we are considering, this something cannot include the conditions that will obtain in nine month's time, namely, the occurrence of an eclipse, but only conditions that obtain in the *present*, for example, the present location of the sun, the moon and the planets, current maps of the solar system showing their previous locations, readings on computer screens, formulations of the laws of motion, and so on. On the basis of these, we can now predict that in nine month's time, when we look up at the sun, we shall see it eclipsed, and in virtue of them, assert that if we then state "The sun is eclipsed now," we shall utter a true statement. Again, the eclipse itself is not part of the conditions the meaning and truth of this last assertion, made in the present, and the subject of which is the future token, are attached to.

However, "the world changes," and with it also "that over which [we] quantify when [we] say 'There *is* something in virtue of which . . .'" (Dummett 1978, 373). So we can also think of this future token of "The sun is eclipsed now" in connection with the conditions that will obtain in nine month's time, that is, the sun's being eclipsed, and say that at that time this future token will be true in virtue of these future conditions, rather than in virtue of present conditions, as was just asserted is the case. There is no contradiction because, as discussed in detail in 3.2, in appealing to conditions that obtain now in saying that the token will be true, and in saying that it will be true in virtue of conditions that will obtain then, *two distinct notions of truth* are being employed.

Thus, we can say of a future token of "The sun is eclipsed now," to be uttered nine months from now, that it will be true, but attach to this assertion two different meanings, each corresponding to its own notion of truth, one attached to conditions that obtain now, the other to those that will obtain in nine month's time. Now, if we look at this last duplicity more closely, we see that it does not consist merely of two sets of conditions, but that concealed in it are two distinguishable meanings of the term "truth conditions." The reason is quite straightforward. In giving the future truth conditions on which a future token of "an eclipse is taking place now" will be true, we describe the *future* eclipse. At the same time, the pivotal claim of Dummett's view is that meaning and truth-values can depend only on what is available to us in the present, that is, that only *present* conditions, in the specification of which the future eclipse would not be mentioned, can figure as truth conditions.

The only way to reconcile the two claims, the claim that only present conditions are truth conditions, and the claim that future conditions will be truth conditions, is by allowing that the term "truth conditions" does not mean the same in each of these assertions. Just as, on Dummett's account, the notion of "truth" comes to bear a temporal index (see p. 54) so the notion "truth conditions" comes to bear a temporal index: "truth conditions$_1$" is associated with what is covered by the expression "That in virtue of which . . ." as it is used *now*; "truth conditions$_2$" is associated with what will be covered by the expression "That in virtue of which . . ." nine months from now. And, as in the case of "truth," the crucial point is that this distinction *itself*, between truth conditions$_1$ and truth conditions$_2$, is made in the present: it is connected to truth conditions$_1$. That is how all this fits with the antirealist's contention that only *present* conditions can be truth conditions.

That the word "true" can have distinguishable meanings is something that Dummett's text itself brings to our attention. But that this is the case also with the notion of "truth conditions" is never mentioned. There is a reason for this, which is that the distinction between truth conditions$_1$ and truth conditions$_2$ is one we simply do not know how to draw. Let us see why.

When Dummett's view was accused of being contradictory, of violating the truth-value link, his rebuttal consisted of pointing out that in the formulation of the alleged contradiction the word "true" is used twice, but that on these two occasions it means different things. Or, paraphrasing Dummett, that the word as it appears in one of these uses cannot be used to say what it says when it appears in the other. Now, when Dummett employs this distinction, and tells us that we cannot now mean by the word "true" what we will mean by it when we use it a year hence, he can specify the difference between a present use and a future use of the word by reference to the difference between the truth conditions each use is attached to: one notion of truth is attached to and derives its meaning from present conditions, and the other from conditions that will obtain in the future.

But this explication is not available to him in connection with the different uses of the term "truth conditions." Fleshing out this difference by referring back to the different uses of "truth" is blatantly circular: the different meanings of "truth" were given in terms of different truth conditions. Nor can he do so by appealing to the difference between present conditions and future conditions, because it is exactly the difference between the meaning of the term "truth conditions" as it is used in relation to present conditions, and its meaning when it is attached to future conditions, that he needs to flesh out. It is utterly unhelpful to describe, for example, the eclipse taking place now, and contrast it with the eclipse that is to take place in nine month's time, for that is simply to point to the difference between present and future conditions, not to explain what the difference consists in. When it comes to the term "truth conditions," there is nothing for Dummett to fall back on in expounding the difference in meaning between its use in relation to present conditions, and its use in relation to future conditions. The dichotomy between these two uses of "truth conditions" is simply not one that Dummett has provided us with means for drawing. But without this dichotomy, the basic tenet of the view, that only present conditions can figure in truth conditions, can no longer be stated, for, on pain of violating the truth-value link, it presupposes this dichotomy.

To be sure, this conclusion does not open the door for the realist to return with her charge of self-contradiction. By invoking the distinction between the different notions of "truth" that figure in her account the anti-realist can reject this charge. And our analysis accepts this distinction and hence is not directed at uncovering contradictions. What we do uncover is a further distinction, one underpinning the distinction between different notions of "truth," namely, the distinction between different notions of "truth conditions." And here, as we just saw, the issue is not consistency, but intelligibility—the inability to meaningfully express this distinction in language.

Could an antirealist reject the above train of reasoning, and deny that she must invoke two notions of "truth conditions" in order to defend her view? Not if she relies on Dummett's text. In Dummett's paper we find rather a confirmation that, indeed, one "cannot by any means at all now express" (1978, 373) what future tokens will express when they are tokened. Dummett says this about the phrase "absolutely true": of this phrase he says that it is impossible to now express the meaning one will attach to it in the future. But this problem is readily projected onto other terms, including the phrase "truth conditions." Dummett himself expands it to include the word "now": "I cannot now say by means of [the word "now"] what I will later be able to say by means of it" (ibid.). Thus, at the moment we cannot use a token of "a solar eclipse is occurring now" to say what we will be saying with a future token of "a solar eclipse is occurring now." In fact, we cannot now assign any meaning to this future token. "A solar eclipse is occurring now," thought of in relation to future conditions, is nothing but a string of marks on paper.

But then it must also be the case that when we say of a future eclipse that it will figure as the condition on which a future token of "a solar eclipse is occurring now" will be true, we are using the term "truth conditions" differently than when we assert that the eclipse taking place now is the condition on which a token of "a solar eclipse is occurring now" uttered now is true. In other words, we cannot now mean by "truth conditions" what we will mean by this phrase in the future. Otherwise, we *would* be able to say now what we will mean in the future when we utter a token of "the sun is eclipsed now." If the phrase "truth conditions" always meant the same, then we could say now that the future eclipse will figure as a condition on which future tokens will be true (or false), and mean by that precisely what we mean when we say of a present eclipse that it is the condition on which present utterances are true (or false), and so attach now the meaning and truth-value of a future token of "the sun is eclipsed now" to these future conditions.

Perhaps the point can be illuminated from a different angle. Note that truth conditions that are not present do not have *any* sentences attached to them, for the meaning and truth-values of *all* sentences are attached to present conditions. Saying that a future token of "a solar eclipse is occurring now" will be attached to future truth conditions is not the same as saying that there is a sentence whose truth-value is attached to conditions that are not present—the second assertion cannot be made sense of for, again, *all* sentences are attached to present conditions. But then what kind of *truth* conditions are these, if we cannot point to even one truth that is attached to them? Thus, in relation to future conditions, the words "truth conditions" are nothing but a string of marks.

Plainly, marks on paper are not something with which the phrase "truth conditions," used to denote present conditions, can be contrasted. For these strings of marks to constitute the other side of a dichotomy of *meanings*, we must *understand* what they say (Dummett himself repeatedly stresses that meaning and understanding are inextricable). And, without the "future side" there is nothing with which to contrast, in the form of a dichotomy, the materials of the present. We thus find that the antirealist's position assumes a dichotomy the stateability of which is prohibited by this very position. So the view is self-refuting. It invalidates its own tenets by stating them in a language that is undercut by those very tenets. It invokes a certain picture of reality—"a solipsism of the present moment"—but it does so with a language that would not be possible in this kind of reality—our language, to which we have no alternative.

It goes without saying that a view that is self-refuting is not one from which we can derive new meanings and uses for the word "real." In fact, the reasoning we've just been following can be used to underscore just how difficult it is to make sense of the idea that the present enjoys some "privileged reality" or "privileged ontological status." Let us return to the association made in section 3.2 (p. 49) between "truth conditions" (in the sense of "truth makers") and what is "real." We suggested there that the idea that *x* is "real" if and only if *x* can be a "truth condition" would seem to square well with the major themes of Dummett's position, even though he himself does not explicitly state it.

With this association in mind, the claim that only present conditions are truth conditions—Dummett's view—could be reformulated as saying that only present objects, events, state of affairs, and so on, are "real." But this assertion only begins to capture the special position of the present. For, bringing to bear the above conclusions, their implication is that we cannot even *think* of other times as *ever* being privileged in this way. We cannot say that the privilege that now holds with respect to the present held in the past with respect to conditions that are now past, or that in the future it will hold with respect to conditions that are now future, for the view does not allow us to call past or future conditions "truth conditions" in the same way we call present conditions "truth conditions," and so does not allow us to say that they are real in the same sense that, according to it, present conditions are real. We can say that future conditions *will be real* and that past ones *were real*, but our words do not have the same meanings they have when we assert that present objects and events are real. That is why it is apt to call this view "a solipsism of the present moment": only present conditions can truly be thought of as "real."

Dummett's own text (and, again, I mean primarily "The Reality of the Past") does not betray the radicalness of the views I have been arguing are enfolded in it. But here and there one runs into statements that resonate with the above. Thus, in a passage that was already partially quoted, Dummett says: "The antirealist takes more seriously the fact that we are immersed in time: being so immersed, we cannot frame any description of the world as it would appear to one who was not in time, but we can only describe it as it is, i.e., as it is now" (1978, 369). The way the world *is* is identified with the way it is *now*. If this is not an empty tautology ("the world as it is now = the world as it is now") then the phrase "The world as it is" must designate all that we can meaningfully think or speak of (and if you can't think or speak of it, than you can't whistle it either, to paraphrase Ramsey). Sure, we speak about the past and the future. But on the version of the tensed view we have attributed to Dummett, the "real" history of the world consists entirely and solely of what is the case in the present.

This picture is incoherent. The somewhat intricate details of its incoherence have been developed above. In much simpler terms, if my childhood is not part of my history in the same way that my typing these lines now is, if my childhood, *as it was then*, is not something I can even *think* about *now*, then my conception of who I am is severely distorted. Similarly, if what I will do in the next seconds—including *completing this very sentence* (or this very thought), is not something I can *now* think about, if I cannot think the sentence I am trying to complete *as it will be when I complete it*, then the very notion of completing a sentence or a thought crumbles. Thus, when history is collapsed, albeit tacitly, onto the present, the activities of thinking and speaking—activities that take place in *time*—fall apart. We live, think, and speak with a language in which time consists of a past, a present, and a future, and which does not recognize that one of these realms is "more real" than the others. Denying this is incoherent because this very act of denial, executed in language and over time, confirms it.

4.6   The "Now" Moves to an Impasse

The final theory we will consider, the "moving Now" doctrine, is, of all the views we've been studying, the least appealing. This is somewhat surprising, given that it is driven and shaped by an attempt to cohere best with our language and experience. Its unforgivable weakness is that it is vulnerable to the accusation of self-contradiction. This view explicitly claims that only the present is "real." To this claim, proponents of this view add—an addition that puts this view in stark opposition to Dummett's position—that the Now runs along the series of moments, momentarily privileging one of them, making it real and alive (see the quotations given in section 3.1). This addition amounts, in effect, to recognizing conditions obtaining at any time, past, present, or future, as truth conditions, as that the obtaining of which establishes the truth or falsity of sentences. And herein lies the contradiction. On the one hand, only the present is real, which means that only present conditions can count as truth conditions. On the other hand, the Now moves, rendering conditions that were future and not real, present and real. The conditions obtaining at a certain time turn out to be both real and not real.

Consider a future token of "The moon is eclipsed now," uttered during a lunar eclipse a year from now. Only the present is real, which means that the only conditions on which this token can be true are present conditions. And at present the moon is not eclipsed. Thus, in relation to present states of affairs, the token is false. So the token is false, for it is false on the only conditions that can function as truth conditions, namely, present conditions. Nothing else is "real." But time flows, and in a year's time other conditions will obtain, which will include a lunar eclipse. In a year's time, then, this token, this very token, will be true. Again, it will be true on the only conditions that can function as truth conditions, namely, what will then be present conditions. This is a contradiction—one and the same token cannot be both true and false. Or, put differently, a state of affairs cannot be both real and not real.

We have met this contradiction before. It is the one McTaggart points to in his argument against the reality of tense. It is also the same contradiction that a violation of the truth-value link yields. Much of Dummett's effort was directed at escaping this contradiction. It's his evasive maneuver that leads to the "solipsism" we have attributed to him. And the gist of this solipsism consists precisely in the rejection of the notion that the Now moves (in the sense that successive moments become "real" consecutively), while retaining the notion that the Now is special.

Schlesinger, we saw back in section 3.1, does purport to offer a way out of the contradiction without surrendering the moving Now. To this end, he recruits the omnipotent "possible worlds" apparatus, and the foliation into worlds which is the hallmark of this metaphysical framework. Each world W_n is in effect static, with the present permanently occupying the time interval designated by m_n. In each such world the truth-value of a token evidently does not change. A token of "The moon is eclipsed now" is not true or false *simpliciter*, but true or false relative to a world W_n. Time's passage is found in this doctrine, not among the moments that make up a world's history, but in the ordering of worlds along the A-series. The familiar relations "earlier"/"later," are bifurcated into two sets of relations ("two different types of temporal characteristics," says Schlesinger [1991, 440]) which are "radically different" (1991, 431) from each other. One set of relations obtains within each of these infinitely many, never changing, possible worlds. Here, the terms "earlier" and "later" have the meanings we are familiar with—they describe the temporal relations among the events that make up the history of that particular world. The other relations, which we shall denote as "earlier*"/"later*," obtain between worlds: W_{n+1} is later* than W_n if the "now" is located in W_{n+1} at a later moment, a later date, than the moment it occupies in W_n. To repeat: "earlier"/"later" temporally arrange events within worlds, "earlier*"/"later*" arrange the worlds themselves.

Thus, the pressure exerted by the contradiction threat results in an ambiguation of the meanings of the terms "earlier"/"later." We, of course, know of no such ambiguity from any other—mundane or scientific—occasions in which we encounter these common words. And remember that the "moving Now" view is supposed to be nothing but a systematic formulation of our ordinary, familiar notions of time. Evidently, the initial desire to structure a theory around these notions rather than fabricate a theory by means of unfamiliar technical terms has already been upset. Can we understand the new theory?

Imagine Jim telling Joan—"James landed twenty minutes ago." Let us call the uttering of this token p, and let us call the event mentioned in it, James's landing, e. On Schlesinger's view, Jim is reporting two temporal facts: that e is twenty minutes earlier than p, and that it is twenty minutes earlier* than p, that is, that the moment in which e is present is twenty minutes earlier* than the moment in which p is present. Or, in Schlesinger's terms, that W_e, the world in which e occurs Now, is twenty minutes earlier* than W_p, the world in which p occurs Now. Moreover, these are two "radically different" facts.

Well, we surely understand that e occurred twenty minutes ago and that it is twenty minutes earlier than p. But the claim that e is twenty minutes earlier* than p prompts disturbing questions. Besides the formal definition, what does it mean for an event to be earlier* than some other event? What content, which can be fleshed out in familiar terms, can be attached to this relationship? Furthermore, if indeed there are two radically different temporal relations here, what exactly accounts for the perfect correlation between them? How is it that, in general, whenever event e is t moments earlier than event f, W_e is exactly t moments earlier* than W_f? And are moments = moments*? For, if anything, W_e is t moments* earlier* than W_f (or should it be t moments* earlier* than W_f)? If indeed moments = moments* then in what sense is being earlier so radically unlike being earlier*? We could be told that W_e is *defined* to be t minutes* earlier* than W_f if and only if e is t minutes earlier than f, and that minutes are by definition equal to minutes*. But what drives these definitions? We would like to have some independent motivation for them, some reason, other than the need to evade self-contradiction, for considering seriously such hitherto unknown temporal relations.

The worse problem with this scheme is, of course, that it does not achieve its goal: that of ridding the "moving Now" from self-contradictions. Schlesinger is not unequivocal in characterizing the relations "earlier*" and "later*." On the one hand he says they are radically different from our familiar "earlier" and "later." He states, for example, that W_{n+1} does not follow W_n in the way that "night follows day" (1991, 431). On the other hand, he does not deny these are *temporal* relations, and he refers to them as such on many occasions. The fact of the matter is that these *must* be temporal relations if his theory is to depict the "moving Now." Nontemporal relations would not yield movement, or transience of the Now. So these relations must be temporal.

On the tensed view Schlesinger is defending, it is of the essence of time that among its elements there be a privileged one, a present element that is alone "real and alive." So if "earlier*" and "later*" are *temporal* relations, one member of the series W_n of worlds must be present, or present*, "real and alive." If there is no privileged present* then time* is not really time, and again the picture is no longer that of the moving Now. What we are left with in this case is nothing but a formal skeleton of a picture that originally was supposed to faithfully systematize our conception of time's *passage*. Moreover, this picture cannot constitute an alternative to the tenseless view. Unless one of them is elevated and privileged, the worlds of the many worlds system are on a par. And this ontological egalitarianism is precisely what the tenseless view stands for. So for transience to be part of Schlesinger's view, there must be a privileged present*.

And the problem is that with this privileged present* we are back to contradictions. The advantage of presentness* would be conferred on each of the worlds successively, and the result: one and the same token of "W_n is present" would be true when W_n is present but false "earlier*" and "later*"—the old contradiction.

Needless to say, a contradictory theory is not where viable new uses for old words are going to be found. Like the theses making up Dummett's antirealism or Mellor's tenseless view, the tenets of the moving Now are expressed by means of uses of the word "real" we do not know how to understand. We do not know what it means for one moment to be "real" and for another to be "not real," or for an event to be "real" at one moment and not real at the next. The theory itself might have endowed these new uses of "real" with a sense, in the way that scientific theories support new meanings of certain words. But, if the theory is inconsistent, it cannot be appealed to for this purpose.

4.7 Transcending Ontology

In section 4.2 we discussed the use that both tenseless and tensed theorists make of the distinction between being *real* and being *not real*, and
concluded that it was unusual to the point of not making sense. We then
raised the suggestion that, in formulating the main tenets of their views,
theorists of both camps are not merely assuming this distinction, but are
in fact striving to make it meaningful in the context of the theories themselves. However, if the conclusions of the last sections are correct, this goal
is not fulfilled. Neither the tenseless theory nor the tensed theory can be
relied on for giving a new sense to these unusual employments of the word
"real." That means that we cannot, in any way, attach a sense to the statements making up the basic tenets of both theories in the metaphysics
of time.

This conclusion should be understood strictly: we do not know what to
make of either the metaphysical thesis that "only the present is real"; or
of the opposed thesis that past, present, and future events are "equally
real." If these theses were supposed to respectively constitute "Yes" and
"No" answers to the question: "Is the present 'ontologically privileged'
with respect to the past and the future?" then our conclusion is that we
have no well-formed answer to this question, or to its twin, "Does time
really flow, or is time's passage an illusion?"

There are, we all know, many ordinary occasions on which we speak of
time's passage, and refer to past things as nonexistent. But when it comes
to *metaphysical* theses that concern such occasions, we do not know how
to understand them. We do not know what to make of the claim that only
present things are real, or of the contrary claim that things that are not
present are nevertheless real; we do not know how to make intelligible the
metaphysical thesis that time flows, that is, the thesis that future things
that are not real become real with time's passage and then lose this advantage when time's flow makes them past; nor do we know what to make of
the contrary contention that all events are equally real and time's passage
is an illusion.

This may initially appear like a negative result. But we will see that the
contrary is the case. That neither theory is defensible, that the only two
possible answers to the question "Is the present 'ontologically privileged'
with respect to the past and the future?" cannot be made sense of, means

that no definite sense can be attached to the question itself. *Tense simply cannot be meaningfully cast in ontological terms*; it cannot be thought of in these terms, or investigated in them. This conclusion is by no means slight. It bears the weight of a long philosophical tradition in which tense *is* analyzed as an ontological matter, a tradition the existence and significance of which are rooted in the naturalness, the spontaneity, and the inevitableness with which, upon crystallizing, philosophical curiosity takes on the form of an ontological investigation, as was described in section 4.1 above.

Prephilosophical discourse, ordinary and scientific, is, as we saw in the beginning of the chapter, innocent of tense-related ontological commitments. Only the philosophical inquiry introduces tense-related ontological claims. The discovery we've just arrived at, that tense cannot be conceived of in ontological terms, does not take us back to those prephilosophical sensibilities. It does not return us to the quiet we enjoyed before philosophical curiosity was first aroused. Rather, it carries us ahead, beyond the unrest and confusion that manifest themselves in the kind of wrestling over ontological issues we (as spectators rather than as participants) have been occupied with. It elevates us to a new phase of the philosophical investigation, to a post-ontological domain, in which the various issues that call for a philosophical treatment are addressed in light of the newly attained recognition that reality claims cannot be part of the articulation of these issues, or of their treatment. In short, the result of the attempt to develop and defend ontological theses in relation to tense is the transcendence of ontology, the realization, to repeat, that tense cannot be cast in ontological terms.

With this realization at hand, we can proceed to distill from the products of the metaphysical labor valid insights concerning tense. To do so we should note that both tensed and tenseless theorists are engaged in two separate tasks, a negative task and a positive task. The positive task of each camp consists simply of defending its conception of time. The negative task consists of undermining the opponents' view of time. Writers on the metaphysics of time do not usually highlight the distinction between the two tasks because they do not regard them as truly separate and distinguishable. They assume that conclusively undercutting the rival view is tantamount to establishing the correctness of their own view, and that, conversely, putting forth conclusive claims in favor of their view suffices for defeating the rival view. They are not entirely unjustified in this assumption—as we observed, the evolution from initial curiosity concerning time to a philosophical inquiry culminates with the by now familiar forced choice between the tensed and the tenseless views. And, confronted with such a choice, the endorsement of one theory means the rejection of the other, and vice versa.

However, having transcended the ontological framework, the negative and positive tasks can be separated and assessed on their own. Let us consider for a moment the negative theses. Tenseless theorists attack the tensed notion that only present things are real, or that present things are somehow "more real" than past and future ones. Tensed theorists argue against the tenseless contention that all things, regardless of their temporal location, are "equally real." *We* can endorse both negative theses. Together they amount to a rejection of the tenseless and tensed attempts to use the word "real" for the sake of analyzing tense, and casting tense in ontological terms. The negative theses are not only compatible with our conclusions concerning the unintelligibility of studying tense by means of reality claims, they jointly express this conclusion.

In contrast, we cannot endorse either theory's positive theses, which are framed in terms of reality claims the intelligibility of which we have rejected. Endorsing either theory's positive tenets would be tantamount to trapping the inquiry in a zone of incoherence. What we can do is focus on the more specific claims that make up the positive theses, and study them afresh from our post-ontological viewpoint. The subtheses of the metaphysical theories function as flags that mark the elements in our conception of time that are wanting in clarity and map the loci of philosophical perplexity. We shall attend to these issues in the next chapter, and, we hope, lay them to rest.

5 Time—As Seen from a Post-Ontological Perspective

In *Physics* iv 10, Aristotle asks "whether time is one of the things that exist [*ontôn*] or not," and proceeds to inquire whether time's parts, and specifically those parts delineated by the tenses—the past, the present, and the future—exist. Thus the ontological inquiry gets underway. In its course, various subquestions come to the fore, each representing a cloud of haziness, which has been engulfing, unbeknownst to us, some aspect or other of our understanding of time. That is the "problem-mapping" process that falls out of the metaphysical enterprise.

A famous issue that Aristotle runs into early on in his discussion concerns the duration of the present. Aristotle presents two arguments to the effect that the present is pointlike. We will use this conjecture as a starting point for the stage we are entering now, namely, reacquainting ourselves with time by revisiting the philosophical challenges it poses and examining them from the post-ontological perspective available to us—we are standing on the shoulders of metaphysics and can benefit greatly from this elevated viewpoint. After discussing the issue of the present's duration, we will move on to other major topics in the metaphysics of time.

5.1 The Duration of the Present

Aristotle's argument to the effect that the present is pointlike occupied the minds of his successors and continues to be discussed today. However, whereas in earlier texts one finds interesting rebuttals, in our day the conclusion of the argument seems to have become entrenched. For many, the notion that the present is confined to a volumeless point is self-evident. One reason for this is, I believe, the widespread use, in numerous contexts and connections, of diagrams in which time is represented by a line: the "time line." Coordinate systems used in the sciences are a very common example of such representations, but there are others. If the question of locating the present in such representations comes up, Aristotle's argument seems to establish that as a matter of logical necessity, the present is to be associated with a geometrical point on the line. However, events and states of affairs that we refer to as present—a hockey game, a mission of a space shuttle, a collision inside a particle accelerator, your reading this chapter—endure over some time interval. Jane complains: "I've caught the flu and am not that well just now." An editorial opens with the assertion that "at present, the French prime minister is a socialist." In none of these examples is the present state of affairs alluded to pointlike.

There is, then, a striking discrepancy between the philosophers' vanishing present and the apparent temporal voluminousness of present events and states of affairs. Two possibilities present themselves: either our apprehension of present events as enduring in time is utterly mistaken, or else the argument that purports to establish that the present is pointlike is invalid. It seems evident to me that there is nothing wrong with speaking, say, of the hockey game—as opposed to some "instantaneous part" of the game—as a present event. If you ask me "Where is Ruth these days?," I am accurately giving her location *at present*, not at any volumeless point in time, when I reply "In New York." Thus, it is the conception of the present as pointlike that is distorted. I believe this distortion is rooted in the ontological language, which, as can be seen explicitly in Aristotle's text, permeates our thinking about time. It is the ontological approach to understanding tense that yields the pointlike present. From our new perspective this approach is no longer defensible, and so neither is the pointlike present.

Aristotle's argument is straightforward. Let us assume that the present consists of an interval and not of a point. In such a case, claims Aristotle, the present overlaps with the past and future, which is a contradiction: a moment of time cannot be both past and present (or future).[1] Therefore, the present must shrink to a point.[2]

Augustine adopts Aristotle's argument but gives it a setting that increases its persuasiveness. Gale's reformulation of Augustine's argument runs as follows:

Suppose we are at a concert and I ask you what the orchestra is playing now, to which you reply "The Eroica Symphony." After a moment of reflection I come back with the query, "But the Eroica has four movements—certainly all four movements are not present *now*." You then narrow your original claim and say, "Only the first movement is now being played," but this is immediately countered with my question, "How can all 691 measures comprising this movement be present *now*?" You restrict yourself further to the 100th measure, but I then ask how all three beats, each being a quarter note, can be present now? Finally in desperation, after I have forced you to pulverize your present down to twelve eighth notes, you give up and say that strictly speaking nothing is present now—*the* present is, as Augustine claimed, an indivisible instant. (1968, 4)

The argument here consists of a series of descriptions, each regarding smaller and smaller segments of a musical piece. It begins with the piece itself, the Eroica Symphony, continues to its movements, then to the measures that make up each movement, the beats, and so on. Each describes an event, and the events correspond to a series of contracting intervals of time that converge to a pointlike moment. The reasoning is that no finite segment can be present, because it consists of smaller segments of which some are past and some are future. Thus we are driven to conclude that *the* present, that which is indivisible and hence has no parts that are not present, is pointlike. The argument is compelling because it succeeds in making us believe that at each stage a better, more precise description is formulated of a present that exists independently of the description. And the picture emerging from it is the familiar one: time, like a geometrical line, is continuous and composed of extensionless points, which are successively occupied, one at a time, by the present.

This argument is misleading in its simplicity. That it is more intricate than it appears can be recognized from the manners in which it can be misconstrued. Thus, according to Westphal (2002), for example, Augustine's error is a case of the standard "fallacy of composition": he erroneously requires the whole to be contained in each of the parts, rather than seeing it as composed of the parts, which, of course, are contained in it. Westphal suggests that this error reflects a misunderstanding, on the part of Augustine, "of a feature of the logic of the concept 'the present'" (2002, 2). Thus, thinking for example of the present crisis, Westphal finds Augustine making the blunder of requiring that it exist, in its entirety, at each of the instants over which it extends. Or, returning to the Eroica Symphony example, the mistake would consist in taking the assertion that the orchestra is now playing the Eroica Symphony to imply that at each instant in which the orchestra is playing, it is playing the entire symphony.

But this diagnosis of Augustine's error makes it appear almost trivial: why would anyone think the whole should be contained in each of its parts? The triviality of such a mistake is indicated by Westphal himself, who, invoking the familiar analogy with space, demonstrates with ease the non-retrenchable character of the spatial "here": it is evident that "here" is not pointlike, that by asserting that she is here, in New York, Dana does not mean that the whole of New York is somehow here, inside her room. But then why would anyone have thought that by asserting that the game is now in progress, one might have meant that the entire game, all three periods of it, are being played now, at this very instant?

It seems to me that to attribute to Augustine such carelessness is to miss what was really bothering him, and Aristotle before him. The key to understanding the argument is to uncover several hidden assumptions underlying it, which belong to the ontological framework. The present needs to be conceived as distinct from the past and the future, and moreover as changing, as "always different and different," to use Aristotle's words. In more familiar terms, time, but not space, *flows*.[3] Or at least everyone agrees, tenseless theorists included, that we experience it as flowing, think of it as such, and speak of it as such. Moreover, we experience this flow, like the flow of the Seine, as something external to and independent of us and of our experiences.

It is important to emphasize that the categories of past, present, and future are being understood here as *ontological* categories. Thus, in the passage just before the one Westphal quotes at length at the beginning of his paper, Augustine states that "the present passes into the past," that is, time flows, and that "the past now is not," and that "the future is not yet" (Gale 1968, 40), or, in other words, that only the present *is*, or that only the present exists. Aristotle likewise couches his discussion in ontological terms: referring to the past and future respectively, he says that "Some of [time] has occurred and is not, while some is going to be and is not yet" (*Phys.* iv 10, 217^{b}33). And, of course, contemporary philosophers are even more explicit in construing the distinction between the past, present, and future as an ontological one.

It is this conception of time, according to which time flows, ontologically privileging moments that become present, which is Aristotle's and Augustine's point of departure, and the source of their worries. From this initial view (which Augustine ultimately abandons for the sake of a precursor of the tenseless view), the retrenchability puzzle is anything but the result of a simple confusion. On the contrary, it seems somewhat inescapable. For nothing can both *be* and *not be* at the same time. Imagine that the present is not pointlike, but rather endures, say, sixty seconds, that is, the duration of the present is sixty seconds (the locution "the duration of the present" is an odd one, which we will return to shortly). And think of two such "presents" that partially overlap, an earlier present P_1 (represented by the gray arrow in figure 5.1), and a later present P_2 (the white arrow), and of an instant t that is inside the overlap. Then there is a time interval during which t is present, but a previous instant, t', which belongs only to the earlier present P_1, is both present and past: present by virtue of belonging to P_1, and past by virtue of preceding P_2. Ontologically speaking, considered from t, that is, while t is present and therefore *is*, t' both *is* and *is not*—a contradiction.

In the Eroica Symphony example, allowing the continuously flowing present to be extended would make, for example, the fifth measure of the second part be both past and present at the time during which the sixth measure is being played. It's this feature of the present—its smooth flow, which ontologically privileges some events over others—that drives the retrenchability puzzle. (There is, of course, no spatial analogue to time's passage, and since no one has ever suggested that the distinction between "here" and "there" is an ontological one, the non-retrenchability of *here* teaches us nothing at all.)

Given that this is the background from which the argument derives its force, countering it requires an objection to some element of this background. One possibility is to challenge the premise that time flows smoothly, or continuously. Thus we find the idea that time advances by leaps appearing in the thought of Diodorus Chronus, a generation after Aristotle, and again in the works of subsequent philosophers, such as Damascius. However, discontinuous time poses difficulties of its own, which are no less daunting than those accompanying the idea of a pointlike present.

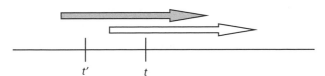

Figure 5.1

Worse than that, it suffers from the same weaknesses as the pointlike present, because it shares with it the supposition that, as it flows, time "ontologically privileges" events of the present.

If we are not drawn to challenging the continuousness of time's passage, then our objection to the retrenchability argument must target the notion that the present is ontologically privileged. And, indeed, once this supposition is transcended, the path is cleared for a sound approach to the issue at hand. Let us begin by observing that our dealings with the present—in speech, thought, and experience—are *always* contextualized. I mean by this that we never encounter—in experience, speech, or thought—"the Present" as such, but always *something* that is present: a hockey game, a mission of a space-shuttle, a collision inside a particle accelerator, your reading this chapter (what makes a certain event present, past, future is a question we will turn to in the next section). To be sure, the context may be described negatively, as in "nobody's using the basketball court now" or "the press conference scheduled for this evening is not being held." Contexts, in short, can also be constituted by states of affairs in which something does not obtain. Still, some context or another is in place whenever the present figures in speech, thought, or experience. Even when we speak of the "present time," or the "present century," it is not a certain time interval that we describe as present. Such expressions are always used in relation to some states of affairs—"the present time is a difficult one for the workers," "the present century is one of new breakthroughs in space exploration," and so on. If we say, "The present hour is crucial," what we mean is that present events taking place at this hour are crucial.[4]

The contextuality thesis supports the following claims. First, the question "how long is the present?" is not one we understand, for it is asked outside of any context, and that therefore, "a vanishing instant" is not an answer we understand either. Second, when a question of duration does arise, it always concerns not "the present" as such, but an event, or state of affairs, which is present, for example, the duration of the first period of the hockey game being played now, which is twenty minutes, or the duration of the current Mars probe mission, which is nine days.[5] It thus turns out that the retrenchability argument offers an answer where a question has not yet been properly posed—we do not know what sense to attach to talk of "the present's duration," be it in asking what its duration is, or in arguing that it is pointlike, or in arguing that it is not pointlike (as West-phal does). The pointlike present ought to be rejected, but *not* in favor of a present that endures over positive intervals of time. Rather, it must be realized that it is events, or states of affairs, that endure, while it is mean-ingless to speak of "the present's duration."

Let us see how these observations dissolve Augustine's argument. We begin by noting that the temporal parts of events are also events: the second day of the probe's five-day mission, the third period of the game, playing the symphony's first movement, or the third chord in the fifth bar of the first movement—all these are in themselves separate, individual events. Such events may also be relevant contexts. Take the succession of events that figure in Gale's story: the symphony, its first movement, the movement's 100th measure. What appears as a narrowing down toward the "real" present is, in fact, a change of context. By zooming in on smaller and smaller events that are telescopically contained in each other, we are not better approaching that which is truly happening *now*. Rather, we successively modify the context in which we are describing what is happening now, that is, the context with respect to which the present is alluded to.

There is no "real" present, any more than there is a "real" context: the entire symphony, its first movement, the movement's 100th measure, are on equal standing, as are the presents associated with the performance of them. All that Augustine shows is that in relation to a certain particular context—that point which is the limit of the converging intervals—the present event is pointlike.[6] Augustine does not show that this context is in any *other* way unique, or privileged. In other words, what Augustine's argument shows is that there are, perhaps, pointlike present events, not that all present events are pointlike, and certainly not that the present itself is pointlike.

In fact, rather than supporting the idea of a pointlike present, conceived of independently of any context, Augustine's argument demonstrates the above claim, namely, that the notion "the present," or the term "now," are always attached to an event, and our understanding of them to our description of the event. For, in the argument there is no mention of the present itself, only of events that are present. That each of the events described—the playing of the symphony, or of the first movement—is referred to as *present* is not a flaw of the language the argument is stated in. It is a reflection of the inextricable connection between the present and particular contexts.

Aristotle's original argument should also be analyzed in light of the contextuality principle. In that argument the claim was that an extended present would overlap with the future and past. But once it is noted that the distinction between the past, present, and future is drawn only with respect to a context, the apparent contradiction vanishes. There is one context in which the orchestra is "now" playing the Eroica Symphony, and another in which it is "now" playing the symphony's first movement. The past, in the first context, ends with the beginning of the symphony, and the future begins with the symphony's end. In the second context, the present event lasts approximately fifteen minutes, beginning with the symphony's opening note and ending when the second movement begins. It may appear as though the second movement turns out to be both present and future—present in the first context, and future in the second. But that is not the case. In the first context no mention is made of the second movement. In particular, it is not claimed that the playing of that movement is present. That the symphony is being played now *does not* logically entail that all its parts are being played now, and is entirely compatible with the playing of its second movement still being future. If we fail to see this, that is only because we have failed to appreciate that by turning our attention from the playing of the symphony to the playing of its second movement we have shifted contexts, whereby a different event gets picked out by the word "now."

Still, a contradiction may be lurking under the surface. Assume the playing of the symphony begins at 8:00 PM, and that the first movement ends and the second movement begins at 8:17 PM. In the first context, 8:20 PM is part of the time interval picked out by the word "now" as it figures in "the orchestra is now playing the Eroica Symphony." In the second context, "the orchestra is now playing the first movement," it is not. Rather, it belongs to the future. So, is 8:20 PM present or future? It surely cannot be both. The answer is that it is neither. In itself, this moment in time, 8:20 PM, is neither present nor future (nor past). A moment in time is not a context. Events, states of affairs, are; times are not. And, to repeat, tense terms like "now" can be meaningfully used only once a context is in place. Some locutions blur the fact that moments in time are not themselves tensely located, for example, "it's now 8 o'clock."

But let us trace the context for this use of "now." Often the sentence would be a more elaborate one: "it's now 8 o'clock, time to turn on the TV for the start of the game." Or else, the token of "it's now 8 o'clock" would be produced in response to the question "what time is it now?," a question which itself is prompted by some interest or need, the specification of which would describe a context. And the answer too would be given in connection to some state of affairs, for example, the position of the arms of a wristwatch. On its own, the instant in question—8 PM—has no tensed properties. It has them only in relation to the relevant interests motivating the question, and the circumstances grounding the answer.

We think of moments in time as themselves tensely located, that is, as present, past, or future, because events and objects are tensely located, and it is easy to slip into attributing to moments in time the tensed location we associate with events that occur at those moments, and then forgetting the events. If the crashing of the *Challenger* is a past event, then 1986, the year of the disaster, is thought of as past as well. But, according to the thesis of this chapter, it is only in the context of the event, the shuttle's crash, that the moment of the crash, is past. There are other events, or states of affairs, that span time intervals that include the year 1986, which are present. For example, the present era of electronic communication includes 1986. Similarly, when we say that the year 2008 is in the future, what we mean is that events that will occur then but have not yet begun (or states of affairs that will obtain then but do not obtain now) are in the future. The year 2008 in itself is not in the future, the present, or the past. Rather, in the context of, say, the first meteorite shower of 2008, it is future. But, the international space-station project is an ongoing, present program, spanning several years, in which the year 2008 is included. In this context 2008 is part of the present.

Granted, initially the suggestion that the year 1453 is not truly, or absolutely, past might sound implausible. But when one thinks, for example, of the age and current state of the Milky Way (e.g., its position with respect to Andromeda), the insistence that 1453 is truly past ceases to seem so evidently reasonable. The 500+ years that have passed since 1453, thought of in relation to our galaxy's history, are like the twinkling of an eye. For the galaxy, these 500+ years are not even what two seconds are for Jane, who is down with the flu. And surely, when Jane says "I am down with the flu," she does not mean that two seconds before uttering this sentence she was well, or thinks of her condition at that time as past. It would be strange if she did. The idea that in the galactic context 1453 ought to be thought of as truly past is just as strange.

I think the initial sense of implausibility has to do with the fact that in the vast majority of cases in which we come across the date 1453, it is indeed the date of events that are past—Gutenberg's invention of print, Charles VII's victory at Castillon, and, of course, that particular rotation of Earth around the sun with which that year is associated. But, there are contexts, albeit few, such as the evolution of galaxies, in which this is not the case. Thinking of *these* states of affairs reminds us once again that it is not the year 1453 in itself that is past. Rather, it is past in relation to events that took place in that year and have now been long over.

There is a misunderstanding the above discussion may invoke, and which must be prevented if we are to gain a sound conception of the present. It might be mistakenly thought that, with all the view's merits, it suffers from a crucial flaw, namely, that it does away with the present altogether. According to the worry we now need to consider, insisting that the present is not separable from a context, and that reference to the present is always done in relation to a context that fixes it, implies that the present is nothing but a verbal or conceptual construct. To dispel this impression, I wish to pause for a moment, and rehearse a distinction Putnam makes between conceptual relativi*ty* and relativi*sm*.

Putnam makes this distinction in connection with the term "object": "Consider a world with three individuals, x_1, x_2, x_3. How many *objects* are there in this world?" (1990, 96). Three, on one count. But if mereological sums are admitted, then the answer is seven: x_1, x_2, x_3, $x_1 + x_2$, $x_2 + x_3$, $x_1 + x_3$, + $x_1 + x_2 + x_3$. So how many objects are there *really*? Is it true or false to assert of such a world that it consists of exactly three objects? Putnam claims that it is meaningless to ask these questions outside of a context that fixes whether or not mereological sums count as objects. And once such a context is in place, there is no difficulty answering them determinately. If at first the existence of two incompatible answers creates the semblance of a contradiction, the observation that the term "object" is context sensitive, that it does not have one "absolute" meaning, explains it away. There is no contradiction in saying, in one context, a context that does not take mereological sums to be objects, that there are three objects in that world, and in another context, that there are seven. There is no contradiction in referring to the Milky Way as one object in one context ("How far is the Milky Way from Andromeda?"), and as billions of objects in another ("How many of the Milky Way's suns are larger than ours?"). Similarly, the question "Which kind of 'true' is really Truth?" is a meaningless one. The statement "there are three objects" is true in one context and false in the other, as is "there are seven objects."

Descriptions of contexts are linguistic entities. And it is often assumed (a highly problematic assumption, we should note) that it is *we* who choose, on a given occasion, according to *our* needs and interests, which description is appropriate for that occasion, that is, it is *we* who select a context in reference to which the meanings of terms like "object" and "true" are fixed. Highlighting this aspect of our verbal practices may raise the risk that objects and truth *themselves* will come to be thought of as linguistic constructs. That is what happens to the notions "truth" or "object" when they are appropriated by the metaphysical doctrine known as *conceptual relativism*. From the viewpoint of that doctrine, whether a sentence is true, or whether something counts as an object, depends solely on and is determined entirely by the description of a context, that is, by language. Objects themselves are rendered, by this view, to be verbal or mental entities.

Similarly, it may appear as though the thesis that our understanding of "the present" depends on a context entails that the present is a creature of the language with which the context is described, or of the mind that generates the description. If which event is present is determined in relation to a humanly fabricated description, is not the present a product of the human mind? Is it not the case that if there were no intelligent beings in the world that developed a language with which they can describe events and objects, if there were no descriptions, there would be nothing in relation to which the present could be thought and spoken of, and thus nothing in relation to which the present could *be*?

The answer is that the present is no more language or mind dependent than the events to which it is attached. Events are not mind dependent just because we access them by means of their descriptions. Whether the orchestra is one object or a collection of objects, or whether the playing of the Eroica Symphony is one event or many events (which it is if we think of each movement separately), depends on a description, on a context. That does not turn the orchestra or the separate entities it is composed of, or the musical piece or the parts it is composed of, into language or mind-dependent entities. The same goes for the present. Whether a sixty minutes long or a fifteen minutes long event is the present event depends on the description with respect to which the present is thought of—the playing of the entire Eroica Symphony or only of its second movement. That does not render the present mind dependent.

If there is any doubt on this matter, the following consideration should suffice to remove it: once a context is set, we still need to go and find out *empirically* how long the present event spans. We need, for example, to measure the duration of the symphony's playing before we know how long this present event lasts. Were the present mind dependent, it should have been up to us to decide how long a present event spans, independently of anything external, anything that is not mind dependent. But if in determining how long a present event endures we need to resort to clocks and other devices that are not mental entities, then the span of that present event, and *ipso facto* the present, are not mind dependent.

Think again about Putnam's treatment of mereological sums. As mentioned, the Milky Way can be viewed as one object, or as a collection of stars. But even though the number of objects denoted by the name "the Milky Way" depends on a context, we still need to go out and count those objects to know their number. And likewise, even though the span of the present event depends on a context, it is still necessary to measure that span, for, like the number of the Milky Way's suns, it is a matter of objective fact.[7]

To recap. The ontological framework yields and sustains an argument establishing that the present is pointlike. Without the support of this framework, the argument crumbles. Hence, in rising above the ontological assumption we leave the pointlike present behind as well. Furthermore, we discover that the general question of the present's duration is ill posed. There is no meaningful way to speak of the duration of "the present" as such. Rather, it is present events that have a duration, and different events have different durations. Thus, present events that last nanoseconds may coexist alongside present events that span millions of years. We may encounter short-lived present events or present events the span of which contains our lifetimes. That our cognitive relation to the present always involves a context does not render the present in any way mind dependent. As a corollary we obtain the discovery that moments in time cannot be thought of as themselves tensely located, as past, present, or future. Rather, it is only in relation to events, or states of affairs, that occupy these moments that they are tensely located. Thus, one and the same instant t can count as past in relation to one event and as present in relation to another. This raises the question: what makes a certain event present, past, or future? In the next section we will familiarize ourselves with further aspects of the present, and lay out the essentials of an answer to this question.

5.2   The Presence of Experience

A short terminological reminder: an event's A-time tells us where, with respect to the present, it is temporally situated. It tells us, in short, what we have been calling its tensed location—whether it is past, present, or future, and perhaps also how far past or future it is. For instance, to say that the space telescope Hubble was launched seventeen years ago, and that the first manned mission to Mars is planned for ten years from now, is to give these events' A-times.[8] Mellor says that we perceive the A-times of experiences:

we perceive them [our experiences] to be present; and on this fact depends all our knowledge of the A-times of other events. When I see a past event, like a solar flare, it is the perceptible fact that my seeing it is present which tells me that the flare must be as far into the past as it is earlier than my seeing it. And as in this case, so in others: it is the self-intimating presence of our observations that enables us to infer the A-times of the events we observe. (1998, 41)

In other words, which are also Mellor's, "It is the directly perceived presence of experience which tells us what the tensed facts of our world are" (1981, 49–50). Evidently, this phenomenon, which Mellor labels "the presence of experience," fulfills a central function in his scheme of things.

We are supposedly familiar with this phenomenon. If we pay attention to the temporal properties of our experiences, we will immediately note that our experiences are present. For instance, "Having a headache, inevitably includes knowing—if one thinks of it—that it is present; and similarly for all other experiences" (Mellor 1981, 49). Descartes opens his *Meditations* with some observations based on information "drawn from the senses: for example, that I am now here, seated in this place, clothed in a winter garment holding this sheet of paper in my hands, and similar things" (Descartes 1996, 13). Russell has his own version of the same kind of description in the opening section of *The Problems of Philosophy*: "It seems to me that I am now sitting in a chair, at a table of a certain shape, on which I see sheets of paper with writing or print. . . . I believe that if any other normal person comes into my room, he will see the same chairs and books and papers as I see, and that the table which I see is the same as the table which I feel pressing against my arm" (Russell 1991, 1). Both philosophers describe their visual and tactile experiences *in the present tense*, using the word "now" to indicate their tensed location. The phenomenon these quotations bear witness to is universal: "Whoever I am, and whenever I believe my experience to be present, that now-belief will be true. This is the inescapable presence of experience" (Mellor 1998, 44).

If indeed temporal *presence* is "a key aspect of experience," if being present is "essential to any experience, i.e. essential to its being an experience" (Mellor 1998, 40), then both tensed and tenseless theorists are confronting a phenomenon they are obliged to explain. Tensed theorists need to explain why experiences are different from other events, why many events are past or future, but "our experiences . . . seem to be confined to the present" (ibid., 44). Tenseless theorists for their part have to say how experiences are possible, if they are essentially present and there is no present: if ϕ is an essential property of x and if nothing can have this property then nothing can be an x.

On the face of it, tensed theorists are in a comfortable position to account for the presence of experience: if only the present exists, then only experiences that are present exist to be experienced. We have had experiences in the past, and hope to have more experiences in the future. But only present ones are "real and alive," so only they can be experienced. The more formidable challenge belongs to the tenseless theorist, who needs to explain how it is that our experiences tell us of their presence despite the fact that none of them is truly present, for there is no such thing as "the present" to which they belong.

Mellor's account, very briefly, is as follows. Experiences are, indeed, not present. Rather, the presence of experience consists in our *believing* that our experiences are present. And the existence of such beliefs can be readily accounted for tenselessly. Let us see how. There are various beliefs we may have about our experiences: that they are pleasant, painful, painless, auditory, tactile, and so on. However, experiences are not always accompanied by the many beliefs one might have about them. To use Mellor's example, as we settle into a comfortable armchair we are not usually aware, and thus do not usually form the belief, that our experience is painless rather than painful, or tactile rather than visual. Yet, had we turned our attention to the painlessness of this experience, we would have formed the belief that it is indeed painless. Similarly, we do not ordinarily entertain the thought "this experience is present" as we experience something. Yet, had we turned our attention to the temporal aspects of the experience, we would have formed such a belief.

There is, however, a striking difference between the painlessness of an experience and its presentness: not all our experiences are painless, but all of them are present. To repeat: "Whoever I am, and whenever I believe my experience to be present, that now-belief will be true. This is the inescapable presence of experience" (Mellor 1998, 44). *That's* the fact that needs to be accounted for. Mellor's explanation is simple. Indeed, not all our experiences are present: we remember past experiences and anticipate future ones. But if we ask about an experience, while it is being had, what is its tensed location, the correct answer is always the tautological "at present." Concerning experiences that are being had, we may find that they are painful or painless, tactile or visual, and so on. That is why there are no equivalent phenomena, such as the painlessness, or the tactileness, of experience. But experiences that are being had are always believed to be present, and never past or future (that is, if we form tensed beliefs about them at all). That is the presence of experience. To complete the account, Mellor needs to provide the tenseless facts that make these beliefs true. These too are ready at hand: the act of posing the question "what is the A-time of this experience?" is cotemporal with the experience the question is about. These are the tenseless facts that ground the tensed beliefs that constitute the presence of experience.

Note in passing that similar accounts are easily given for the pastness of remembered experiences and the futurity of expected experiences. The pastness of remembered experiences consists in the fact that whenever we turn our attention to the A-time of a remembered experience, an experience we have had, we find that it is past. And the explanation is the same: the act of posing the question "what is the A-time of this remembered experience?" is always later than the experience that it is about. Similarly for future experiences. Thus, experiences tell us directly of their presence; memories tell us directly of the remembered experiences' pastness; and expectations tell us directly of the expected experiences' futurity.

But wait. We started with something that seemed unique and surprising, namely, that whoever I am, and whenever I believe my experience to be present, that "now-belief" will be true. Now we see that this holds only for experiences that are had cotemporally with the formation of the now-belief. Other experiences are correctly believed to be past and future. Bringing these other experiences into the picture dims the uniqueness of "the presence of experience." Moreover, it brings to our attention the odd ring accompanying this discussion. There is something distinctly strange about the thought that the pastness of remembered experiences, or the futurity of anticipated experiences, are phenomena in need of explanation (we will attend to this oddness in the next section). Noting this can help awaken us to the peculiarity of accounting for the so-called presence of experience. Indeed, we will now proceed to see that the "presence of experience," the "pastness of the remembered," and the "futurity of the anticipated" are ghosts of phenomena—there are no such things, and nothing to account for. More importantly, and not surprisingly, we will see that these ghosts appear only upon entering the ontological framework in which Mellor's theory is set. Uncovering this fact and exorcizing the ghosts will further enhance our understanding of the present.

Let us begin by stating the self-evident fact that the presence of experience, as Mellor conceives it, is *not* part of experience. In Russell's report, quoted above ("It seems to me that I am now sitting in a chair"), there is no allusion to any now-beliefs, beliefs concerning the presence of his experiences. Rather, such a belief would have presumably been formed in him had he been requested to answer the question "what is the A-time of the experiences you are having?" But this question would have probably struck him as quite curious. Compare it to "What color is the sheet of paper you are looking at?," or "Is there a noticeable scent in your room?" There are normal circumstances in which such questions would actually come up. But "what is the A-time of the experiences you are having?" is a question no one who has not read Mellor's book has ever encountered ("No one but a philosopher doing philosophy talks in this way," to quote Broad [Gale 1968, 136]). It is a question that comes up in the service of a philosophical agenda of a very particular kind, and after ordinary descriptions have been superseded by a specialized jargon. In short, the so-called presence of experience is not part of experience, but part of a philosophical inquiry. Indeed, we will see that it does not exist outside it.

The presence of experience consists, we are told, in now-beliefs of the form "Experience *e* is present." But there is a deep problem with the idea of such beliefs. To explain the difficulty, I wish to digress for a moment and look again at one of the most intensely debated sections of Wittgenstein's *Philosophical Investigations*. In §50 Wittgenstein writes:

There is one thing of which one can say neither that it is one metre long nor that it is not one metre long, and that is the standard metre in Paris.—But this is, of course, not to ascribe any extraordinary property to it, but only to mark its peculiar role in the language game of measuring with a metre rule.—Let us imagine samples of colour being preserved in Paris like the standard metre. We define: "sepia" means the colour of the standard sepia which is there kept hermetically sealed. Then it will make no sense to say of this sample either that it is of this colour or that it is not.

That asserting of *S*, the rod in Paris, that it is one meter long is not like asserting of, say, some table that it is one meter long, seems quite evident. For one thing, contrary to all other reports of length measurements, the statement that *S* is one meter long is not based on a comparison. In fact, it is not based on a measurement at all. In all other cases, the length of a thing *x* must be measured, and that is done by comparing *x*'s length with that of something else, a ruler, for example. As for the ruler, it is taken to be an authoritative device because its length as well, or the distance between its indices, has been established by comparison to a standard. But *S is* the standard for the unit meter, and so its length is not fixed by comparison to anything else. Is such a comparison with something *else* essential to measurement? Can a standard not be applied to itself? Another famous passage in the *Investigations*, §279, illustrates the awkwardness of such an idea: "Imagine someone saying 'But I do know how tall I am!' and showing it by laying his hand on top of his head." The nonsensicality of this gesture is indicative of the meaninglessness of employing a unit of length that is defined in relation to a certain object—the meter rod in Paris, or one's body—in order to assert the length of that very same object.

Just as it is strange to assert of the rod in Paris, *S*, that it is one meter long, so it is strange to assert of *S* that it is *not* one meter long. If we cannot say of the rod in Paris that it is not one meter long, that is not because such a statement is false. There is nothing to prevent us from uttering false-hoods and still making sense. The problem here again would be that the term "meter" is applied to S, to that which serves as a standard for that very unit of length. So of S one can say neither that it is nor that it is not one meter long. Now, these reflections about the exceptionality of S seem quite plausible. On the other hand, contrary to Wittgenstein's own assessment of them, according to Kripke (1980, 54), Wittgenstein's remarks point to "a very 'extraordinary property,' actually, for any stick to have. If the stick is a stick, for example, 39.37 inches long (I assume we have some different standard for inches), why isn't it one meter long?" And Kripke's wonderment also sounds plausible. But how can Wittgenstein's remark and Kripke's rejection of it both be plausible? Answering this question will help us elicit from Wittgenstein the insights we need for our purposes.

The first thing that needs to be made explicit, and which Kripke seems not to be attentive to, is the context in which Wittgenstein is making his remarks. The context, he tells us, is one of a philosophical discussion, the subject of which is the role standards have in the language games they figure in. There are *other* contexts in which we could quite straightforwardly say of S that it is one meter long. Imagine that you are in the room where S is kept, and that you need to keep a container, which is full to the rim with a highly poisonous substance, perfectly horizontal on a one-meter high table, one leg of which is broken. You are frantically searching for a fourth leg when your friend shouts "But the rod in the vault is one meter long!" Your problem is solved. Here, then, is a case where we can use ordinary linguistic practices to say of S that it is one meter long. Thus, the observation that of S it can neither be asserted that it is one meter long nor that it is not one meter long is either wrong (Kripke says Wittgenstein "must be wrong") or philosophically illuminating, depending on the context in which it is made.

What Wittgenstein is drawing our attention to is the fact that the string of signs "S is one meter long" does not *always* constitute a meaningful proposition. Whether or not it does depends on the context in which it appears. In some contexts, such as the poison jar case, it does. In others, it is only misleadingly of the appearance of a proposition. We made above the quite straightforward observation that it is not possible to measure S's length in meters, for, being the standard meter, there is nothing else its length can be compared with, and it is also not possible to apply a standard to itself. That explains the assertion that it cannot be said of S either that it is or that it is not one meter long. Thus, one context in which "S is one meter long" does *not* constitute a proposition is that set by the idea of establishing S's length by measurement. In general, the idea of establishing S's length seems vacuous. None of the procedures with which we go about establishing the lengths of objects are applicable to S.

What we just said concerning the question *what* is the length of S is true also of the question *why* S is one meter long. Evidently, asking for an account for S's being one meter long would also be meaningless. Of course, if the person asking does not know that S is the *standard* for the unit meter, she may want an explanation for why it is said of S that it is one meter long, as happens, for example, in the poison jar case. To repeat, performing a measurement would not do in this case. Rather, one would have to simply inform her that S is the *standard* for the unit meter. If after that she persisted and wanted a further explanation for S's being one meter, it would be impossible to make sense of her request. At this stage, repeating that S is the *standard* for the unit meter would not be answering her, but rather pointing to why her question is meaningless. In this situation too, then, "S is one meter long" would not count as a proposition. Otherwise, it *would* make sense to ask why it is true.

It may be useful to highlight the peculiarity of the string of signs "S is one meter long" from yet another angle. Can we imagine S being not one meter long, or, to put it in other words, is "S is one meter long" informative in that its truth excludes other possibilities? Kripke thinks the answer to these questions is "Yes": "is the statement 'stick S is one meter long' a necessary truth? Of course its length might vary in time" (1980, 54). Now, in a sense Kripke is right. Speaking of the rod in Paris long before Kripke, Reichenbach remarked that "if an earthquake should ever throw it out of its vault and deform its diameter, nobody would want to retain it as the prototype of the meter" (1957, 20). Even without a change in its length, the Paris rod to begin with might have been half the length that it actually is, or a different rod of a different length might have been placed in Paris as the standard meter. Surely these are possibilities. But these are *not* possibilities that, now that stick S is already in place as the standard for the unit "meter," the sentence "S is one meter long" excludes. On the contrary, in describing these counterfactual situations we (tacitly, perhaps) rely on the term "meter," which is available in virtue of S's being the *standard* for the unit meter. By asserting that S is one meter long, as though we could imagine things differently, we would be divesting it of its role as standard, whence we would lose the means for articulating the above possibilities. So "S is one meter long" excludes no alternatives. That is not to say that it is therefore always meaningless. Such an inference would constitute a gross example of an application of the notorious "contrast theory of meaning" or "contrast principle" (discussed above, see p. 78). It does mean, however, that asserting "S is one meter long," as though we are thereby excluding other possibilities, makes this string of signs into something that, while appearing to be a proposition, in fact is not.

Finally, it should be noted that if regular, ordinary procedures and explanations do not apply to S, that does not mean that metaphysical theories can be called on instead. The reason is simple: regardless of where the explanation comes from and what form it takes, we do not know for *what* exactly an explanation is being sought. Imagine the ceremony at which S is singled out and designated as the standard meter, and imagine that on that occasion one of those present remains unsure and asks that it be explained why S is one meter long. Would we seek an explanation, or would we suspect that he has failed to understand that which he had just witnessed, and is making a senseless demand? We may put forth metaphysical theses, according to which "S is one meter long" is true *a priori*, or *necessarily*, or *by definition*, or *by convention*. But we'd be overlooking the fact that posing the request for a philosophical explanation to which one of these theses could constitute a response would already make for a context in which "S is one meter long" is not even a proposition. To put it differently, the above theses would be introduced as explanations in contexts in which the notion of "explanation" cannot be made room for.

So much for the Wittgensteinian digression. Returning to our subject—"the inescapable presence of experience" (Mellor 1998, 44)—we will now see that an experience's presence is like S's meterhood: it is a ghost of a phenomenon, not something in relation to which the idea of an explanation, or an account, can be given any sense. The phenomenon, we recall, consists in the fact that if x asks himself what is the tensed location of an experience e he is having, his answer will invariably be—"e is present." But, I will argue, for x to pose this question makes for a context in which "e is present" does not so much as constitute a meaningful proposition, even if initially it has the appearance of one. On the other hand, just as stick S

has a vital role in making available in language the term "meter," so our experiences have a vital role in making available tense terms. Thus, the analogy between (1) "*S* is one meter long" and (2) "*e* is present" has two aspects that will be pursued. First, in the context of seeking philosophical explanations, neither string of signs constitutes a meaningful proposition. Second, in other contexts, *S* and *e* have vital roles, *S* as the anchor for the term "meter," *e* as one of the anchors for tense terms.

In discussing *e*, the relevant context will be one in which a person considers her own firsthand experiences. For the sake of convenience, I will be speaking of the auditory experience that I am having now, that of the phone ringing next to me. For me, *e* will denote this experience. You, the reader, are invited to let *e* stand for some experience you are having now, as you read these lines.

To begin with, we need to realize the meaninglessness of the idea that *e*'s presence is something that is determined by some act, by employing some technique. We certainly do not establish that *e* is present by *comparing* its temporal location with that of some other event. Which event would that be? The ringing of the phone? Other events seem to be utterly irrelevant. And the ringing of the phone does not tell me that the auditory experience of hearing the ring is present; rather, if anything, it is the experience that tells me that the phone is ringing now. Besides, and more importantly, the idea of establishing that *e* is present by *comparing* its temporal location with that of some other event is just as meaningless as the idea of using a comparison to establish that *S* is one meter long. A comparison could have been relevant only if the outcome might have been that *S* is not one meter long, or that *e* is not present. And just as it is meaningless to think we could discover *S* is not one meter long by comparing it with another object, so it is meaningless to suppose I could discover that my hearing the phone ring is not a present experience by comparing its temporal location with that of some other event. So the act of measurement by comparison is not one with which *e*'s presence could be ascertained.

Could the discovery that *e* is present be made by other means? Again, this question makes sense only if I can imagine *e* being not present. A technique for determining whether or not x is ϕ could be employed only if x could turn out not to be ϕ. Otherwise there is nothing for the employment of the technique to determine. Well, can I imagine that *e*, the auditory experience I am having *now*, is not present? The wording of this question answers it. Here it is inconceivable that things are not what they seem. *e* may not be the sound of a phone ringing—I may be hallucinating it. But what alternative is there to *e*'s being *present*? Since the idea of establishing that *e* is present elliptically introduces the suspicion that it is not, and since this suspicion is not one we can intelligibly entertain, the idea that there is something here to be accounted for or explained is, *ipso facto*, vacuous.

The meaninglessness of the idea of measuring, or determining by other means, *S*'s length, helped us a while back to flesh out the assertion that of *S* it can be said neither that it is nor that it is not one meter long. Using this formulation we can rephrase the above claim, and state that of *e*, the auditory experience I am having now, it can be said neither that it is nor that it is not present. This, to continue the paraphrase, would not be to ascribe any extraordinary property to *e*, but only to mark its peculiar role in the language game of tensely locating events, a point we shall get to shortly.

As before, the context in which these observations are made is crucial. There are other contexts in which saying of *e* that it is present is utterly unproblematic. "No, the pain isn't over, I'm in pain *now*" is an utterance one might use if the doctor on the other side of the phone is having hearing difficulties (if he still does not understand one might try the otherwise awkward locution "it's *at present* that I'm in pain"). This is analogous to the poison jar scenario. But recall that in that scenario it was possible to state that *S* is one meter long thanks to the availability of the term "meter," which in turn relies on there being a standard for the unit meter. Likewise, the possibility to refer to *e* as a present event is due to the availability of the term "the present," and, as we will shortly discuss, the fact that this term is available is also rooted in something like a standard. And the analogy continues: just as in the poison jar scenario the standard for the term "meter" turned out to be *S* itself, so here, the "standard" for the term "the present" will turn out to be *e* itself. At any rate, let us stress that once we have turned our attention from such ordinary situations back to a philosophical study of the availability of the terms in question, we shift into a context in which we *cannot* assert of *S* that it is or that it is not one meter long, and we *cannot* assert of *e* that it is or that it is not present.

Similar remarks pertain to counterfactual possibilities. Recall Kripke's comment that *S* could have been, say, half a meter long, and that there-

fore Wittgenstein is wrong to claim that one cannot meaningfully say that
S is one meter. Such an assertion would be both meaningful and informative: it would tell us, for example, that S is not half a meter long. The
problem with Kripke's comment, we already saw, is that it too is blind to
the context. Two contexts, that must be kept separate, figure in describing
clearly the mechanism that is at work in the counterfactual case. In one
context, we counterfactually describe S as, say, half a meter long, and thus
implicitly imply that it is not one meter long. If we can do so, however,
that is because we already possess the term "meter." And we possess the
term because there is a prior context, one in which S's role as a standard
is established. And once we shift attention to this prior context, "S is one
meter long" ceases to figure as a proposition in the way it does in the
context of the counterfactual possibility.

Analogously, imagine John murmuring to himself as he leaves the
dentist: "I'm in such pain! I wish I had gone to the dentist yesterday, the
pain would have been gone and over by now." Here John is entertaining
the counterfactual possibility that e were past and, therefore, not present.
Does this show that "e is present" could be asserted meaningfully and
informatively, for example, for the sake of excluding this hypothesized
alternative state of affairs? No it does not. Here as well two contexts must
be kept separate. "e is present" is meaningful in the context of John's mur-
murings—"I am in such pain (at present)." But it is made meaningful by
the availability of the term "present." And the making of that term available, something in which e plays an essential role, is, as it were, a prior,
separate context. In this prior context "e is present" is meaningless. Thus,
whether or not "e is present" constitutes a proposition depends on the
context in which it appears. In ordinary ones it does. But in a philosophical context, the subject of which is e's role in making the term "the
present" available in language, it does not.

Let us now focus on e's role in making the term "the present" available
in language and, more generally, in the language game of fixing the
tensed locations of events. If the analogy I am drawing between e and
S is valid, then e figures as a kind of standard, or a *quasi standard*: it
is in relation to the tensed location of e that the tensed locations of certain
other events are fixed. There are present events that I will judge to be
present by ascertaining that they are cotemporal with e, for example, the
ringing of the phone. Other events I will judge to be past because they

ended before *e*. In general, my thesis is that our firsthand experiences figure in roles akin to those of standards: we determine the tensed location of events by comparing these locations with those of our firsthand experiences, just as we determine the length of objects by comparing these lengths with that of *S*.[9]

There are obvious differences between *S*, which is a standard, and our firsthand experiences, which are only quasi standards. For example, only one object, *S*, has the role of the standard for the unit "meter," whereas each of us employs a multitude of experiences as quasi standards. Also, *S* is public, whereas our firsthand experiences are, in some sense, private. My quasi standards are not yours, and vice versa. So in establishing something's length we all always refer back to *S*, but we do not all always refer back to *e* for establishing something's tensed location. In fact, you never refer back to *e*, which for you is not a firsthand experience at all. And even I refer to it, if at all, in only a very limited number of cases. Thus, in asking about the tensed location of an event, we encounter a twofold multiplicity. First, we need to determine *whose* experiences serve as the measure; and, then, assuming we are focusing on *x*'s experiences, we need to say something about *which* of *x*'s many experiences is to be appealed to on a given occasion. Given this multiplicity, what, if anything, guarantees agreement among a person's numerous tensed beliefs, and between the tensed beliefs of different people?

These queries are less discouraging then they appear. Starting with the second question—in relation to which of *x*'s experiences are the tensed locations of events determined—the answer is: one of *x*'s present experiences. All and only those events that are cotemporal with that experience are present. In a moment we will say something about which of *x*'s present experiences can serve as *x*'s quasi standard. But given that on a certain occasion a present experience *e** serves as *x*'s quasi standard, those events that ended before *e** are past, and those that have not yet begun are future. Most important: for *x there is no further question* as to which of her experiences are present. In particular, *x* cannot meaningfully ask whether *e** is present. As shown above, such a question constitutes a context in which "*e** is present" is not even a proposition. To revert again to our analogy, for *x* to query as to the presentness of *e** would be like inquiring into *S*'s length—not something she would know how to do.

As to which of her present experiences can serve as her quasi standard, we need to be aware of the following complication. It stems from the conclusion of the previous section, namely, that different present events are of different durations. That applies in particular to present experiences, which are themselves present events. Thus my experience e, hearing the phone ring, is cotemporal with another experience I am having, E, watching the news on the television. The first experience lasts a minute, but E continues for thirty minutes. The complication is obvious. Let's say that the news program began fifteen minutes ago (remember there is no contradiction between the fact that the program began fifteen minutes ago and its being a present event). Now imagine that five minutes before the phone started ringing a dog barked out in the street. That event preceded e, my hearing the phone ringing, but was cotemporal with E, my watching the news. And both e and E are present. If E serves as my quasi standard, then the barking turns out to be present, which it is not. If e is the quasi standard, the barking turns out to be past, as it should be.

Thus, not just any present experience can serve as a quasi standard for the determination of the tensed locations of events. Still, the determination is quite simple. It suffices that *at least one* present experience started after an event ended for that event to be classified as past, and it suffices that *at least one* present experience be over before an event commences for that event to be future. That the barking was over before e began makes that event past. Experiences are not pointlike events. But they are often made up of events that are of brief duration, and in some contexts we may want to turn our attention to such short-lived parts of experiences when determining the tensed location of an event. In other contexts lengthier present experiences will do. For example, I apprehend the Olympic games as a present event by apprehending their cotemporality with my hour-long experience of watching a live broadcast from the games.[10]

A related clarification concerns present events or states of affairs that endure over relatively long stretches of time. For example, Mars is now in its closest position to Earth, a proximity that repeats itself every seventeen years. I classify this event as present because of its cotemporality with my present experiences, for example, with my hearing the phone ring. That the ring is over does not entail, of course, that the present state of affairs in question—the proximity of Mars to Earth—is over as well. Events or states of affairs can be cotemporal without being equal in duration. Today I discern the planetary state of affairs as present owing to its cotemporality with experiences I am having now; tomorrow it will be tomorrow's experiences that will serve as standards, just as yesterday it was yesterday's experiences that had that role.

Now on to the question of *whose* experiences serve as the measure. The tensed location of an event is obviously not determined by comparison with a particular person's experiences. I know that the phone is ringing now, that is, that the phone's ringing is a present event, through *my* experiences. My wife knows of the same event that it is present through *her* experiences. In general, each person's experiences are her own quasi standards, or "tense rulers." But the worry about agreement between these individual rulers is as vacuous as the previous worry. Take the phone's ringing. My hearing the phone ring, e, is cotemporal with my wife's hearing it ring, e' (assuming she is here in the apartment with me, and not on some distant star, listening to a radio transmission from home). This cotemporality can be easily ascertained by means of verbal exchanges, watches, and the like. And these experiences are cotemporal with the ringing itself. To be sure, it is not always the case that an experience is cotemporal with the event experienced. Sometimes the temporal relation between an experience and the event experienced can be determined, if at all, only with the aid of instruments and theory.[11] But in many other cases, such as the one we are considering, this cotemporality is apprehended almost directly. After one has been around for a while and has gained (perhaps tacit) knowledge of the velocity with which various signals propagate, such direct apprehension becomes almost automatic.

At any rate, this cotemporality is all that is required to guarantee the agreement we are concerned with. Thus, my wife and I will both judge the phone's ringing to be a present event, each of us by means of her or his auditory experience, her or his quasi standard; and since our experiences are cotemporal, we will identically tensely locate the ringing as present. As before, there is no *further* question as to why e, my auditory experience, or e', my wife's auditory experience, is present. So, indeed, tensed locations are determined in a relation to a multitude of quasi standards and not in relation to some one standard. But, just as there is no question as to *which* of one's experiences ought to figure on a given occasion, so there is no question as to *whose* experiences ought to figure on a given occasion. Your experiences will serve you, mine will serve me, and, barring mistakes in ascertaining either the cotemporality of our experiences or their temporal relation to the event experienced, the determinations yielded by our quasi standards will be in accord with each other.

The above discussion concerning which and whose experiences count as quasi standards for tensed locations may be the source of a serious mis-understanding, which must be dispelled. It should be clear that placing our experiences in such a prominent place in the scheme *does not* imply that tensed locations are derived from, or are in any other way dependent upon, experiences. Tensed locations are not perspectival or subjective. Even if there was no one at home to experience the ringing of the phone, this event would still be present. Assuming otherwise would be akin to con-cluding that the length of an object is dependent on the length of *S*, the rod in Paris. But, obviously, Everest would be 8,847 meters high whether or not there was a rod in Paris serving as the standard for the unit "meter." The rod (or whatever serves as the standard) is essential for making the term "meter" part of our vocabulary, and thus in making talk of spatial lengths and distances possible. But it has nothing to do with fixing these lengths and distances. Similarly, we tensely locate events by reference to our quasi standard, to the tensed locations of our experiences, but that does not make tensed locations depend on our experiences.

Does the fact that the rod, in contrast with experiences, is a material object, the properties of which are independent of our experiences, and even of our existence, destroy my analogy? I think not. What's important is that the rod was *chosen* for the role of being the standard. And this choice is as blatantly a part of our human lives as are our experiences. With no human beings to select and use the Paris rod as a standard, the meter unit would never have come into existence. But, to repeat, that would not render Everest heightless—it would still be 8,847 meters high. Likewise, with no human experiences the term "the present" would not have come into existence and there would be nothing in relation to which it could be established that the merging of the clouds taking place now over the Everest is a present event. But that would not render that event devoid of a tensed location—it would still be present.

There is another difference between the standard rod *S* and our quasi standards that should be addressed. The rod in Paris was chosen *arbitrar-ily*. If, on the other hand, I choose to look up at the sky, I cannot help seeing the clouds merging, and being in my room now, I *unavoidably* hear the phone ring. And it is these experiences, or others like them, in relation to which events are determined to be present. This difference is grounded in deep features of space and time, in particular, in the fact that time, but not space, flows (it should be obvious that stating that time flows is not in contradiction with the conclusions of chapter 4, where we established that, *viewed as an ontological matter*, it is meaningless to assert either that time flows or that it does not; how to conceive of time's passage non-ontologically is the subject of section 5.4). We experience this difference, for example, in our ability to move about freely in space, and not in time. This, in turn, makes it possible to carry a measuring rod and, by placing it alongside another rod, compare their lengths. Such an exercise is not even thinkable in relation to time—we cannot "carry" a one-hour-long event and place it alongside another event to compare their durations. We cannot even attach a clear sense to the words of the previous sentence. This means that we cannot arbitrarily select a "tense ruler" and take it along with us. Rather, we are forced to resort to the quasi standards available at each given situation—those experiences that are present in that situation. This fact about our "tense rulers" does not, however, undermine the scheme outlined above or, in particular, the pivotal role of our experiences in it.

A final elucidatory note on the above scheme. We are not conscious of conducting any comparisons in order to determine the tensed locations of events. No apparent computations are involved in cognizing that the dog's barking is a past event, or that the phone's ringing is a present event. Yet, supposedly, comparisons and computations do figure in establishing the tensed locations of events. Well, much of our knowledge is based on cognitive processing we do unconsciously. Our automatic assessments of distances, sizes of distant objects, velocities, and more, are the product of complicated computations. It may appear somewhat odd to describe the apprehension of the speed and distance of an approaching truck as the result of a "computation"; the truck is apprehended directly, with no trace of the workings of some internal processor. But, even if the details are not known to us, such a processor is at work. Sometimes the computation becomes explicit, for example, when greater precision is required or when it involves a theory. Then actual measurements and comparisons take place. But often they remain hidden.

Finally, let us return to the issue that got us started with all of this—Mellor's attempt to account for the so-called presence of experience. Two things are evident in light of the above discussion. First of all, there is no such phenomenon. It is not the case that all our experiences are present—some were had in the past, some will be had in the future. And it is not the case that "whoever I am, and whenever I believe my experience to be present, that now-belief will be true." It is not the case because once we frame the question "What is the tensed location of e?" the context becomes one in which the chain of marks "e is present" does not even constitute a proposition, and so obviously does not express a belief that can be explained or accounted for. Like S's meterhood, e's presentness is not something about which our judgments are always correct; rather it is something about which we never make judgments at all. To repeat, it is a ghost of a phenomenon, and no more.

Mellor is compelled to account for the so-called presence of experience because, as a tenseless theorist, he denies that events, and among them experiences, are tensely located. But he cannot deny that experiences figure in giving us the tensed locations of events, and that they do so in virtue of their being themselves tensely located. Reflection on the fact that experiences appear tensely located though they are not leads precisely to questions such as: in virtue of what is the belief expressed by "e is present" true? We see, then, that Mellor's metaphysical commitments yield, quite straightforwardly, the problem of the so-called presence of experience. But they also suggest a description of this pseudo-phenomenon that suits Mellor. In this description, tense turns out to concern not our experiences, but only the beliefs we may form about them. Once the presence of experience is relegated to this realm, a tenseless account of it readily follows: the now-beliefs that make up this supposed phenomenon, the beliefs that our experiences are present, are always true because they pertain only to experiences that are cotemporal—a "tenseless relation"—with them. The explanation offered by Mellor's theory is, indeed, elegant, but the important point is that what is being explained is just as much a product of that theory as the explanation itself (and it is worth mentioning, as we did in the opening of this section, that the ontological commitments of tensed theorists compel them to account for the "presence of experience" as well).

But the second thing that is evident in light of the above discussion is that much is gained from contending with the theses Mellor puts forth on this matter. Taking on his challenge—the challenge of accounting for the presence of experience—resulted in the scheme we now have of the workings of experiences as quasi standards for the determination of tensed locations. We again witness how entering the ontological venue puts us before issues that, outside this venue, cannot be stated in words. How, without the tenseless view, could it become necessary to explain the "presentness" of the headache one is suffering from now? And yet without contending with this issue, it would not be possible to properly analyze the intricate manner in which firsthand experiences figure in facilitating the incorporation of tense into our practices and language. Of course, the key to success here lies not in contending with this issue from within the tenseless theory—that's what Mellor does—but in having transcended it.

5.3 The Pastness of Remembered Experiences

We know the American Revolution is a past event. But whence do we obtain the understanding of what it is *to be past*? Here too our experiences play a vital role, which is different in nature from their role in providing us with other types of knowledge. We know that the sky is blue, that the Golden Gate Bridge is long, and that bears huff. We know these things because we have had visual experiences in which we saw the sky's color and the length of the bridge, and auditory experiences of bears huffing. But we do not take our experiences themselves to be colored or spatially lengthy or to sound huffing. In contrast, our experiences themselves are tensely located. In the previous section we suggested that our firsthand experiences serve as "tense rulers": it is in relation to the tensed locations of our experiences that the tensed locations of other events are given. In this section we will add to this that our apprehension of the tensed location of our experiences is also the basis for our understanding of what it is to be tensely located. To develop and explain this thesis, let us turn our attention to our past and future experiences.

I mentioned in passing that frameworks such as Mellor's give rise not only to the so-called the presence of experience, but also to issues concerning the pastness of remembered experiences and the futurity of expected experiences. Mellor does not deal with these latter issues, but other thinkers do. Thus, one occasionally encounters the question: why is it necessary, if indeed it is, that we should remember only the past and anticipate only the future? Why can we not have, for example, memories of the present or of the future?

Unsurprisingly, and in accordance with the spirit of the previous sections, I will argue that these are pseudo questions that concern pseudo phenomena: there is no such thing as the pastness of remembered experiences or the futurity of expected experiences. More generally, there is no question as to why all the experiences we have had, whether we remember them or not, are past, or why those we will have are future. If m is an experience one remembers having had, and f is an experience one anticipates having, then contexts in which such questions arise are contexts in which "m is past" and "f is future" are not even propositions. In these contexts, we cannot say of m either that it is past or that it is not past; we cannot say of f either that it is future or that it is not future. Since the arguments in support of these claims are similar to the arguments of the previous section, they will be presented very briefly.

Let us begin by seeing how the tenseless and tensed theories invite the articulation of pseudo-theses about the pastness of remembered experiences and the futurity of anticipated ones. We will focus on remembered experiences (the treatment of future experiences requires some modifications, but proceeds along analogous lines and will not be delved into here). Mellor describes "the causal machinery of recollection" as follows:

To recall something that I have perceived is in effect to perceive it again via my original perception of it. So as a kind of indirect perception, recollection has its own causal mechanism, that of memory. Suppose I recall an event e that I have seen. To enable me to do this, my perception of e must have left a trace in me.... (1998, 122)

In his *Phenomenology of Perception*, Merleau-Ponty is a bit more elaborate:

This table bears traces of my past life, for I have carved my initials on it and spilt ink on it. But these traces in themselves do not refer to the past: they are present; and, in so far as I find in them signs of some "previous" event, it is because I derive my sense of the past from elsewhere.... If my brain stores up traces of the bodily process which accompanied one of my perceptions, and if appropriate nervous influx passes once more through these already fretted channels, my perception will reappear..., but in no case will this perception, which is present, be capable of pointing to a past event. (Westphal and Levenson 1993, 180)

According to this passage, the carving in the table does not "refer" to the past, and traces in my brain do not "point" to the past; these are *present* objects or states of affairs, which "in themselves" have nothing to do with the past. The "sense of the past" comes from "elsewhere," from within us, Merleau-Ponty later adds. It is *we* who use present materials in a manner that yields images, thoughts, and utterances about past events. "Pastness" is a cloak in which certain *present* perceptions are wrapped. Memories are such cloaked perceptions. They are present perceptions, whose content is that of previous perceptions, and which are distinguished from other present perceptions by carrying with them this "sense of the past." In Dummett's jargon, we learn to recognize certain present situations as justifying the assertion of past-tense statements. I am now looking at the reproduction of Ingres's *La Grand Odalisque* that hangs above my desk, and at the same time I'm also remembering seeing the painting a year ago in the Louvre. These are very similar perceptions; both are had in the present, but the latter is wrapped in "pastness," while the former, the direct perception, is not. I can also anticipate having a similar perception tomorrow, and this perception is differentiated from the first two by the hue of "futurity" that varnishes it.

Granted, this characterization of what it is like to remember or anticipate experiences that are not present may not be universally accepted. But it seems indisputable that there is a tense-based qualitative distinction between experiencing, remembering, and anticipating. If we are tenseless theorists, such a distinction calls for explanation. With no event or experience really being present or past or future, a reason must be given why certain events and experiences, and not others, appear as past.

We're familiar with Mellor's explanations: we need beliefs about the *A*-times of events in order to succeed in our actions, and so we are evolutionarily equipped with mechanisms for the formation of such beliefs. As for which experiences will be believed to be past, the answer relies on the simple tenseless fact that experiences that are remembered precede the remembering. There is a *causal* relationship between the early experience and the later memory: the former is among the causes of the latter. Since causes always precede their effects (barring backward causation, against which Mellor has a detailed argument), a remembered experience is always earlier than the remembering. So when the remembering occurs the remembered experience is necessarily believed to be past. Moreover, that among the causes of the memories there are previous experiences may explain the distinguishing quality of memories, a quality we pictorially referred to above as the "cloak of pastness."

Tensed theorists for their part (and, again, by tensed theorists I mean those who hold that there are ontological differences between the past, present, and future, regardless of how they understand this claim) seem to be better positioned to deal with the qualitative difference between experiencing and remembering an experience, for they assert, rather than deny, an ontological difference between the past and the present. According to them, remembering involves past materials. These materials are, ontologically speaking, qualitatively different from present ones. Their qualitative peculiarity manifests itself in experience as that flavor of "pastness" that remembering possesses. Since these materials are essential to memory, the remembered must always be past. Similarly for anticipating, which involves future materials, with their unique quality of futurity. Thus, for tensed theorists, the qualitative distinction between remembering, experiencing, and anticipating is but a natural reflection of the ontological differentiation between the past, present, and future.

But tensed theorists do not escape difficulties that conveniently. Elliott Jaques states that "records, artefacts, memories exist as part of the only world we can know—the world of now" (1982, 38). This statement seems, on the one hand, to square with the tensed theorist's commitment to the present's ontological supremacy. But it brings out an undesirable corollary to the theory—a restriction of our knowledge to present events and states of affairs. And, though we did not put it in these terms, our treatment of Dummett's antirealism clearly gestured in the same direction (recall Dummett's observation that "we can only describe [the world] as it is, i.e., as it is now" (1978, 369), the wording of which is very similar to Jaques's comment). Tensed theorists would not admit their theory entails such a restriction. But they face a real challenge in showing that it does not, and the reason is simple. If, indeed, memories involve past materials—that's what distinguishes them from other experiences—how could there be memories, given that only the present exists, and all that is available are present materials?

This difficulty is highlighted by the following consideration. That my memory of seeing *La Grand Odalisque* concerns a past experience is manifested in the fact that unlike, say, my experience of seeing a reproduction of it now, it comes along with a "sense of the past"; it is, as it were, immersed in a "haze of pastness." Yet this "haze" is *itself* present, and so cannot "point" to the past any better than can a coat of red paint covering a bicycle. Indeed, Jaques is pessimistic about the prospects of overcoming this difficulty: "memories are alive in the present," he says, but "how their meaning relates to their meaning at the earlier time of their occurrence can never accurately be known" (1982, 63).

That our epistemic horizon comes to include other times, that memories reach beyond the present materials from which they are conjured up, are facts that tensed theorists must contend with. Regardless of the degree of success with which they do so, the important point for us is that tensed theorists, no less than their tenseless counterparts, need to contend with the pastness of remembered experiences.

Here then is another philosophical issue that grows out of the metaphysical framework. Both the tenseless theory and the tensed theory lead to questions regarding the pastness of remembered experiences, the first because it claims there is no such thing as "the past," the other because it places the past hopelessly out of reach. Yet, "the pastness of remembered experiences" can easily be shown to belong together with "the presence of experience" and "the meterhood of the Paris rod": it is another thing that cannot be explained because it cannot even be described. Let us proceed to see why this is so. Again, I'll be echoing some of the claims made in the previous chapter, so I will keep it brief.

Choose some remembered experience *m* (in my case, I am thinking of the pain that followed the dislocation of a shoulder in a skiing accident). Now ask yourself: could you imagine *m* not being past? In a sense, yes: one can imagine that the event did not happen at all, that one's imagination is deceiving one into seeming to remember something that never happened. Plainly, in such a case, one is not really remembering. But is it possible to imagine that one *is* remembering, and yet that one's memory is deceptive, not about *m*'s occurrence, but about *m*'s being *past*? To put it differently, could there be an issue of establishing that *m* is indeed past? Could some technique or other be employed for the sake of ascertaining that it is past, or of verifying that "*m* is past" is true? The problem with these questions is that, like their counterparts concerning the presentness of experience, we do not understand them. It is unimaginable that, in some way, *m* is not past but rather present or future. If a suspicion that it is not past does arise, that can only be from within a metaphysical theory that challenges the way things seem. The tenseless theory does this by denying that there is a past, which implies that *m* is not *really* past, but is only subjectively or perspectivally apprehended as past. The tensed theorist for her part demotes the past ontologically to such a degree that it seems to simply drop out of the world altogether, so that what we do cognize, whatever it is, cannot be past.

Note that the above observations concerning past experiences (and similar remarks apply to future experiences) introduce a qualification to the theses of the previous section. We said there that the tensed locations of events are given in relation to our firsthand present experiences. This claim does not apply to those past and future events that consist of our past and future firsthand experiences. We do not tensely locate any of our experiences, past, present, or future, by a kind of comparison, or by the employment of any other technique. When it comes to our firsthand experiences, there simply is no issue of tensely locating them.

The pastness of remembered experiences is, then, another puzzle that the tenseless and tensed theories purport to untangle, but which can be described only from within these theories and does not exist without them. But, like the presence of experience, studying it uncovers the nature and centrality of the role experiences play in relation to tense. Just as the geometrical features of *S* equip us with the term "meter," which we can then apply to other objects, so it is from the tensed features of remembered experiences that one derives the tensed notions that are then applied to past events. A child's memories from a visit to the zoo can, in the appropriate context, serve as anchors for the meaning of the phrase "a week ago." Telling a child "In the past you used to suck a pacifier" can, in conjunction with the appropriate memories, give her an initial notion of the meaning of the term "the past." Once these phrases and terms are integrated into one's vocabulary and conceptual stock, they can be employed in other contexts, with various variations. When we learn how to extrapolate them we can begin to think and speak of events that date back to before our birth. Without the experiences which anchor these terms—the remembered experience of visiting the zoo or of sucking the pacifier—we would not be in possession of these tense terms at all. Similar remarks pertain to terms that serve us in thinking and speaking about the present and the future.

That's what I meant when, in the beginning of this section, I said that, not only are our experiences the "tense rulers" with which we tensely located events, they are also the basis for our understanding of what it is to be tensely located. What being past means is given to us through the unique quality that distinguishes remembered experiences from other experiences; what being present means is given to us through the unique character of present experiences; and what being future means is given by the unique quality that accompanies anticipating future experiences.

Needless to say, remembering, experiencing, and anticipating all happen in the present. But, in the case of the past and the future, it is not our present experiences of remembering and anticipating that anchor our understanding. Rather, it is the past, remembered experiences and the future, anticipated experiences that fulfill this role, even if, at present, these past and future firsthand experiences are themselves accessed by present experiences of remembering and anticipating.[12]

Of course, we are not usually aware that terms like "past," as it figures, for example, in stating that the American Revolution is a past event, or "ago," as it is used in saying that the planet Neptune was first seen a century and a half ago, are given to us through our acquaintance with experiences we have had. Nor, for that matter, are we typically conscious when we use the term "meter" to speak of the length of an object that the term is rooted in, and is made available through its relation to, the standard in Paris (or whatever serves as its standard). These are discoveries we make as part of a philosophical inquiry, in the course of contending with queries raised by metaphysical theories. And let us note, once again, that these discoveries underscore the usefulness of making acquaintance with the problems that emerge when tense is analyzed ontologically, assuming, that is, that we have realized that the real solution of these problems is the dissolution they undergo when the ontological enterprise is transcended.

In closing this section let me describe what I believe is another important feature of memory. It concerns the objects of memory. According to many models, from Cartesian "storehouse" models to contemporary distributed, interrelated, and dynamic neural networks, the input memory feeds on are traces in the brain.[13] These traces are ordinarily, and plausibly, assumed to have been left in the brain by previous experiences. But nothing about them, or about the mechanism that then uses them, guarantees that this is indeed their origin. It is not essential to them that they be the results of previous experiences. On the models in question, the world could have come into existence five minutes ago,[14] containing from its inception all the data we find in it now, and from which we learn about the past: texts, fossils, archeological cites, old tapes and films, and, of course, our living memories, that is, our "memory traces." Models of memory that take the mnemonic apparatus to work on traces in the brain portray memory as an internal affair, a kind of flipping through an internal album.

However, I believe models that render memory an internal affair in the above sense—as a cognitive activity that has, as one author put it, "no direct access to the extracranial causes" (Sterelny 1991, 35)[15]—misconstrue it. The objects of memory are not in the head; they are not mind-internal, "intercranial" photo-slides. Rather, they are the very objects perceptions of which left the trace behind. Recalling, for example, the Statue of Liberty, which I last visited some thirty-five years ago, I experience something that is akin to seeing it—I see before my mind's eye the greenish lump of bronze, one of whose arms is stretched upward, holding a torch, while the other arm embraces an open book. Zooming in on the torch, I see a round, open porch, to which visitors can exit, which is the torch's base. It seems obvious to me—though in order not to veer off the course of the discussion I will not argue for this conviction—that the objects of this "mnemonic perception" are the Statue of Liberty and its parts, and not something in my head.

Visual recollection differs, of course, from eyesight, most evidently in that one's eyes do not figure in it. But, although this difference is indeed blatant, it is also the *only* significant one. To look at a friend who is sitting facing me, and to remember how he looked twenty years ago, is to have two percepts of the same person—as he is and as he was. But it is not the case that one is "direct" in a way the other is not. Likewise, it is not the case that one percept but not the other is "inferred," or that one is precise and trustworthy whereas the other is deceptive, inaccurate, misleading. It is certainly not the case that one is inherently veridical and the other fallible. Both can be all of the above—accurate and deceptive, trustworthy and misleading, veridical and fallible. Nor is there a necessary difference in terms of the existence of the object or event perceived: I have more confidence that the Statue of Liberty, the features of which I am now recalling, exists, than I do that the red giant Alpha Orionis, noticeably visible outside my window and lying some 310 light-years away, does: it might have gone supernova fifty years ago.

As just remarked, recollection differs from eyesight in that the eyes are operative only in the latter (though they indispensably figure in the visual experience from which the memory trace comes into existence). Recalling comes into play when one visually cognates objects or events, visual signals from which are prevented from reaching one's eyes, either because of a spatial or temporal distance that separates one from the object, or because of some obstruction hiding the object, or because of a physical condition such as blindness, or an environmental condition such as darkness, and so forth. Memory is a faculty that broadens our field of vision to include objects and events that (at a given moment) are not visible to our eyes. Thanks to it, our present field of vision is expanded way beyond the horizon defined by the straight lines along which travel photons that now impinge upon our retinas.

Needless to say, memory cannot bring into our field of vision just anything. Like other perceptual faculties, it is subject to various constraints, some of which are dictated by our physical makeup, others by our personal histories. In particular, our past history determines which temporally and/or spatially distant, or hidden, events and objects are accessible to our memories—only those which we have been previously exposed to. Such exposures leave traces, and these traces, in turn, facilitate recollection. But again, the objects of recollection are events and things in the world, not in the head.

Remarks in the same spirit, but different in detail, can be made about the anticipation of future experiences. Thus, imagining what it will be like to return to Boston in two weeks time involves images of the Prudential tower, the Charles river, and the dome over MIT's library. These objects do not belong to my mind, but to the world, just like the objects of perception and memory.

Time flows, but in so doing, it does not place the things that become past beyond our cognitive reach. Nor do we need to wait until time's passage makes future things present for us to cognize them.[16] We can access conditions that obtained in the past or will obtain in the future, though we always do so from our present vantage point.

These brief remarks will have to do for now. They are somewhat peripheral to the discussion—which is why they have been presented more or less without defense—but keeping them in mind will help us in our efforts to lucidly grasp time's passage, a task we turn to now.

5.4   Time's Passage

Time's passage is probably the hardest nut in our basket. As already amply observed, naively, prephilosophically, we have no difficulties with it. But, when brought under philosophical scrutiny, a thick sense of indistinctness materializes around our comprehension of the passage of time, as weighty considerations expose gulfs in our understanding of its nature and lead to real doubts about its reality. Tenseless theorists turn these doubts into theses, in which time's passage is reduced to psychology, for example, to our awareness that our *A*-beliefs change and that our memories accumulate. They portray it as a mental phenomenon, a "subjective" product of our own constitution. It resides in our heads, they say, where it is kept away from "reality," our understanding of which it appears to threaten otherwise. Tensed theorists, on the other hand, answer the conceptual challenges with ontological theses in which passage, conceived as a change in the ontological status of events, is coroneted as the essence of time. Time, for them, is a global ontology machine, the flow of which consists in the carrying of unreal future events into the limelight of the "real and alive" present, and then ejecting them to the unreality of the past.

However, as we know, both positions are not tenable, and hence, insofar as these are the only conceivable answers to the question "Is time's passage real or is it an illusion?," we cannot regard the question as an intelligible one. Thus, as we transcend the theories that answer it, the theories in the context of which it is initially framed, we leave this question behind as well. More important, the term "time's passage," in its theoretical uses, is also left behind. In contrast with ordinary exclamations such as "How time flies!" and sentences such as "So much time has gone by since I last saw him," which allude to time's passage, the term "time's passage," as it figures in the tenseless/tensed debate, functions as the name of a natural phenomenon, which, like other phenomena, invites a theory that would explain it. However, once we transcend the ontological debate it becomes evident that passage is to time like meterhood is to *S*, the rod in Paris, or presence is to our experiences: it cannot be affirmed or denied. And so it cannot be the subject for an explanation.

Realizing this brings us close, no doubt, to the edge of the philosophical woods. Expressions such as "How time flies!" are thus lifted out of the swarm of queries they initially occasion. We are no longer worried as to whether such expressions refer to an illusion or, conversely, to some onto-logical occurrence which elicits embarrassing questions concerning, for example, its rate and nature. In general, most of the disturbing questions concerning time's passage are rooted in one of these ontological concep-tions of it, and are dissolved with the abandonment of these conceptions.

Thus, from naive, prephilosophical clarity concerning time's passage we are led, by philosophical probing, to perplexity, which then gets dissipated. That surely marks progress. The clarity we now enjoy is no longer naive: we can satisfactorily address the bafflements that upset our original under-standing of the issue. More important, the flip side of rejecting the ques-tion "Is time's passage real?" is our ability to answer in the affirmative the question "Does time really flow?" We can assert that time really flows, without being bogged down by the tenseless contention that time's passage is an illusion, or by the tensed theory's ontological thesis that time's passage "is real" in that it changes the ontological status of things.

But now we'd like to say more about time's passage. From establishing that of a firsthand experience e we can say neither that it is nor that it is not present we attained insights concerning the crucial role of experiences in our apprehension of time. What insights can we attain from the real-ization that of the flow of time we can say neither that it is "real" nor that it is "not real" (when these are taken to be the ontological claims of the tensed and tenseless theories respectively)? To seek these insights, let us return to the relationship between time's flow and truth.

This relationship is brought to the fore by that damning contradiction McTaggart famously showed was concealed within time's flow, an argu-ment which presumably demonstrated the *logical* impossibility of time's passage. Our aim now is to obtain a new understanding of how to recon-cile the permanency of truth with the mutability of reality. We do so by studying how transcending the ontological framework undermines the argument.[17]

Back in section 2.1 we discussed two versions of the argument: McTag-gart's original formulation, and Mellor's regress-free rendition of the argu-ment. We now start with Mellor's version. In a nutshell, it consists in the observation that, if tensed tokens are made true or false by tensed facts (Mellor speaks of facts and of truth makers rather than of truth conditions, and, in this context, we follow suit), and if time really flows, thereby con-stantly changing such facts, then each tensed token is both true and false.

Take, for example, a token of "John left for Paris yesterday." Suppose that the date of the event in question, John's departure, is June 16, 2007, and that the token is uttered the next day, June 17, 2007. The theory Mellor's argument is directed at says that tensed facts are responsible for the truth and falsity of such tokens, and that these facts change as time passes. Thus, up to June 17, 2007, and after this date, the tensed facts are such that the token is false. For example, on May 1, 2007, the tensed facts are that John's departure is still future, and so the token in question, which speaks of John's departure as a past event, is false. On June 17, 2007, the tensed facts are such that this very same token is true. But one and the same token cannot be both true and false. Thus, it cannot be that tensed facts, which change with time's passage, are what endow a given token with its truth-value. The conclusion Mellor draws is that tenseless facts do this job.

But let us be clear: the doctrine targeted by this argument is one in which facts obtaining at present constitute truth makers for *all* tokens—those tokened now, as well as those that have been tokened in the past or will be tokened in the future. This is, of course, the "moving Now" doctrine, in which the Now glides down the series of moments which constitute time, eliminating present facts and replacing them with new ones that, for the duration of their presentness, are crowned as "real and alive." Indeed, if only events and states of affairs that are privileged by the Now are "real and alive," then only they can function as truth makers. So if the events of May 1, 2007, are present and thus qualify to constitute truth makers, then the token is false—John's departure to Paris yesterday is not found among the facts obtaining on May 1, 2007. If it is the events of June 17 that we have to look at, then the token is true—John's departure to Paris yesterday is among them. So this supposedly natural picture of a Now that moves along time false prey to Mellor's argument.

But this picture is deeply routed in the ontological assumption. More explicitly than all other doctrines, perhaps, it ontologically elevates the present with respect to the past and the future. This picture tempts us into thinking that we can, and should, consider a given token from various points in time—those successively occupied by the Now—and assess its truth-value from these different temporal locations. And this thought, we already know, is confused. As we observed, we can say what a token's truth-value will be (or was) at the time of its tokening; but we cannot say what it is now, because now we do not have the token. Now, all we have are replicas of past and future tokens. Tokens are, by their very nature, tokened only once. They cannot be reproduced, only replicated, and it is crucial to stress that the replica is a *different* token. So we cannot now access tokens that are not present and assess their truth-values in light of present conditions.

Once we have left the ontological assumption behind and are no longer committed to it, we no longer feel drawn toward assessing the truth-value of tokens in light of conditions that obtain now. We are no longer committed to the claim that only the present is "real" and that therefore only present facts can figure in making tokens true or false. This frees us to suggest instead that a token's truth-value is determined not by conditions obtaining where "the Now" is located—by what obtains at present—but by the conditions that obtain at the time of its tokening. It is the conditions obtaining at that location that give it its meaning and truth-value.

Imagine that a week ago NASA scientist Joan said: "Our robot is scheduled to land on the surface of Jupiter in three days." What is the status of that token now, a week later? Would we say that it has changed its truth-value from being true to being false (false because now it is not the case that our robot is scheduled to land on the surface of Jupiter in three days)? For it to be false, it, that very same token, needs to be reproduced now, that conditions that falsify it obtain. But tokens cannot be reproduced—of each token there can be only one specimen. What we would say, rather, is that the token in question was true on the day it was uttered, and that today, a week later, it is still the case that that token was true then. The only reason we might not endorse this simple option is if we are "Now theorists" who hold that only what exists now is real and can figure as a truth maker. Then we are truly committed to assessing all tokens, including the one Joan tokened a week ago, in relation to present facts. Indeed, considered in light of conditions that obtain now, that token, which was true then, is now false. But if we stick to the view that a token is attached to the conditions that obtain at the time of its tokening, and that neither the token nor these conditions can be transported to other locations in time, we escape Mellor's argument.

A defender of Mellor's McTaggart might agree that taking the conditions obtaining at the time of the tokening to be a token's truth conditions removes contradictions. But she may want to point out that such conditions are not really tensed, but are rather never-changing tenseless conditions, for it is always the case that on such-and-such a date, such-and-such conditions obtain, and not others. That on the day Joan tokened the above token it was the case that the robot was scheduled to land three days hence is a fact today, and it was a fact a thousand years ago. So this fact is a static, tenseless fact, claims Mellor's defender.

But her claim is based on confusion. The facts in question—that the robot is scheduled to land *three days hence*—are as *tensed* as any fact can be: they concern the robot's *future* landing. In general, the facts that we are claiming make a token true or false pertain to events' being *past, present, or future*, with all the ramifications that follow from possessing one of these tensed determinants rather than another (some of which are yet to be discussed). True, these facts do not change—the conditions obtaining on a certain Tuesday are always the conditions that obtain on that Tuesday. No one has ever suggested that that particular Tuesday comes to be occupied by new conditions as time passes and it becomes Wednesday. Rather, as it becomes Wednesday—as Wednesday dawns—a new set of conditions becomes present, namely those of Wednesday. Tuesday's conditions remain as they are; they only cease to be present and become past. They do not cease to exist, nor do they continue to exist. They do not cease to be "real," nor do they continue to be "real." Changes in tensed facts cannot be reduced to ontological categories, or framed by reality claims. Changes in tensed facts consist simply in that, with time's passage, events that were future become present, and present events become past. Once we recognize this, we are out of the straits of Mellor's version of McTaggart's argument, because we are no longer confined to finding truth conditions only among conditions obtaining at present.[18]

Now back to McTaggart's original formulation of the argument. This formulation does not involve truth makers, but consists simply in the observation that past, present, and future are incompatible "determinants," which each event supposedly has. Since "in reality" events cannot have incompatible determinants, McTaggart's conclusion is that "in reality" there is no distinction between the past, present, and future, that is, events are really not past, nor present, nor future. The traditional rejoinder, we remember, is that events have these conflicting determinants at different times, so for an event to possess them is no more contradictory than it is for a cherry to be green all over and then, after it ripens, to be red all over. I suppose we all feel there is some validity to this rejoinder.

Yet, as we saw (section 2.1), it is easily repelled by McTaggart, who observes that introducing three different times—one in which the event is past, one in which it is present, and one in which it is future—is to no avail because these times are themselves past, present, or future. So now instead of one contradiction we have three. This leads immediately to the infinite regress, which, McTaggart claimed, does not eliminate the contradictions, but rather multiplies them and shows them to be omnipresent.

Dummett makes McTaggart's point even more impressively. By introducing these three new times McTaggart's opponent replaces simple tenses with complex ones: instead of saying that e is past, present, and future, we should say that it *was* future, *is* present, and *will be* past (assuming that now e is present). But, Dummett points out, there are now nine complex tenses: e will be future; e will be present; e will be past; e is now future; e is now present; e is now past; e was future; e was present; e was past. And all nine complex determinants, among which not one but several contradictions are found, are possessed by e. So the contradiction is revived, as is the spiraling down the infinite regress.

What is it then that renders the traditional response ineffective despite its seeming to move in the right direction? What's lacking from it, that makes it fall short of its mark? I think that the traditional rejoinder fails to dismantle the tacit ontological assumptions sustaining McTaggart's argument. Just as we did with Mellor's version of the argument, we need to expose these assumptions, and take them on. But these assumptions need to be approached from an angle that is different from the one from which they were tackled when Mellor's argument was addressed. There, the assumption we had to undermine was the tensed theory's tenet that only the present is real. Here it is the tenseless tenet that all times are "equally real." It is on this tenet that McTaggart relies in rebuffing the traditional rejoinder. Let us see how he does this.

McTaggart's opening move consists in stating that an event e is past, present, and future. The rejoinder is that it is past at t_1, present at t_2, and future at t_3. In essence, McTaggart's response is to claim that these three times, t_1, t_2, and t_3, are, as it were, on an ontological par; they are "equally real," there is no privileged time among them. So the tensed determinants e has in each of them are also on an ontological par: e is not more attached to the tensed determinant associated with t_1 than it is to the ones associated with t_2 and t_3, and so on. Rather, it is equally attached to all three determinants. In other words, e is ("equally") past, present, and future—the original opening move. This, of course, is not how McTaggart words his rejoinder. But by pointing out that each of these times is itself past, present, and future, he is essentially saying that they are on an ontological par, and that hence the determinants associated with them are "equally real."

I think, by the way, that this is precisely how Dummett, whose rendition of McTaggart's rejoinder was presented above, understands this rejoinder. He invokes the notion of "a complete description of the world," one that is "of what is really there, as it really is." And he says that such a description "must be independent of any point of view. . . . of anything which is real, there must be a complete—that is, observer independent—description" (Dummett 1978, 356). In such a description all moments are on an ontological par, and the significance of this fact is that, in light of it, so are the tensed determinants e has in each of them. Hence the contradiction.

The ineffective rejoinder counters that only one of these times is "real" and that therefore e has only one tensed determinant, the one that comes together with the time that is "real": it is past if t_1 is "real," present if t_2 is "real," and future if t_3 is "real."

This showdown repeats itself at every level of the infinite regress. Each side repeatedly declares its position about the reality of past and future times, McTaggart stating that all times are "equally real" and that hence e possess all complex tenses that belong to that level, his opponents that only the present is "real" and that therefore e's only tensed property is the one it has in relation to the present moment.

Thus, the key to the proper response to McTaggart lies in the rejection of the reality claims of both sides. Instead of insisting that only the present is "real," we block McTaggart's access to other times by refusing to acknowledge that all times are "equally real." An event that is occurring now can be said to have been future. But no viewpoint is available from which it *is* future, or will be future, or was past. These complex tenses do not apply to the event now, and other temporal perspectives, from which they supposedly would apply, are not available, not because only the present is real, but because we do not know what to make of the idea that other times are "equally real" as the present one, which they have to be, if they are to constitute viewpoints equal to that of the present.

This response is analogous to the above rejoinder to Mellor's version of the argument. There we rejected the notion that a token tokened at t_1 can be somehow retokened at some other time t_2. Here we are rejecting the notion that a tensed determinant e possesses at t_1 can somehow be reapplied to it at t_2. In both cases, the rejection builds on our ability to repudiate the idea that different moments in time, or events located at different times, are "equally real," without thereby embracing the opposite notion that only the present is "real."

Our response to McTaggart's argument also bears some resemblance to Dummett's solipsism of the present moment. In essence, both block the argument by denying access to those temporal locations in which an event's tensed determinant is different from its determinant in the present. However, consisting of ontological claims, Dummett's move renders those other times too inaccessible. On Dummett's doctrine, we recall, we cannot say of conditions that obtained a year ago that they established the truth or falsity of a token tokened then. Or, to be more accurate, we can say this, but we cannot mean by such an assertion what we mean when we say of present conditions that they are the truth conditions of tokens tokened now; and in fact we cannot really say what we *do* mean by such an assertion. It's not merely that those past conditions are no longer a part of the world; it's that we cannot give a sense to the notion that those past conditions *ever were* a part of the world. But if, unlike Dummett, we do not think of tense in ontological terms, then we can regard past and future conditions as truth conditions in just the sense in which we think of present conditions as truth conditions, while emphasizing that we can only apprehend them from our present viewpoint, and not actually occupy them in a manner that would enable us to utilize them at present as truth conditions. If we do not utilize them at present as truth conditions for tokens uttered at other times, we do not generate the contradictions McTaggart's argument highlights.

Let me restate one more time the scheme concerning truth conditions that has been recurring in the last few pages. The truth conditions for a token p tokened at t are those obtaining at t. However, they include tensed conditions—in specifying them, the *tensed* locations of events, some of which may not occur at t, are given. In the example discussed a few pages back, that the robot is scheduled to land *three days hence*, is the condition on which Joan's token of "Our robot is scheduled to land on the surface of Jupiter in three days," uttered now, is true. The condition obtains now, but involves a future event. We cannot access that future event now; we can only access the present tensed condition, namely, that the robot will land in three days' time. When John tells his friends that he returned from Paris three weeks ago his token is true on the tensed condition that he returned three weeks ago, and not on some "de-tensed" condition, some tenseless "return from Paris" that has no tensed location. But the past event of his return is mentioned when this present condition is given. So in this scheme truth conditions are not those of the tenseless theorist: they are definitely tensed. Nor are they those of the tensed theorist: they do not consist exclusively of present materials, but rather of present conditions, which, being tensed, involve events and states of affairs that are not present. Again, the key to avoiding confusion here is refraining from either attributing or denying some kind of "reality" to future or past events. They are not "not real," as tensed theorists would have them be; nor are they "equally real," as tenseless theorists would have them be.

This connects with the remarks made at the end of the previous section in connection with the objects of memory and anticipation. We said there that cognizing past and future events and states of affairs is not a mind-internal affair, but rather one the objects of which are those "external" past or future things. The obstacles to understanding this come from the thought that to be cognizable x has to be "real," which leads to the tenseless view; or from the tensed theorist's thought that only the present is "real and alive," which makes the cognizing of a nonpresent x a mystery. Once we are free from either form of ontologizing tense, we can set straight the issue of cognizing past and future things. For David to remember seeing a space shuttle touch down at Cape Canaveral a year ago is for him to recognize conditions that obtained then. To foresee seeing Niagara Falls is to cognize future conditions. There is no difference between these cases, and, say, David's seeing an airplane passing overhead. And when we describe the truth conditions for his utterances and thoughts, they will be present conditions the specification of which will involve past, present, and future events: the landing of the shuttle, the passing of the airplane overhead, the future visit to the Niagara Falls.

Perhaps a short summary of all this can be useful. Not counting the tenseless view, which denies time's passage altogether, we have three positions concerning the relationship between a token p tokened at t and the present moment t' (assuming $t \neq t'$).

• On the "moving Now" view, the conditions obtaining at t are the truth conditions for *all* tokens, including p. This position is shown by Mellor to be contradictory.

• On Dummett's solipsism of the present moment, the conditions at t are p's truth conditions. But these are what we called (p. 104) "truth conditions$_2$," a term we had difficulty attaching an intelligible sense to. This made it impossible to satisfactorily incorporate time's passage into Dummett's doctrine.

• On the position I'm advocating, the tensed conditions at t are p's truth conditions, just as the tensed conditions obtaining at present, at t', are those of tokens tokened now. Relieved of ontological commitments, this position does not allow present conditions to constitute truth conditions for tokens that are not present and so is not implicated with contradictions; nor does it "solipsize" the present by ontologically demoting conditions that are not present to a position from which they can no longer constitute the history through which time flows.

McTaggart's great contribution to the modern discussion in the philosophy of time was in articulating more sharply than before the contradiction that supposedly nestles in the idea of time's passage. Since his conclusion, that time's passage is a fiction of our minds, is one that prompts resistance, we are driven by the argument to expose its hidden assumptions. We thereby discover that ontological presuppositions that initially appear natural are in fact prejudices that are the roots of philosophical confusion. Freeing ourselves of these prejudices lets us retrieve time's passage from the gallows of the tenseless theory, without having to surrender it either to the self-contradictory "moving Now," or to the straitjacket of Dummett's solipsism of the present moment.

Having removed this conceptual challenge to the idea of time's passage, we can begin to see it clearly, as something that renders future things present rather than "real," and present things past rather than "not real." Time's passage is not the movement of some *thing* that gives birth to events, states of affairs, and objects that are not yet but are becoming present, and demolishes those that are present but are becoming past. It does not "materialize" present things *ex nihilo* and inject them into history, nor does it obliterate them *ad nihilo* and remove them from history. Rather, with time's passage, things that make up this history's future become present and then become this history's past, an evolution that has nothing to do with ontology, and which cannot be described or explained by reference to the ontological status, or changes therein, of things.

I wish to return now briefly to the question of the rate of time's passage. We observed at the beginning of the section that once we overcome thinking of time's passage in terms of some *thing* that moves the question of rate evaporates. But our appreciation of the above claims concerning passage can benefit from taking another, closer look at this issue. We tell a child who has just bruised herself, "The pain will soon go away." There is nothing that we, or the child if she is old enough, do not understand on such an occasion, or that can or ought to be explained by a metaphysical theory. Presumably, hearing this reassurance will ease the child's alarm. And for good reason: with time's passage her pain *will* soon go away. Far from confounding her, it is through such occasions that her conception of time is *developed*.

Next the child may want to know how soon the pain will go away. "In a couple of minutes," would be a good answer. But what if a philosopher, who is standing by, interrupts and explains that what the child really wants to know is at what rate time passes? In contrast with the child's question, the philosopher's interpretation of it rings queer. And by now we are in a position to say what is queer about it. At the basis of this question there is again that nagging urge to "ontologize" the present, to think of it as a kind of *thing* that runs down the series of moments that make up time, much like water runs down a hose. The "moving Now" picture indeed invites questions concerning the rate at which this "ontologically endowed" thing moves. Schlesinger makes this question vanish somewhere among the hyper-times that arrange the worlds of his many-worlds scheme, times that are not exactly temporal, and that at any rate remain utterly unknown to us. Others, such as Prior (1962), submit the seemingly uninformative idea that time passes at a rate of an hour per hour. Imagine someone dismissing the common wisdom that "The happier the time, the more quickly it passes,"[19] claiming that time cannot pass more quickly on occasion of one's happiness because its rate is fixed to be one hour per hour. Alternatively, think of someone setting out to design a time machine that accelerates the rate of time's passage from one second per second to two seconds per second. Could we reproach him for wasting his time? But, outside the context of the "moving Now" picture, the issue of passage is much less ludicrous, and if it is inquired at what rate does time pass, the onus is on the inquirer to explain the question. Quite likely, the "moving Now" will resurface in one form or another in his response.

The simple question "At what rate does time pass?" can be embarrassingly baffling. One does not have to be a philosopher to pose it or to become intrigued by it. But its simplicity is misleading. There are no simple answers to it, and no quick ways to dismiss it offhand. Tenseless theorists can circumvent it by rejecting the notion that time passes. If time does not really pass, there is no real question about the rate of its passage. But this can't count as an easy answer—becoming a tenseless theorist is no easy feat. Tensed theorists are cornered into giving awkward answers of the kind mentioned above, the unattractiveness of which taints the appeal of their theory and reveals that behind its commonsensical façade lurk cumbersome metaphysical structures.

We have proposed a different approach to this question—we answer it by transcending the ontological assumption that gives rise to it. And this is not an easy answer either, given the naturalness of this assumption, and the work that goes into transcending it. But once we have accomplished this move, and the conceptual frameworks that could provide meaning to the question are superseded, it dissolves. We commonly say things such as "This year went by so fast!" or "Three weeks have passed since she asked him to open the envelope," or more poetically, "On wings of Time grief and sorrow fly off and away," as in La Fontaine's attempt to encourage a young widow. We introduce the name "time's passage" to stand for something that we encounter in locutions such as these, and we then turn to the task of theorizing about it. In the theoretical context questions concerning the rate of passage are in place. But having transcended this context, we can no longer give sense to the question. "How soon will the sorrow fly off and away?" is a straightforward question that has a straightforward answer. "At what rate will the sorrow fly off and away?" is not.

What has just been said may be misunderstood as suggesting that talk of time's passage is metaphorical. So let me repeat the clarification made at the end of chapter 3: it is not metaphorical. The similarity between "This year went by so fast!" and "This cyclist went by so fast!" can easily mislead us into thinking that just as it makes sense to ask at what velocity the cyclist went by, so it makes sense to query about the velocity, or rate, at which the year went by. And the realization that this latter question is meaningless can get us to conclude that, therefore, speaking of time's passage is "metaphorical": if it does not have a rate, then it is not really passage. But this is nothing but an arbitrary stipulation. In court, "John was last seen three weeks ago" would be accepted as a purely descriptive piece of testimony. If this sentence is true, then it is, as they say, "literally" true: indeed, three weeks have passed since John was last seen. It makes no sense to ask at what rate they have passed; but neither does it make sense to deny they have passed, or to suggest they did so only metaphorically—what "nonmetaphorical" means would there be for conveying this piece of testimony? The witness could say, "John was last seen on the fifth of May." If the prosecutor then pressed: "so you mean to say that three weeks have passed since you saw him last, metaphorically speaking, that is?," the question would be thrown out as "intentionally misleading."

We close this section with Parfit's argument in defense of the tenseless view. In a way this discussion is superfluous. Parfit's position is structured around the notion of "tenseless relations," and we've already considered the problems that plague this notion and theories it figures in. But, first, we must become convinced that Parfit's argument does not give this term new meanings we must contend with. Second, dealing with Parfit's argument will give us occasion to examine another veil philosophy throws over the notion of time's passage, namely, the claim that the tenses and the flow of time are *perspectival*.

Parfit, we recall, bases his argument on a notion encountered before in this section, that of a "complete description of the world." Like Dummett, Parfit takes such a description to be one that is "given from no place within this universe" and is therefore thoroughly nonperspectival. Nothing pertaining to the describer's particular viewpoint can be reflected in it. Think of a map of Europe, in which Paris is shown to be west of Prague. A token of "Paris is west of Prague" would supposedly constitute a true description, irrespective of any facts about the spatial location of its tokening. Tokens of this kind are paradigms of the sort of items that would make up a "complete description of the world." In contrast, "Paris is west of here" could not belong to such a description. This token is markedly perspectival. It contains information pertaining to the subjective perspective of some observer, and its truth depends on where it is tokened. Being "here" is a property a random observer happens to have in relation to a certain location, not a property intrinsic to that location, or any other location on the map. Bilbao does not have, in addition to the property of being north of Madrid, the property of being "here" or "there." Saying that it is here would merely be stating its location from someone's subjective, accidental position.

Projecting this moral onto its temporal equivalent is supposed to illustrate Parfit's argument. June 13, 2007 does not have, in addition to the property of being later than June 12, 2007, the property of being past, present, or future. Saying that today is June 13 would be stating the temporal location of June 13 as it is apprehended from our subjective, accidental position. "Now," like "here," is perspectival. Realizing this is tantamount, according to Parfit, to realizing that the tenses are subjective, and that time's passage is part of "mental reality," or, to put it more blatantly, is an illusion.

However, as I now wish to point out, there are some essential disanalogies between space and time. So even if the spatial example gives us a sense of what a "complete description" would look like, and thus of the perspectival nature of "here," this idea cannot be carried over to the temporal "now." Let us observe, to begin with, that there really are "complete," nonperspectival descriptions of spatial locations. (1) "The Empire State Building is in New York" is true regardless of where in space it is tokened, and it contains no information that could be spelled out by means of "spatial tenses" such as "here" or "there." Although the copula "is" in (1) is temporally inflected, as verbs always are (with the exception, perhaps, of statements of mathematics, which form a separate category that is not relevant to this discussion), this "is" is not spatially conjugated. Indeed, we would be at a loss were we requested to conjugate it spatially. Because verbs are truly spatially "tenseless"—there are no spatial inflections of verbs—we can, using proper names rather than occasion-sensitive words such as "here," obtain *purely* (spatially) tenseless descriptions of spatial locations, descriptions such as (1). Moreover, it is the availability of such truly tenseless descriptions that *makes meaningful* the distinction between "perspectival" and "nonperspectival" descriptions. Only against such genuinely nonperspectival descriptions does it make sense to say that (2) "The

Empire State Building is here" is perspectival. If not for sentences such as (1), what would the assertion that (2) is perspectival come to? It would be perspectival as opposed to *what?*

In contrast, as we already know from section 4.3, there are no temporally tenseless sentences. Descriptive sentences always betray tensed information concerning the temporal location of the events or states of affairs they describe. Events and states of affairs are always thought of and spoken of as being either past, present, or future. Temporal inflections simply cannot be eliminated from our thought or spoken tokens. "Paris is west of Prague," for example, is *not* temporally tenseless. The "is" is temporally inflected: the sentence is in the present tense. This token is not true regardless of *when* it is tokened. For example, tokened before the creation of either Paris or Prague, it would be false, if not meaningless. In the absence of a temporal analogue of (1), with "purely tenseless temporal descriptions" being an empty term, the condition under which the distinction between "perspectival" and "nonperspectival" descriptions can be drawn does not obtain.[20]

Following the discussion of chapter 4, it should be clear that these remarks do not pertain to the "surface grammar" of English. Perhaps we could artificially introduce spatially inflected verbs, or means for spatially inflecting existing verbs, so that the verbs of our language would be both temporally and spatially inflected. Such a modification would only alter the surface of our grammar. We would still have the means of producing spatially tenseless descriptions. And the converse—neutralizing temporal tenses so that the verbs of language are no longer temporally inflectable— is not an option.

That Parfit's defense of the tenseless view relies on the notion of a complete description of the world renders his argument circular, for this notion, in the temporal context, assumes the availability of temporally tenseless relations and descriptions. Only tenseless relations could figure in a complete description. But, outside the tenseless theory, which the argument is supposed to make viable, there are no such relations. So his argument relies on means that would become available only if the argument was successful. And his use of the analogy with space fails as well, because of the relevant disanalogies between space and time.

Believing in the idea of a complete description of the world, then, is one way of expressing commitment to the ontological assumption. In such a description all events in the history of the world are on an ontological par. The notion that they are not "equally real," in view of such a description, can only betray one's perspectival prejudices. And, plainly, once one has endorsed the idea of a complete description in which the properties of being past, present, and future are perspectival, one is bound to regard time's passage as perspectival as well, as something that is apprehended from our own subjective viewpoint, not something that pertains to what we are apprehending. Thus, the notion of a "complete description" becomes the source for another idea that could fog our thinking of time's passage—the idea that time's passage is "subjective" in the sense of being "perspectival."

But this obstruction to our understanding is removed when we transcend the ontological assumption and relinquish the ontological parity that underpins the idea of a complete description of the world (once again, not for the sake of some ontological imparity, but for the realization that tense cannot be captured in these terms at all). In particular, as we saw, the attendant perspectival/nonperspectival distinction is shown to be inapplicable to the notion of time's passage.

To sum up: transcending ontology enables us to view time's passage perspicuously. Time's passage simply consists in future events becoming present, and present ones becoming past. This truism is, of course, by no means a triviality. Here's a list of the formidable challenges it faces: Does time really pass, or is time's passage merely an illusion? Does denying that time's passage is an illusion commit one to a tensed metaphysics, to the movement of some ontologically privileged "Now"? Is the notion of passage self-contradictory in the way McTaggart thought it was? If not, how are we to handle the issue of ever-changing tensed truth conditions? At what rate does time pass? And why is it not merely perspectival, merely part of mental reality?

To defend the above truism, and, what's more important, to begin understanding the intricacies concealed within it, we need to contend with these questions, something we have strived to do in this section. The next step involves taking the above simple (not to say simplistic) characterization of time's passage and elaborating it. Ultimately, as will be discussed in the next chapter, this requires turning to phenomenology. But, before that, there is still more we can do with our post-ontological explorations of tense and passage.

5.5 Tense-based Biases

A quick reminder. All our experiences are tensely located; they are all either past, present, or future. Past ones are remembered (some of them, at any rate), present ones are had, (some) future ones are anticipated. And these experiences have a crucial role in our apprehension of the temporal aspects of reality, a role akin to that of a standard. Here again is our analogy: it is in relation to the standard meter that the length of objects is determined by us; and it is by means of the standard that the term "meter" is introduced into language. Likewise, it is in relation to our present experiences that the tensed locations of other events are determined by us; and the tensed terms that serve us in language and thought derive their content from the tensed features of our experiences.

Of course, an event is not present *because* it is cotemporal with one of one's experiences, or future *because* it succeeds that experience, just as a table is not one meter long *because* it is the same length as the standard meter. But these firsthand experiences, these quasi standards, are the basis for establishing tensed locations; they are the anchors of the terms that express tense in thought and speech.

I wish now to broaden our acquaintance with these "tense rods" and hence with tense by examining some of their features. Specifically, I wish to look at differences in our attitudes toward our firsthand experiences, differences determined by the tensed location of these experiences. I have in mind the well-known and varied sentiments that accompany our experiences, such as the thrill and impatience that accompany the anticipation with which we await a meeting with a friend whom we have not seen for a long time; or the pleasant gratification we feel when we remember that meeting several months later. These sensations—thrill, impatience, and then gratification—are a second layer of experiences that ride, as it were, on top of the primary experience, in our example, that of the reunion with an old friend.

Clearly, which second-layer sentiment accompanies the primary experience depends on the *tensed location* of the primary experience. The upcoming reunion is a source of thrill while it is *future*, and of gratitude when it is *past*. As both tensed and tenseless theorists point out, the meeting's merely being *later* or *earlier* than a given moment cannot be the reason for the thrill or gratitude, for (regressing for a moment back into "tenseless" talk) the meeting is *always* later than or earlier than the moment in question. So this "tenseless" fact cannot be the source of the relevant sentiment at a given moment but not at another. If we are thrilled about experience *e* that is because *e* is *future*, not because *e* is later than *t*; why would *e*'s succeeding *t* be something we'd care about? It is always later than *t*; but it is not always future.

Evidently, then, sensations that are associated with a given experience are *tense based*, that is, they depend on the tensed location of the experience. Likewise, shifts in such sensations, such as the shift from thrill to gratitude, or from anguish to relief in connection with an unpleasant experience, are *tense based*: they occur as, with time's passage, *e* turns from being future to being past.

Tense-based sentiments and shifts of this kind are something tensed theorists celebrate because they supposedly provide weighty evidence in favor of their view. Moreover, these sentiments and shifts are something tensed theorists can easily explain: time flows and brings the future experience closer and closer to the point where it becomes "real and alive," or to the point where it actually is experienced, and then it removes it farther and farther into the past. If the experience is a pleasant one, we will want to experience it and so will impatiently await it as it approaches us from the future, and miss it once it becomes past. Our sentiments will be inversed with respect to unpleasant experiences.

But more than they are interested in laying out their own explanations (to which we will return momentarily), tensed theorists are eager to challenge their tenseless opponents with these quintessentially tensed biases. Indeed, given the tenseless denial that in reality events and experiences are tensely located, tenseless theorists are certainly under the obligation to explain the pervasiveness of sentiments that are markedly connected to the tensed location of experiences. The demand for such an explanation was made most famously, perhaps, by Prior (1959). For Prior, exclamations such as "Thank goodness that's over!," something we say when an unpleasant experience is over and past, decisively tell against the tenseless view, for, again, they express distinctly *tense-dependent* sentiments. No one would make such an exclamation with respect to a painful experience that is still future; nor would it make sense to utter such an exclamation in a tenseless world (see section 3.1), a world in which the painless experience is, again, not future. In a tenseless world, a world in which the only kind of temporal facts are of the kind "*e* occurs at *t*," it would make no sense to feel one way about an experience at one moment and differently at another—in a tenseless world, "*e* occurs at *t*" would always be true.[21]

Schlesinger, in the book we have already discussed, *Aspects of Time*, also employs this line of reasoning. Posing these questions as challenges to the tenseless theorist, he asks: "when an unpleasant experience occurs at a given temporal distance from the time at which this token occurs, why should it matter in which direction this experience lies?" Furthermore, "why should our attitude to the event of our birth differ from our attitude to the event of our death?" (1980, 35). Like Prior, Schlesinger regards "our very different attitudes that prevail towards the future and the past" (ibid., 34) as offering strong "evidence" in the favor of the tensed theory of time.

Tenseless theorists acknowledge that there is an issue here for them. Parfit, to take one example, also raises the question whether "if my ordeal is in the past rather than the future, that [does or does not] give me a reason to be glad" (1996, 20). Utterances of the type "thank goodness that my ordeal is in the past rather than the future" (ibid., 27) express an attitude he calls the "bias towards the future," which he also describes as consisting of the sentiment that "past pain matters less." Another form of sensitivity to tense that he discusses is the "bias towards the present," which consists in one's being "glad that my ordeal is not occurring now" (ibid., 16). The question Parfit concentrates on is whether, given that "in reality" there is no difference between the past, present, and future, it is *rational* to care more about a painful experience that is (mistakenly being perceived as) future, or whether we have *reason* to be glad that an ordeal is (perceived as) now past. If experiences are not past, present, or future, it would seem irrational to treat them as though they were, for example, by succumbing to sentiments that are derived from their supposedly tensed properties.

Indeed, from within the tenseless/tensed debate, the need for theories that would explain these biases seems very natural: we want to know what it is about time and about our position in it that makes us sweat and shiver before the shrill of the dentist's drill begins and smile victoriously as we leave her office. We seek a theory that will explain and, more importantly, *justify* this shift in our feelings. I shall argue, however, that the question of the justifiability—of the rationality—of these biases is itself not rational, since it is not even coherent. First, it will be useful briefly to examine the types of justifications offered by supporters of each of the metaphysical theories.

We already saw that tensed theorists are well positioned to account for the biases in question. That only what exists now is real, and that time flows, seem to entail these biases quite straightforwardly. First, they seem to entail the bias toward the present: that "only when events are present they are fully real" (Parfit 1996, 18) seems to *explain* why we are glad that an ordeal is not occurring *now*. After all, we should certainly be glad that something unwanted is not real. That only what exists now is real and that time flows also seem to provide a *justification* for the bias toward the future: the closer a pain is, the more troubling it is. And time's passage brings future pains closer and takes past pains farther away. This tensed fact gives us *reason* to dread future pains and all the more so the closer they get and to be relieved with respect to past pains. Pleasant experiences call for a similar type of account. Thus, Schlesinger explains that

pleasant experiences of the past are recalled with nostalgia, and we regret their passing; that is, we are sorry that they are getting away from the "NOW," which is the point in time at which events occurring at that time are real to our experience. On the other hand pleasant experiences are being looked forward to with joy, for they are approaching the "NOW" and are about to overtake us. (1980, 36)

How can tenseless theorists, who deny the passage of time, account for these biases? Here we meet two basic approaches. One is based on the fact that, as J. J. C. Smart puts it, even if we are tenseless theorists, "certainly we *feel* that time flows" (1980, 3). Mellor too stresses that we all experience time's passage and possess *A*-beliefs, beliefs about the tensed locations of event and about time's passage. But, as we saw, his theory fully accounts for these beliefs and experiences tenselessly. In addition, Mellor relies on his theory of causation, which provides him with the difference between the tenseless relations of "before" and "after" and hence with the directionality of time.[22] It thus becomes fairly simple for Mellor to explain the biases: we all *believe* that with time's passage, events from the future approach us, become present, and then recede into the past. And we believe that we experience only what is present. These beliefs explain our tense-based biases. Moreover, since, according to Mellor, possessing tensed beliefs is not merely a convenience but a necessity, his account, like that of the tensed theorist, constitutes a *justification* of the biases in question. These biases turn out to be grounded in the facts of reality—not in tensed facts, to be sure, but in tenseless facts, as well as in the facts of causation, which support our tensed experiences and beliefs. Since it is rational to act in accordance with the basic facts of reality, it is rational to experience and to act in accordance with the above biases.

Keith Seddon, in his book *Time*, also invokes causation as a basic fact of reality, a fact that, among other things, gives tenseless time a direction. But Seddon highlights a different consideration: "The fact that we cannot now do anything to avoid a past painful experience will obviously be intimately involved in explaining how our anxieties differ depending upon whether they are forward-directed or backwards-directed" (1987, 76). He goes on to say that

past circumstances matter to us, if indeed they now matter at all, in a completely different way from that in which anticipated future circumstances matter to us, for the simple reason that there is often something that we can do now to influence how those future circumstances turn out. It looks to me as though this is why we find that our attention is concentrated upon the future in a way in which it is not concentrated on the past. (Ibid., 87)

It is not necessary for us to engage in an assessment of the merits and shortcomings of this explanation. Let us merely note that the tenseless approaches outlined above strive to offer explanations and justifications that can compete with those put forth by tensed theorists. Their failure to do so would, indeed, turn tensed-based biases into a significant consideration in favor of the tensed theory. Conversely, succeeding in tenselessly accounting for these tensed-based biases would strengthen the standing of the tenseless theory.

There is another kind of tenseless response to these biases, however, one that bites the bullet and proclaims them to be irrational. Speaking of our bias toward the future, Parfit concludes that there is no "independent reason to believe that this bias is not irrational" (1996, 27). Parfit imagines a person, whom he calls *timeless*, and who, in the absence of any theory justifying tense-dependent biases, resolves to adopt a "temporal neutrality," the only view he deems in accord with his conception of himself as a rational being. It consists, for example, in that

he is not relieved when his ordeals are over. "Why should I be?" he asks. "My ordeal is just as long and just as painful, and just as much part of my life. Why is it good that my ordeal is in the past rather than the future?" Similarly, when he is about to die, he is not concerned. More exactly, he may regret that his life is finite. But, although he will soon cease to exist, he is no more concerned than he would be if he had only just started to exist. "Why should I be?" he asks. "Though I now have nothing to look forward to, I have my whole life to look backward to." (1996, 30)

We encountered a similar train of thought in Schlesinger's story of Denisovitch. Schlesinger claimed that, from a tenseless viewpoint, Denisovitch should not care whether it is one week after his incarceration or one week before his release—in tenseless terms, his distance from freedom is in either case the same. From a tenseless viewpoint, "a true philosopher ought to face the future with no less equanimity than the past. The enlightened thinker will view events ahead with the same detachment as the ordinary person views past events which have no further repercussions" (Schlesinger 1980, 37). Schlesinger, who, of course, does not defend this position, reports that "in conversation, Smart has suggested—tentatively—this as a possibility" (ibid., 37fn.). Parfit, as we just saw, appears to actually endorse it.

Needless to say, theorists from either camp are not impressed with the explanations offered by their opponents. Seddon says that "Schlesinger's understanding is wrong because the idea of temporal movement is an absurdity" (1987, 82). Schlesinger, for his part, holds that causal explanations such as Seddon's, in which our ability to shape the future and inability to affect the past play a vital role, "will surely not do, as we dread no less the calamities of the future which are absolutely unpreventable and look forward no less jubilantly to great pleasures which are sure to materialize without our help" (1980, 37). Discontent with the causal explanation is not expressed by tensed theorists alone. Parfit too rejects it: "Suppose we believe that we shall be tortured later today. After trying to escape, we conclude that we have no hope, since our torture is inevitable. Would we think 'Thank goodness!,' regarding such future pain as giving us, because we can't affect it, as little reason for concern as past pain? We would not" (1996, 29). Objections of this nature do not apply to Mellor, whose explanations of the biases rely not on our inability to affect the future, but merely on the temporal directionality induced by the direction of causation. Still, tensed theorists would find his explanations unpalatable because of his rejection of time's passage and of the reality of the tenses. And Parfit would be displeased by the justification Mellor gives to attitudes that, upon inspection, emerge as irrational.

As for Parfit's (and perhaps also Smart's) "temporal neutrality," the position illustrated by *timeless*, who shuns the biases as irrational, this position, says Schlesinger, is "a most unlikely solution. . . . Nor does it seem helpful to summon to mind the traditional notion of the philosopher as being calm and unperturbed at all times; to cite the example of Socrates, who was without fear, even of death; to refer to the fortitude of the Stoics, and so on. The special attitude that has been typical of some philosophers, which we feel is appropriate and even admirable, is based on something entirely different. . . . [on ideas such as] life after death, the possession of virtue, and so on" (1980, 37), and *not* on a metaphysical theory of time. He concludes by saying that when such sentiments are required by a doctrine of time, "they seem contrary to human nature" (ibid., 38).

As insightful as these criticisms may be, they are not the real issue. There is a deeper problem with the various explanations of the biases, which is, to invoke a formulation we have used before, that the biases are not something in relation to which the notion of an explanation can be given any coherent sense. We already saw that the impetus for such an explanation comes from *within* the tensed and tenseless theories themselves. This is evident in the case of the tenseless view, which denies there is a past or a future, and which therefore denies any real differences between the past and the future. From within this stance, the existence of the tensed-based biases discussed above must be explained. As for the tensed theory, explaining these biases is how the theory turns them into an argument in its support.

But I want to claim that, furthermore, not only the impetus but also the *intelligibility* of the request for an explanation of the biases comes from within the theories. Outside these theories, it is impossible to state what it is we are seeking an explanation for. Supposedly, the question is: (1) Why should it matter whether an experience lies in the past or in the future? Perhaps it does not matter. Let us reformulate the question: (2) Does it or does it not matter whether an experience lies in the past or in the future? Tensed theorists say it does matter. Some tenseless theorists, such as Mellor, say that although there are no tensed facts, tensed beliefs nevertheless matter. Other tenseless theorists, such as Parfit, claim that it does not matter where an experience lies in relation to what we call "the present." Given that in reality there are no tensed facts, it would be irrational to suppose there are and to let our attitudes toward an experience be determined by this supposition. That is Parfit's temporal neutrality.

It should be obvious that if the second formulation of the query is meaningless, so is the first. For, if we can answer (1) and say *why* it matters where an experience is tensely located, we automatically get an affirmative answer to (2), the question *whether or not* it matters where an experience is tensely located. And I wish to argue that (2) is indeed meaningless: we cannot make sense of the idea that it does not matter where in relation to the present an experience lies, that is, we cannot make sense of Parfit's temporal neutrality. Hence, we cannot make sense of the question whether it does or does not matter where in relation to the present an experience lies, and so neither can we make sense of the idea of accounting for our tense-based biases. Thus, by exposing the incoherence of Parfit's temporal neutrality we establish the unintelligibility of the project both tenseless and tensed theorists undertake when they put forth explanations of our tense-based biases.

To see why temporal neutrality is not an intelligible stance, I want to suggest two lines of thought, a minor and a major one. Let's begin with the minor argument. Imagine Jane being asked why she fears the pain she will have to endure in the course of an operation scheduled for the next day. She would be giving a perfectly direct answer (to a rather impolite question) if she simply stated that pain is an unpleasant, fearful experience.[23] Suppose we are not satisfied with this answer and demand a *further* explanation of *why* she fears the experience, as though its being *painful* were not enough. We'd be like that person who, having witnessed the ceremony in which *S* is designated as the standard meter, then questions whether *S* is one meter long. If we are questioning Jane's explanation, then we are questioning whether pain is truly unpleasant and fearful.

And that's exactly what Parfit's *timeless* does—he questions her explanation. According to him, one ought to be neutral as to where in time a painful experience is located. If Jane would have a certain disposition toward an experience she counts as past, she should have the same disposition toward a similar experience she counts as future. And since she would not fear a "past" operation, she should not fear the "future" one either. Such an asymmetry in dispositions would violate temporal neutrality. Parfit's idea of temporal neutrality, then, seems to entail that Jane's explanation—that pain is unpleasant and therefore fearful—does not constitute a good reason for her dreading tomorrow's operation, and so seems to be underpinned by the supposition that pain is not fearful. Indeed, turning to one of *timeless*'s own pains *P*, which occurs at *t*, when would *timeless* fear it? Certainly not before *t*, when *P* is "future," nor after *t*, when it is "past"; and at *t* he experiences it, which is something different from fearing it. So, again, for *timeless* pains are not fearful.[24]

Perhaps *timeless* would rephrase his question and ask Jane, not why she fears tomorrow's pain, but why she fears only pains that are "future." The second argument I will turn to in a moment will establish that this request for a further explanation does not make sense. And at any rate, posing it would not change the fact that *timeless*'s position involves questioning whether pain, any pain, is fearful. And that's truly problematic. It's not like questioning whether having one's skin scorched by fire is fearful. There is something contingent about the fact that getting burnt is painful. Perhaps it is conceivable that some organisms actually enjoy exposure to dangerous temperatures, and do not experience them as painful. But there is nothing contingent about pain being unpleasant and therefore fearful (in some cases, at least).[25] It is of the essence of pain that it, initially, at least, triggers a reaction of repulsion toward it. *Timeless* is peculiar precisely because, unlike the rest of us, for him even acute pain is not fearful, and so (assuming we fear what is extremely unpleasant) it is not unpleasant, which raises the question weather for him pain is painful. Hence the intelligibility issues with "temporal neutrality."

But there are other intelligibility issues, which are more important for us to pursue because they lead to the insights concerning tense I wish to draw from this discussion of the biases. So let us turn to the second argument. First of all, let us note that not everything about *timeless*'s story is incoherent. Evidently, we *can* imagine someone *not* fearing a future painful experience. Being feared is not constitutive of being pain. Imagine Jane, who is stranded on the tenth floor of her blazing building. She has to jump out the window, it is her only chance to survive, and she is terrified to the point of paralysis. There are many ways we can imagine this fear being eliminated. She might be drugged, or dealt a hefty blow on the head. Perhaps her officemate can rapidly convince her of the actuality of an afterlife. Or, as the last quotation from Schlesinger pointed out, she might be reminded of the serenity with which Socrates drank his poison or of the martyrs who bravely stepped up to the stake. There were schools—the

Stoics were such a school, perhaps, and the samurais—whose members learned through lengthy and strenuous training to not dread certain (or any) pains. But of course their methods had nothing to do with Parfit's temporal neutrality. To the contrary, the need for such methods *underscores* the differences between our attitudes to the past and to the future. These methods pertain solely to future pains, not to past pains. And they presuppose future pains *are* dreaded; otherwise, it would not be necessary to train in order not to dread them.

We can highlight this difference between temporal neutrality and, say, stoic indifference to pain by rehearsing a point already made above. Temporal neutrality has to do not with the dread we feel before a painful experience per se, and not with the relief we feel once the pain is over, but with the *contrast* between the two. Temporal neutrality is the thesis that this contrast is groundless, that there is no basis in reality for having one attitude toward an experience when it is past and another attitude when it is future, for there is no past, present, or future. In particular, there is no reason not to have toward an experience that is yet to come the same attitude that we ordinarily have toward it when it is over. So, if we do not ordinarily dread pains that are over, we should not dread pains that are yet to come either. That's the temporally neutral stance *timeless* adopts.

But this idea, of symmetry between our dispositions toward pains that are yet to be experienced and toward those that are over, is untenable. Returning to Jane, the relevant kind of fearlessness that temporal neutrality could endow her with is precisely the fearlessness she displays with respect to past ordeals. Imagine that, against all odds, firefighters manage to rescue her. She would probably feel great relief, and, though she would be shaken up for a while, she would no longer feel the fear that gripped her while she was trapped next to the smoky window. It is *this* sensation, *this* kind of fearlessness, the one typical of *past* experiences, that, if she were temporally neutral, she should have experienced *before* being rescued.

Now remember that, supposedly, "our bias towards the future is an attitude . . . to time itself" (Parfit 1996, 31). Temporal neutrality could therefore be achieved by nothing else but working on transforming our conception of time. And we all agree that this work is constrained by the fact that, to repeat Smart's observation, "certainly we *feel* that time flows." So suppose I have a painful experience planned for tomorrow. How can I bring myself to eliminate the dread the prospect of this experience induces in me? How can I attain before the experience the calmness I expect to feel when it will be over? I can imagine what it would be like for the experience to be past, but that evidently will not do. I do not want merely to *imagine* the anticipated calmness, but to actually experience it. Nor, to repeat, would it help to become a samurai or a religious ascetic. That would secure calmness, but of a very different kind, the kind that comes along with a change in one's attitude toward *pain*, not toward *time*. The calmness that has to do with *time*, the only calmness that is grounded in the *temporal* properties of experience, is the calmness we feel toward *past* pains. So, to acquire this attitude toward the experience planned for tomorrow I must treat it as a past pain.

Again, it would not be enough to merely think of it *as if* it is past. That would only give a sense of what it would be like for the pain to be past. To actually feel no dread with respect to tomorrow's pain, it must actually be conceived *as* past. But it is conceptually impossible to conceive of a future experience as a past one; it is as impossible as it is to conceive of *S*, the standard meter, as being half a meter long. I can imagine the *counterfactual* possibility that *S* is half a meter long, or that something I'm about to experience has already been experienced and is now past. But I cannot imagine that *S is* one meter long, or that my future experience *is* past. In the context of such exercises, "*e* is future" simply ceases to function as a proposition, as does "*e* is not future" or "*e* is past." Language—ordinary, scientific, or philosophical—does not possess the means with which one could speak of an experience about to be had as past. But then we cannot express the conditions underlying the idea of temporal neutrality: it is only by thinking of a future experience *e* that it is past that I could state what such neutrality actually comes to. So, again, the idea is unintelligible. This should come as no surprise. We have already encountered several times the tenseless predicament of having to think that events and experiences are not future (or present or past) while being told that we cannot help thinking that they are.

But the unintelligibility of temporal neutrality is an important discovery for us, one that enriches our understanding of tense. Our fundamental resource for the task of explicating the difference between the past, present, and future is found in the differences between what it is for one of our experiences to be past, present, or future. And the differences in our experiences concern, foremost (though not exclusively, as we will see in the next section), the differences we've been tracing in the sentiments that accompany our experiences.

That an experience e is future is not something we can or should explain or justify (as we saw in section 5.2). Likewise, we cannot make sense of the notion of explaining or justifying, with a theory of time, e's being, for example, feared while it is still future. But its being feared can figure in characterizing what it means for it to be future. Our notion of the future is derived, among other things, from the sentiments that accompany our anticipation of future experiences. Similarly, that we abhor a certain ongoing experience and want it to be over is not something a theory of time can explain, because by framing the request for such an explanation we deprive of meaningfulness the description of what needs to be explained. But that we want the experience to be over may be what, on a particular occasion, characterizes it as present. And the relief felt once an unpleasant experience is over cannot be the subject of a theory of time, but it can be that which characterizes that experience as past.

Our notion of what it is for an experience to be past, present, of future is derived from the sentiments that accompany our cognition of the experience. These characterizations are then projected from our firsthand experiences to events in general. Our apprehension of what it is for an event to be past, present, or future is given (again, in addition to things we will discuss in the next section) by the kind of sentiments that accompany our apprehension of the event.

The sentiments we are speaking of come in an immense variety. Dread, thrill, relief, nostalgia, gratitude, pleasure, abhorrence—these are just a few items in a vast and rich array of sentiments. Since studying our sentiments is central to the study of time, exploring this array—discovering nuances, comparing and highlighting elements of it that often go unnoticed—are among the aims of the investigations conducted by phenomenologists. But more on that later.

To sum up, our experiences figure not only as "tense rods," which enable us to tensely locate events, and as anchors for the tense terms of our language, but also as differentiators between the unique qualities that make the past, present, and future what they are. By means of the "second-layer" sentiments that almost unfailingly accompany them, our experiences, as it were, "color" the past, present, and future and bring us the differences between them. And we now enjoy the advantage of being able to tap into this endless resource without being hindered by worries about the "subjectivity" of our characterizations of tense, or about the "unreality" of tense, or the like. We use the elements of this resource in quite the same way as we use rulers to measure objects. Space is not "subjective," and it is certainly not in some way "dependent" on measuring rods, even though it is not given to us independently of the rods *we* designate as standards. Likewise, time and tense are not "subjective" and do not depend on our experience, even though our conception of time and tense is inextricably tied with experiences we have in time, and with tense-based sentiments that accompany these experiences.

5.6 The Future's Openness; The Past's Fixity

Alongside the "sentimental colors" of the previous section there is what we may call an "epistemological palette" that provides another important resource for the characterization of the differences between the past, present, and future. We are familiar with the claims that "the future is open" and "the past is fixed." Like the phrase "time's passage," these terms are somewhat specialized. We don't routinely use them, and we encounter them mostly in contexts of a theoretical nature. But they stand for something we do encounter routinely, for example, when we compare our uncertainty as to whether it will rain next week in Vancouver with the certainty with which we know that it rained there last week. Most young children already know that there's a difference between *speculating* what the outcome of tonight's game will be and *wanting* to know how the previous game ended. There is a difference, that is, between the future game, whose outcome *is not yet determined*, and the previous game, the score of which *is fixed*.

Let us look at some more examples. We quite often qualify sentences about the future in manners that have no past tense parallels:

If all goes well, the shuttle will land in three hours.

True, in certain circumstances we might also say:

If all went well, the shuttle has landed three hours ago.

But the qualification here has an utterly different meaning. It expresses ignorance, while in the first sentences it expresses a hope, and has nothing to do with ignorance—short of Divine assurances, there is no information someone could obtain that would set our minds at ease (we'll get to Laplacian demons and determinism shortly). Or compare:

A hurricane is expected to hit the coast tomorrow,

with

A hurricane was expected to hit the coast yesterday.

To the latter token we can add something like "but it didn't," whereas there is no equivalent future-tense clause that can be added to the first token. Also, there is a difference that concerns action: the first token, but not the second, may prompt us to take certain cautionary measures. We could say "I may go to Japan next month, I have not yet decided," but it is impossible to conjure up a past-tense sentence that would express a similar kind of "openness." We can only report in the past tense that such "openness" obtained at the time, something like "At the time, I was not sure whether I would be going to Japan or not." More generally, we are taught early on that the future is what we make of it but that what's done is done; one cannot change the past.

Suppose you and a friend are playing a series of three chess matches. You have just played the first two and are about to play the third. You are mulling over the mistakes you made in the previous matches and planning a strategy for the last one. There are various contrasts in attitudes and sentiments that accompany your thinking about the past matches and the future one, contrasts of the kind we have studied in the previous section. For example, you're frustrated about the second match but optimistic about the third. In addition, however, there are other contrasts, not discussed hitherto, which pertain to knowledge. For example, you know the outcome of the previous matches but not of the upcoming one. You are confident that the previous matches took place but worried that your friend (a doctor on call, let us say) may leave before the third game terminates.[26]

It's contrasting sentiments of this latter kind, which we encounter on numerous occasions, that ground the notions of the past's fixity and the future's openness. But, if it is relatively easy to illustrate these notions by pointing to everyday situations that manifest what, in theoretical contexts, we would refer to as the "past's fixity" and the "future's openness," it is quite a challenge to analyze the contrast between the past's fixity and the future's openness and say what it consists in.[27] We cannot, for example, reduce the contrast to the difference between knowing and not knowing. There are contexts in which this latter difference gets blurred and yet the contrast obtains. For example (we'll see more examples later), Jane and her NASA team have sent two probes into Saturn's rings. The first was launched a month ago and was supposed to go into orbit two weeks ago; the second was launched a week ago and is supposed to go into orbit next week. Data from the first probe will be transmitted for the first time in three days, from the second probe three weeks later. In terms of knowledge and ability to act, there is at present no difference between the team's position with respect to the first probe's entering into orbit—a past event—and their position with respect to the second probe's entering into orbit—a future event. Still, Jane and her team apprehend the first event as belonging to a past that is fixed, and the second one as belonging to a future that is open, these notions having been made available to them through contexts in which the contrast in "epistemic sentiments," for example, the contrast between knowing and not knowing, does figure. In other words, the contrast between the past's fixity and the future's openness is carried over from contexts where the sentiments that ground it are manifest to those in which they are not.

Note, however, again, that the past's fixity does not consist in our knowing everything about the past, and the future's openness does not consist in our not knowing what the future holds. There are many past facts, including facts pertaining to our own personal histories that, owing to the absence of records and memories, are not known to us and will never be known to us. And there are many future facts that are known to us. We know that a lunar eclipse will start one hour from now, that Bush will begin another evening as president of the United States, and that there will be enough oxygen in the atmosphere for us to breathe. It is simply not the case that about the future we have no knowledge but only guesses.

In the chess match example, the results of the third game were not known, and this exemplified the absence of knowledge about the future. Just now, however, I gave examples of future facts that are known to us. Let us pause for a moment and alleviate the tension between these examples. We do so by highlighting, yet again, the role of the context. You do not know that the third chess match will be played to the end—you're concerned your partner will be called back to work. But you do know that whenever he leaves, the door of your apartment will open so that he can exit. Now, you can shift contexts and become worried that maybe the doorknob will not turn. Perhaps, while you were absorbed in your chess match, a prankster jammed the doorknobs of several doors in the neighborhood. Thus, a fact that in one context is the subject of one's knowledge can, in a different context, be something about which one is uncertain.[28] But even if you become uncertain about the door's opening, you do know that when your friend will go to the door and find it jammed, the moon will exist and will be orbiting around Earth. It is possible to get fanciful and raise doubts as to whether you really know that as well. This sort of exercise belongs to the kind of shadowy territory painstakingly explored, for example, in Wittgenstein's *On Certainty*. However, as fascinating as this territory is, we cannot in the course of the present discussion veer into it.[29]

For our purposes we ought to remain focused on mundane contexts in which both the future's openness and our knowledge of the future figure ordinarily. Your uncertainty as to whether you and your friend will complete the third game is the manner in which the future's openness presents itself in this context. And your knowledge—not your belief, or your guess, but your knowledge—that when your friend will get up to leave he will do so on two feet and through the door is one of the many items of knowledge you possess concerning the future.

We now go back to the observation that the contrast between the past's fixity and the future's openness cannot be analyzed in terms of what we know: we know a great deal about the future, and there are many things about the past we do not know. Nor can it be explicated by claiming that statements about the future are "contingent" and lack a definite truth-value, whereas those about the past always possess a definite truth-value. It is just not the case that statements about the future always lack a truth-value (and it is not obvious that those about the past always possess one—as we know, Dummett, for one, thinks that many of them do not). At noon, "The sun will not set for another two hours" is a true sentence. Imagine your cosmologist friend telling you "There will be a total eclipse of the moon in two days." You're surprised and you ask: "Is this true, do you *know* this for a fact?" He'd be giving a clear-cut answer if he said: "Yes, I made the calculations myself." He'd be giving a strange answer if he said; "No, the future is open and my statements about it lack a truth-value." If the meteorologist says "It will rain tomorrow in New York," her statement is either true or false (if by some calamity New York will no longer exist tomorrow then the sentence is certainly false).[30] We may say that "It will rain in New York tomorrow" is neither true nor false. But that cannot be squared with the universally recognized fact that either it will or it will not rain in New York tomorrow.[31] Or consider the sentence "England will beat Germany in tomorrow's soccer match." It could be supposed that this sentence lacks a truth-value, for the future is "open" and the game's outcome will only be decided tomorrow. But what does it mean for a sentence to possess or to lack a truth-value? Presumably, a sentence has a truth-value if and only if it is either true or false. But then "England will beat Germany in tomorrow's match" is, just like "It will rain tomorrow in New York," also either true or false (again, if the game does not take place for some reason, or ends in a tie, then the sentence is false).

When Jack says "It's true what Ruth said, her son will definitely pay the bill tomorrow," he's making no blunder in ascribing a truth-value to Ruth's utterance "My son will pay the bill tomorrow." Of course, it may turn out that Ruth's son will not pay the bill tomorrow—he may fall sick or forget, or the sun may go nova before he gets to the bank. But should any of these possibilities actualize, then the sentence "Ruth's son will pay the bill tomorrow" will have turned out to be false, not to have lacked a truth-value. In short, that event *e* is future, does not mean, or entail, that a future-tense sentence describing the event lacks a truth-value. So the contrast between the past's fixity and the future's openness cannot be drawn by claiming that future-tense sentences lack a truth-value whereas past-tense sentences possesses them.[32]

More generally, framing the contrast between the future's openness and the past's fixity in terms of general theses concerning knowledge seems undoable. Such attempts are by nature reductive. They tacitly assume that the difference between being past and being future can be reduced to some epistemic category. But what needs to be exposed is not merely the failure of these reductive attempts, but more deeply, the misguided motivations behind them. As we shall see, these attempts are expressions of a quest for a metaphysical account and justification of the contrast between the past's fixity and the future's openness. Going beyond the metaphysical quest will enable us to employ the contrast for the sake of furthering our understanding of the differences between the past, present, and future.

We can frame the question driving the metaphysical quest as follows: is the contrast between the future's openness and the past's fixity part of reality, or does it belong to our psychology, to the way we apprehend things, but not to the way things are? One of the above examples concerned the contrast between tonight's game, the outcome of which, we said, *is not yet determined*, and the previous game, whose score *is already fixed*. Let us pose the above question in relation to this example: is tonight's game really "open," or is the thought that it is merely a consequence of our at present irremediable ignorance concerning its result, which is actually fixed? There is a somewhat subtle issue here that is central to our investigation. There are two readings of this question, only one of which pertains to the philosophy of time. Let me say something about the other reading. There are well-known answers to this question that seem to challenge the future's openness: determinism, fatalism, and preordination. Each of these doctrines is supported by arguments, which, if valid, would seem to render the future fixed. However, perhaps surprisingly, these doctrines *have nothing to do* with the metaphysics of time. Let me explain.

These doctrines by no means challenge the future's openness because they *assume* it. It is only against the future's openness that these doctrines are contentful. If the future were not open, there would be nothing for the laws of nature, or of logic, or of Divine preordination to fix. God would not have to destine a future if it was a feature of *time* that the future was already predestined. It would not occur to us to appeal to logical considerations for raising the possibility that the future is fixed if reflecting on time would have already presented this possibility to us. And Laplace would not have to invoke physics to challenge the openness of the future if time itself told us the future is not open. It's because our understanding of *time* tells us that the future is open that these doctrines make a substantial claim. If we have to appeal to these doctrines, that is precisely because the future, as we know it prior to and independently of this appeal, is open.

This becomes abundantly clear when we note how happily we embrace the past's fixity *without* any appeal to determinism, fatalism, or religious belief. Just as these theories say nothing about the past's fixity, so they say nothing about the future's openness. It's a feature of *time* that the past is fixed and the future open. It's against this fact that doctrines can be conjured up that would render the past mutable and the future fixed. Moreover, in spelling out the claims made by these doctrines we assume the past's fixity, for it is (implicit) reference to this fixity that tells us what the "fixing" of the future would amount to. What it means for the future to be fixed is explicated by pointing to the fixity of the past—it's this kind of fixity that the doctrines impose on the future. And were we to become interested in a theory that "opens" the past we'd invoke the future's openness as a reference point to the kind of "openness" we'd be attributing to the past.

Thus, insofar as our interest is *time*, these doctrines are not what we should be looking at. The challenge to the contrast between the future's openness and the past's fixity that we should be concentrating on must concern *time itself*, not the laws of nature, or of logic, or of the Divine. We find such a challenge in the tenseless view, according to which there is no past and no future and thus no contrast between them. If all events are "equally real," then all events are equally fixed, or equally unfixed (though this possibility would seem to correspond to the idea that all events are "unreal," and not to the tenseless claim that all events are "real"). On this view, the contrast in question, like time's passage, belongs to mental reality, to the way we think, speak, and experience, and not to the way things are in reality.

The tenseless theorist does not have to regard the contrast as utterly groundless. We already know tenseless methods for retrieving tense-beliefs, and these methods can be used for reconstructing the contrast between the past's fixity and the future's openness as well. Mellor, to return to our stock example, argues that temporal order is fixed by (though not reducible to) causal order, which means, first, that causes always precede their consequences (no backward or simultaneous causation); and second, that events we count as future are causal consequences of those we count as present or as past. Furthermore, according to Mellor's theory of causation, causes do not necessitate their consequences, they only raise the chances that these consequences will actually occur. Equipped with these theses, the future's openness and the past's fixity can be reincorporated into the tenseless picture of how we think and experience in time. States of affairs we call past and present do not determine those of the future. Rather, they increase the odds that certain future states of affairs and not others will occur. The increase may be significant, in some cases significant enough to rule out all but one course of events, but in other cases it does not guarantee the realization of any given possibility. To take an example: David, who is anxiously watching the landing of the space shuttle, is right to regard the question whether touchdown will go smoothly as an open one, for the conditions obtaining several moments before touchdown do not fix the occurrences of the subsequent moments, and so do not secure a safe landing. In this respect, what for David, from his subjective perspective, counts as future is open. Conversely, the past is fixed in the sense that nothing that occurs "now," or will occur in the "future," will have any bearing on the odds of the occurrence of an event we call "past."

This account, however, does not really preserve the future's openness or the past's fixity, for, again, Mellor denies there is a future or a past, and so in particular, an open future or a fixed past. The contrast he offers is not between the future and the past, but rather, at each moment *t*, between those moments preceding *t* and those subsequent to it: events at *t* can be causes of subsequent events and results of previous ones, and the causal asymmetry between causes and consequences manifests itself, among other ways, in the above tenseless rendition of the "future's openness" and the "past's fixity." Openness, then, belongs, not to the future, but to later moments as viewed from earlier ones. And fixity is a feature not of the past, but of earlier moments as viewed from later ones. Indeed, if, according to Mellor, in general tensed language cannot be reduced to tenseless claims, the contrast between openness and fixity can very well be described in tenseless terms because it actually has nothing to do with the tenses. "Openness" and "fixity" are simply names for probabilities with which events transpire; "openness" designates the (perhaps smaller than 1) probability calculated from moments that are earlier than the event in question, "fixity" the certainty perceived from moments later than the event in question.

But let us return our attention to the hidden assumption underlying this account, namely, the idea that the contrast in question should be accounted for. Tensed theorists share this assumption, of course, the raison d'être of their view being its ability to describe and explain such tensed contrasts. According to them, by becoming present an event becomes "real and alive," which means, among other things, that it gets "congealed," as it were. The past simply consists of such "consolidated" events and states of affairs. Future things, in contrast, are amorphous, waiting to take shape when their time to become present arrives. The common assumption that the contrast between the past's fixity and the future's openness is something that can and should be accounted for is but another offshoot of the more fundamental assumption the views share, the ontological assumption. It's the ontological assumption that underpins the tenseless claim that events are not past, present, or future, and specifically the denial of the contrast in question, which in turn generates the need for accounting for the presence of this contrast in thought, language, and experience. And for tensed theorists the ontological assumption, or rather the tensed theses it sustains, are developed into ontological accounts of the various manifestations of tense, the contrast in question included.

Accordingly, it can be expected that, as before, transcending the ontological assumption will lead us to a vantage point from which the idea of an explanation—in this case, an explanation of the contrast between the past's fixity and the future's openness—no longer makes sense. The form of the argument is familiar. You are playing roulette, repeatedly putting your money on the number seven. You have already lost three rounds, and now the wheel is spinning for the fourth time. You may think that now, some thirty seconds before the ball comes to a rest, the lucky number it will fall on has already been determined: you may be a determinist or a fatalist, or believe that your prayers have been heeded. These possibilities reflect your belief in the future's *openness*—if it was closed you would not need the laws of nature, or of logic, or of the Divine, to secure this future result. To repeat, in asserting that the past is closed, one does *not* need to rely on any of these doctrines. If with regard to the future one *does* need to resort to one of these doctrines, that could only be because one does not believe the future is closed.

So here we have the contrast laid clearly before us: the results of the previous roulette spins are fixed; that of the current spin is, insofar as *time* is concerned, undetermined. Let us now focus, not on the contrast between the results, but on your experience of this contrast. It consists of several elements: you are disappointed with respect to the previous rounds, hopeful with respect to the present one (these are the tense-based sentiments of the previous section); you know the results of the previous rounds, but not of the present spin; you think of the previous rounds as fixed, and experience the present one as still "open." We have shifted from looking at past and future results of roulette rounds to looking at experiences we have with respect to these rounds, and in particular, at the contrast between our treating the previous results as fixed and the future one as undetermined. The crucial question is this: can we, without resorting to the laws of nature, logic, and the like, imagine an alternative to this latter contrast, and in particular, imagine treating the future result as fixed? Of course, we can imagine what it would be like for this result to already be past and therefore fixed. But we are not interested in exercises with counterfactuals. What we need to know is whether it is possible to actually treat the upcoming result the way we standardly treat past results, that is, as fixed, even though it is still future.

In trying to perform this experiment, we find that we encounter resistance; we need to impose on our attitude to the future result something foreign to it that will nullify the sense of openness that initially accompanies it. This novel element can be provided by determinism, or fatalism, or religious belief. But, again, that only shows that there is a sense of openness that needs to be overcome. Otherwise, the only way to treat the result as fixed without having to struggle with the openness that relentlessly engulfs our attitude toward it is to come to think of it as actually past— not to think how we would treat it if it were past, but think that it *is* past and then treat it accordingly. And that is not something we can do. It would involve believing that our future experience is a past experience, a belief that cannot even be stated coherently. So the contrast between the past's fixity and the future's openness is not one we know how to negate; we do not know how to do this any more than we know how to negate the claim that S is one meter long. And in both cases the quest for an explanation is a hollow one: in the context of such a quest the words expressing the claims that are to be explained cease to function as meaningful propositions.

There are further elements that go into this contrast. As noted, concerning future experiences, there is a doubt that they will actually come to pass. Suppose you are anxious about a tooth removal scheduled for next week, an operation you know to be painful from a similar experience you had the week before. There is an outstanding contrast here: while you have no doubt that you have had a painful experience, there is a possibility that you will be spared the painful experience scheduled for the future: contrary to your plans, you may not live to experience it, for example. Now imagine challenging this contrast, imagine, that is, acquiring a conviction that the future experience will be experienced, identical in nature to your conviction that you have experienced that past experience. Imagining the expected experience to be past will not do. That will only give a sense of what it would be like to have the conviction in question; it will not actually create it. To actually possess this conviction, one needs to think the future experience *is* past—a thought the wording of which displays its incoherence.

This applies not only to our experiences but also to our attitudes to all events. We cannot suspect that past events did not transpire in a manner analogous to, and deriving from, the doubt we might have concerning the coming to pass of future events. And vice versa, we cannot think of future events as bound to transpire in a manner that derives from the way we know past events to have happened. We know that the sun rose above the eastern horizon yesterday, and also that it will rise tomorrow. But while we know that it did not go nova yesterday, we do not know that it will not go nova tonight. Here are two very similar events, one of which is past, the other future. And there is a tense-based difference in our attitude toward them: one can imagine the latter not coming to pass but cannot imagine the former not having occurred. To this difference, one can conceive of no alternative. Or, and this is the real point, we cannot conceive alternatives to this contrast *without making metaphysical assumptions*. Specifically, as we saw, the ontological assumption invites conceiving alternatives to this contrast. And since metaphysical speculation inevitably channels us to this assumption, we inevitably come to challenge the contrast between the past's fixity and the future's openness. This is where the notion of accounting for this contrast comes in. If we are tenseless theorists, we will deny the reality of this contrast, and either attempt to remove it from our apprehension of the world, or else provide a tenseless explanation for its occurrence in our minds. If we are tensed theorists, we will reaffirm this contrast by providing ontological grounds for it.

But if we have transcended the ontological assumption, we no longer have the means, *or the motivation*, for challenging the contrast or for explaining it. Rather, this contrast gets added as another element in that second layer of sentiments and attitudes that accompany our cognition and give us a handle on what it means for something to be past or future. There are contexts in which, together with anxiety, hopefulness, anticipation, and other sentiments that "spice" our cognition of future experiences, we become aware of uncertainty as to *how* things will transpire, and even *whether* the thing expected will transpire. You plan to execute a certain strategy in the third round of your chess match, but you're not sure that the way the game will unfold will enable you to do so. And you're still worried the game will not even take place. Doubts of this kind express the future's openness. And alongside relief, emptiness, satisfaction, and other sentiments that accompany our cognition of past experiences come various certainties that make up our sense of the past's fixity: tapes, photographs, memories tell us *how* things happened and *that* they happened. You remember vividly the excruciating maneuvers with which you tried to evade checkmate in the first round.

To be sure, as already stressed, the notions of the future's openness and the past's fixity cannot be reduced to or identified with the uncertainty sensed with respect to some future experiences, or with the certainty sensed with respect to past experiences, or with the absence of knowledge with respect to the future or the possession of knowledge of the past, and so on. Rather, the sense of uncertainty that accompanies our cognition of some future experiences and the sense of certainty that accompanies our apprehension of some past experiences become the bases of our notion that the future is open and the past fixed, respectively. These notions are then applied to experiences and events in general.

Looking at the road ahead of me I am certain that the bridge I am approaching will still be there thirty seconds from now, when I will come to cross it. And thinking five weeks back, I am utterly uncertain whether I drove my car that day or not. But the contrast between the future's openness and the past's fixity is unaffected by observations such as these. Even when I think of the future experience of crossing the bridge, though I am certain the bridge will be there, I still apprehend this experience as belonging to a future that is open. Feeling certain that the bridge will be there does not contradict my sense that the future is open. The sense of openness that builds on experiences that are characterized by uncertainty with respect to the future is projected onto situations in which uncertainty is not present. If need be, one can recruit one's imagination and artificially induce a sense of uncertainty on the situation at hand. For example, I can conjure up scenarios in which the bridge will not be there in thirty seconds, or in which it will be there but, for whatever reason, the car will not reach it. But this will merely highlight what is already there—the apprehension of an experience that belongs to a future that is open. Likewise, my uncertainty as to what happened five weeks ago has nothing to do with my apprehension of the past as fixed. I know that whatever happened in such cases is fixed in exactly the same sense that I am familiar with from cases in which I have clear evidence of what happened: I project the sense of fixity from the cases in which I can ground it in evidence to those in which I cannot. And, again, with my imagination, I can induce a sense of certainty with respect to the past even when it is absent: if I imagine that five weeks ago I did drive the car, then the kind of fixity I recognize from occasions in which there is evidence to ground it presents itself in relation to the imagined event.

This should be clear, but let me emphasize that I am not suggesting that the notions of the future's openness and the past's fixity denote anything "subjective." That we perceive the past as fixed and the future as open is not constitutive of the difference between the past and the future. Rather, the sentiments and attitudes that accompany our experiences are among the things in terms of which the difference between the past and the future is given to us, very much in the way that the notion of the distance between points in space is given in terms of the term "meter," though the length of S is not constitutive of the distance between, say, Los Angeles and New York. To put it differently, our conception of the differences between the past, present, and future depends on our experiences, but the differences themselves do not. This is not surprising: our conception of the distance between Los Angeles and New York depends on our experience, but the distance itself does not. What makes time peculiar, and so hard to study is the fact that, unlike the study of space, which involves assessing the properties and roles of a single, simple, public rod, to understand time we have to expose and scrutinize the properties and roles of a multitude of intricate, personal experiences. Still, what we obtain is not merely a mapping of the properties of our experiences, but a conception of time itself.

5.7   Relativity Theory

Events that belong to a future that is open become, with time's passage, present, and are then appropriated by a past that is fixed. This old claim stands now on fresh ground that was obtained by contending with the tenseless attempt to uproot it (and with the tensed theorist's attempt to metaphysically ground it). But there is yet another attack on the contrast between the future's openness and the past's fixity: the argument from relativity theory to the tenseless view. A discussion of this argument is not entirely necessary: our remarks concerning the tenseless view pertain with equal force to the version of the view that this argument purports to sustain. In particular, the problems afflicting the attempt to flesh out tense in ontological terms, and those surrounding the notion of tenseless relations, plague the position alleged to emerge from relativity theory as well. Nevertheless, the impact of relativity theory on our conception of time has been, and still is, the subject of so much research and controversy, that the argument from relativity theory deserves separate treatment.

Relativity theory tells us, quite surprisingly—this claim would have been treated as unintelligible before the theory—that simultanety is a relative relationship, that is, that two events that are simultaneous according to one observer, may be observed to be not simultaneous by another observer. We discussed this back in section 2.3. Relativity theory also teaches us the no less astonishing fact that the temporal length of an event is also relative to a frame of reference. A soccer game that is measured to go on for 90 minutes according to the spectators in the field will be measured to last 180 minutes by an observer moving at 87 percent the speed of light with respect to the field. These are indeed genuine and startling discoveries. But is it the case that, as we are often told, relativity theory has in addition revealed that time does not flow, that, to quote Einstein again, "the distinction between the past, present and future is merely an illusion"? In section 2.3 we rehearsed the arguments that purport to show that, in light of relativity theory, we need to (1) abandon the common belief that "All and only things that exist now are real" (Putnam 1975a, 198) and accept instead the tenseless claim that "All future things are real, and likewise all past things are real, even though they do not now exist" (ibid., 204); and (2) abandon the contrast between the future's openness and the past's fixity, and accept instead that the future is not open, but that "the outcome of future events [is] determined at the present time" (ibid., 201), and "that contingent statements about future events already have a truth-value" (ibid., 204), that is, they are already true or already false.

I would like now to reexamine these arguments. Let us start with the argument for the first thesis. Recall the dialectics of the argument. First we are presented with a choice: either (1) "All (and only) things that exist now are real" or else (2) "All future things are real, and likewise all past things are real, even though they do not now exist." Then relativity theory is used to rule out (1), and so we are left with (2). Plainly, (1) and (2) respectively constitute "No" and "Yes" answers to the question "Are past and future events and states of affairs real or not?," the fundamental question arising from the ontological assumption. In other words, (1) and (2) belong to the framework constituted by the ontological assumption, and, as we have repeatedly pointed out, we are forced to choose between (1) and (2) only as long as we are committed to this framework. Otherwise, a rejection of (1) *does not* entail an acceptance of (2).

Thus, the first thing to establish when interpreting the philosophical ramifications of relativity theory is that, without invoking metaphysical assumptions that have nothing to do with the theory, the theory does not "prove" that past and future events are "real," nor does it give a sense to this claim. This may sound obvious by now, but that's because of the time we've spent exposing, analyzing, and transcending the ontological assumption. And transcending the ontological assumption is not an obvious move. Indeed, perhaps the best-known rebuttal of the argument from relativity still takes place within the framework of this assumption. Its original formulation is Stein's (see Stein 1968, 1991). Stein uses the notion of "becoming" to represent the tenses and time's passage, and argues that this notion can be accommodated within the structure of Einstein-Minkowski spacetime. The gist of the conception of tense that emerges from his argument consists in relativizing the notion of "becoming" to a point in spacetime: given an event e—a point in spacetime—all and only events that are in e's past light-cone have "already become" and are "ontologically fixed and definite" (Stein 1991, 148)[33] with respect to it.[34] Stein derives as a theorem the conclusion that this relativized relationship of temporal "becoming" is the only one that satisfies certain constraints, among them a transitivity requirement, which we will return to shortly. In essence, on Stein's picture the boundaries of an event's past consist in its past light-cone; its future lies within its future light-cone; and the present is conceived as that which is both *now* and *here*.[35]

A fuller conception of Stein's view of local becoming is obtained when "becoming" is thought of in reference not to a pointlike event, but to an event that endures over some interval of time. Thus, the "here" that Stein is speaking of is not a point in space; rather, it is a region, and quite a sizable one: it is the region that is located around the event, and whose borders stretch as far as light can travel within the time that the event endures. Still, sizable as it is, the present on Stein's view is *spatially restricted*: it has spatial boundaries. Events that are so distant from each other that signals from one cannot reach the other within the time interval occupied by these events are not copresent. Thus, to take an example, a concert in Boston can be copresent with a soccer match in Sydney, but not with a soccer match on, say, Alpha Orionis: the present as it is defined relative to the soccer match extends some ninety light minutes into space, and so includes Sydney, but not Alpha Orionis, which is several hundred light years away.

Most events we ordinarily think of as copresent are spatially proximate enough to continue counting as copresent also on Stein's conception of a spatially restricted present. As we saw, the concert still is copresent with the soccer game. If we are attending one of these events we can state without hesitation that the other one is also taking place *now*. In the vast majority of cases in which we say of distant events that they are taking place now, we are correct—on Stein's picture they are indeed taking place now. This feature of Stein's local becoming certainly makes it more palatable. But if we consider truly distant events, certain critical weaknesses of this picture surface. Consider an event that is space-like separated from a certain observer, that is, an event that is outside the region that at a given moment constitutes the spatial component of that observer's present. On Stein's picture such an event is in a dubious position. For, it was previously part of the observer's future, and it will be part of that observer's past: the future and the past are not spatially restricted.[36] But since that event is too distant to enter into the observer's present, it switches from being future-for-that-observer to being past-for-that-observer *without ever being present-for-that-observer*!

Moreover, it is far from clear how events that are space-like separated from a given observer are tensely located with respect to her. Since they have not yet become, they are neither past nor present, from which it should follow that they are future. But they are outside that observer's future-cone as well. It could be stipulated that events that are space-like separated from a given observer do not have a tensed location altogether; that is the position of many of Stein's followers. But this stipulation is problematic. First, with time's passage the event in question will enter the observer's past light cone, so this solution either lands us back in something similar to the previous conundrum, namely, the conclusion that events that have no tensed location become past without ever having been future or present; or else it forces us to regard some events in our past as not being past at all. Worse, this solution constitutes a partial acceptance of the tenseless view, and of the most unacceptable aspect of it, namely, of the notion that (some) events are not really tensely located. But even the staunchest tenseless theorists accept that we cannot make sense of this notion; all agree that when we think and speak of events, *any* events, inescapably, we think and speak of them as tensely located.

Consider the following scenario. You are at the control center in Houston, where the monitors are showing pictures of an astronaut inside a spacecraft, preparing for a space walk, in the course of which she will repair a telescope. She is some ten light-hours away, and so the pictures you see are ten hours old. You glance at the large clock ticking on the main screen. It indicates that the reparation has just begun. You pray everything is going well. Of course, it will be almost ten hours before the first report from the mission will reach Earth. Still, you know that, unless something unexpected happened, the reparation is taking place *now*, at this very moment. From Stein's viewpoint such a thought is misguided—the reparation is too distant to count as present. But can we so much as think of this event as anything *but* present? Yesterday, when we communicated with the astronauts and discussed the details of the mission, they and we spoke of the mission as future; and tomorrow, during the debriefing, we will refer to it as past. But is it never present? Is there no moment in which we, on Earth, can truthfully say or think: "The mission is taking place now"? How are we to speak and think of it now—in this tenseless limbo? It seems to me obvious that, contrary to Stein's view, there is nothing wrong or misguided about thinking and speaking about what's happening *now*, in *any* spatial location. To the contrary, some situations, such as the space walk just described, make it inevitable to do so.

Stein's local becoming is not merely stipulated, but is rather derived from an argument that relies on certain premises. One of these premises is that "becoming" is a transitive relation, namely, that if b has "already become" for a and c for b, then c has "already become" for a. But, it should be asked, what is the rational behind this principle? Why does the "already become" relationship have to be transitive? As far as I can tell, the sole motivation driving this transitivity requirement derives from the ontological assumption. That Stein is committed to the ontological assumption is evident from his manner of parceling out the distinction between the past, present, and future: all and only events that have "already become" with respect to *a* are "ontologically fixed and definite" with respect to it. In general, future events have not yet become and have no "definite ontological status," whereas past and present events are "ontologically endowed." These characterizations make it plain that, like his tenseless rivals, Stein regards tensed statements as *reality claims*: statements that tell us whether or not an event is "real."

Once this prejudice is capitulated to, the transitivity demand presents itself. It cannot be allowed that different observers will disagree as to what physical reality consists of, which, in the context of the ontological assumption, means that they cannot disagree as to whether or not an event, or an object, or some state of affairs, is "real." That is not to say that events, objects, and states of affairs that made up reality for George Washington are exactly those that make up reality for Bill Clinton. Kennedy has "already become" and is thus "real" for Clinton but not for Washington. The claim is rather that when two observers have "already become" for each other then they share the same physical reality, that is, whatever has "already become" for one of them and is thus ontologically "real" is ontologically "real" for the other as well. That is particularly true of two observers when they intersect in space and time and are thus "real" for each other. As far as I can tell, it's this idea, the idea that if an event is "real" for one observer, and that observer is "real" for a second observer, then the event is "real" for the second observer as well, that yields the transitivity of "already become." In fact, we find here at work a transitivity principle much akin to one of the premises in Putnam's original argument: "If it is the case that all and only the things that stand in a certain relation *R* to me-now are real, and you-now are also real, then it is also the case that all and only the things that stand in the relation *R* to you-now are real" (1975a, 198).

Thus Stein's rejoinder to the tenseless theorists relies on the same metaphysical prejudice that damns the position he criticizes. The result is a spatially restricted present that, for the reasons given above, does not hold water. But Stein's argument, like other products of the ontological assumption, leads to an important discovery concerning tense, namely, that *cop-*

resentness is not transitive. The transitivity of copresentness is a private case of the transitivity of "already become." If a is present for b and thus has "already become" for b, and if b is present for c and thus has "already become" for c, then, by the transitivity of "already become," a has "already become" for c, which means that it is either past or present with respect to c. In the latter case we have transitivity of copresentness. Hence, by leaving behind the ontological assumption motivating the transitivity of the more general relationship of "already become" we also undercut the motivation for the transitivity of copresentness.

In fact, relativity gives us a decisive reason for renouncing the transitivity of copresentness, for it teaches us that simultaneity is a frame-dependent relationship. And, plausibly, if α and β are simultaneous and α is occurring now, then so is β; and, conversely, if both α and β are occurring now, then they are simultaneous. If this association of simultaneity and copresentness is correct, as it seems to me to be, then, like simultaneity, copresentness is a frame-dependent, and therefore nontransitive, relationship. Let us consider what this nontransitivity of the present amounts to.

Recall the scenario presented in section 2.3: three observers, α, β, and γ, who are moving at relativistic velocities, intersect. We call this event e_1. Another event e_2 occurs at a distance. The observers' velocities are such that for α, e_1 and e_2 are simultaneous, while β measures e_1 to precede e_2 by 32 minutes, and γ measures e_1 to succeed e_2 by 32 minutes. In other words, at the moment of their meeting, which the three agree is a present event, α asserts e_2 to also be present, while β takes it to be past, and for γ it is still future. Now let us assume (as we did back in section 2.3) that event e_2 is the closing of the ballots in some intergalactic elections. So, at the moment of their intersection, for β the ballots were closed 32 minutes ago, and the election's results are already fixed; in α's frame of reference the ballots are closing, and for her as well the results are fixed; γ on the other hand takes the race to be still open, with 32 minutes remaining before the outcome is decided.

Imagine that Wolf, an acquaintance of α, β, and γ, is one of the candidates in the elections, and that as they meet β muses out loud "I wonder how Wolf is feeling now." What would happen if the three were to share their thoughts on the matter? If we were to accept some version of local becoming, we would have to reject the question "How is Wolf feeling now?" as meaningless. Since Wolf is space-like separated from α, β, and γ, it would be meaningless for them to speak and think of him in tensed terms. If we reject local becoming but insist on the ontologically motivated transitivity of the present, we would be at a loss trying to answer this question. β would have to think of the closing of the ballots as a present event even though it is past for her, and γ would have to think of it as present even though for her it is future. If, on the other hand, the three know that copresentness is not transitive, a straightforward exchange between them can take place. α might think that "Wolf is probably very tense, now that the ballots are closing," while γ would guess that "knowing Wolf, she's probably still trying to persuade hesitant voters, and will continue doing so in the half hour left until the ballots close"; β tries to imagine how Wolf is coping with the result, which β believes she has learned a few minutes earlier. The three will have very different thoughts on the matter, but there will be no disagreements between them. Each will know the others' temporal relation to the closing of the ballots, and will understand why the question "I wonder how Wolf is feeling now" prompts the different reactions that it does.

Admittedly, the scenario described constitutes a curious state of affairs. But this is just another instance of the unexpected features of the world emerging from relativity theory. We know that our three observers would give diverging answers if asked about a distant event's duration, or about the length of a distant object, or its mass. For a pre-relativistic sensibility, that is, for our ordinary sensibility, this scenario is no less odd. And consider the question "which is earlier and which is later—the closing of the ballots or our meeting?" It too would draw three different answers. Is this less peculiar than the disparity in the answers they give in relation to e_2's tensed attributes? Are we to conclude that the temporal relations "earlier than" and "later than" are "not real"[37]? It seems more plausible to maintain our familiar notions of temporal order, duration, mass, spatial length, and distance, while realizing that these are not "absolute" but rather relative to a frame of reference. It seems more plausible because we do not really have an alternative. What could temporal duration be other than what it always was? Or mass? Or spatial distance? Even simultaneity is what it always was: e_1 and e_2 are simultaneous if they occur at the same time. The startling revelation is that whether or not they are simultaneous depends on the frame of reference with respect to which this question is asked.

Similarly, I claim, tensed attributes are what they always were, just that they too turn out to be frame dependent. Relativity theory does not teach us that "in reality nothing is past, present, or future," or that tense is "merely an illusion." Rather, it tells us that whether a distant event is past, present, or future depends on the frame of reference with respect to which the question is asked. This is undoubtedly surprising, and requires that we, who experience the world nonrelativistically, adapt ourselves to facts about reality that, prior to relativity theory, were unimaginable. But it does not impose on us new "ontological truths." Without the ontological assumption, we do not get from relativity theory an argument against the reality of tense. Scenarios such as the above tell us nothing about the ontology of tense. They merely illustrate the nontransitivity of copresentness, which is an immediate consequence of the first result of relativity theory, namely, the nontransitivity of simultaneity. Once a frame of reference is fixed, events are past, present, and future in the regular, pre-relativistic sense we are familiar with, a sense that, I have been arguing, never consisted in reality claims.

In general, having gone beyond the ontological framework, we can smoothly import the understanding we *already* have of the difference between past, present, and future from non-relativistic to relativistic situations. That includes our understanding of the contrast between the past's fixity and the future's openness. To see this, let us proceed to the second argument that is based on relativity theory.

Like the first argument, this argument too presents us with a choice between a tensed and a tenseless conception, and uses relativity theory to establish that only the tenseless option is viable. The choice, more specifically, is between the tensed view that there is a difference between the past and the future, consisting in the fact that sentences describing the past have fixed truth-values whereas those describing the future lack one, and the tenseless claim that there are no past and future, and *ipso facto* no differences between them. In particular, according to the tenseless conception it is not the case that the future differs from the past in that sentences describing it lack a truth-value. Rather, as the argument supposedly proves, statements about the future *already* have a definite truth-value, they are "already true or already false" (Putnam 1975a, 201).

In response to this argument, we rehearse the familiar observations. To begin with, it tells against a conception of tense we have abandoned anyway, one grounded in the ontological assumption. True, on the tensed view, the future contrasts with the past in that it has not yet been touched by that "ontological quality" that makes things "real." Hence, with respect to the future, there is nothing to describe, and so sentences describing future events and states of affairs must lack a truth-value. But once we have transcended the ontological assumption, we are no longer bound by this picture and its conclusions. As discussed in section 5.4, we can now regard past and future conditions as the truth conditions of tokens that are contemporaneous with them. And in the previous section we gave several examples of sentences that both describe future events or states of affairs and possess a truth-value. So the argument from relativity theory is redundant—we do not need it in order to realize that sentences about the future may be true or false.

But it is worse than that. The argument is circular, for it assumes a "tenseless language." Recall that in the example through which the argument was expounded back in section 2.3, the conclusion was derived by means of the sentence "The light pulse is, or will be, red." We saw that *this* sentence is already true or already false for γ even though according to her the elections are still future. But plainly, this artificially concocted disjunction is archetypically tenseless! It is true, if true, regardless of where in time it is tokened—before, during, or after the event.[38] And as Putnam points out, "It is unfair to assume a form of language which presupposes Aristotle was wrong and then to use the assumed correctness of this linguistic formalism as an argument against Aristotle" (1975a, 201; Aristotle represents in this context the tensed contention that sentences about the future lack a truth-value).

As with the first argument, unless we are committed to one of the options dictated by the ontological assumption, rejecting the tensed view does not force on us the tenseless alternative. So, although we indeed reject the notion of "future contingents," of future tense sentences that lack a truth-value, we have a different, post-ontological alternative to it. Recall that we have established that the contrast between the past's fixity and the future's openness has nothing to do with whether or not a descriptive sentence possess a truth-value, and that, consequently, the claim that future-tense descriptive sentences have a truth-value is compatible with the notion that the future is open. Thus, in contrast with the tenseless denial of the future's openness, our alternative is one according to which future-tense descriptive sentences are either true or false (at least many of them are), and yet the future is open, in the sense formulated in the previous section. To illustrate this alternative we can look again at the galactic elections case.

Let us first note that although the three observers perceive the situation differently, contrary to Putnam's assertion that they "cannot [all] be right" (1975a, 202; Putnam says it in connection with the example he uses, of course, which is different from ours), they *are* all correct, and, moreover, despite the differences, *they do not disagree*—none of them takes any of the others to be wrong. That is, they agree that the closing of the ballots is present for α, for whom the results of the elections are already decided, and that it is past for β, and yet future for γ, for whom the race is still open. Since tense is not reducible to other facts, and in particular, not to ontological facts, or to epistemic facts, they will not quarrel about the ontological status of the event, nor will the differences in how they apprehend the event be the source of disagreements.

Of course, for this harmony to obtain, there must not be a disagreement concerning the elections' results. Here, we are helped by the same fundamental stipulation of relativity theory that yields such unusual scenarios, namely, that there is an upper bound on the velocity of light and of the transmission of information. Thus, since in α's frame of reference the elections are taking place one billion kilometers from where she momentarily crosses paths with β and γ, and since she is at rest with respect to the election's location, she can receive the radio announcement of the results no less than fifty-five minutes after the intersection. If α then decides to radio the results to β and γ, her transmission cannot reach them before they receive the original transmission from which she herself learned the results. The same is true of β and γ: they cannot inform their fellow observers of the results prior to the arrival of the official announcement transmitted from the ballots. So it cannot happen that one of the three will know something the others do not know concerning the results. This means that the experiences, sentiments, and reactions of the three observers will be the ones familiar to them from nonrelativistic situations. A severe disruption of the three observers' conception of tense and time would ensue only if their different tensed stances with respect to the closing of the ballots would entail unusual, inversed sentiments and reactions. I mean, for example, a situation in which γ, for whom the race is still open, could be made to already feel the thrill of victory or the frustration of defeat; or a situation in which γ creates in β a heartfelt hope for success in a race that β knows has been lost; or a case in which γ induces in α and β future-tense worries that the elections will not end as planned, or in which α and β instill in γ a past-tense certitude that the elections ended successfully. Such cases, if they can be imagined at all, would result in a destruction of the observers' understanding of tense.

However, these scenarios are not of course part of relativistic reality any more than they are of nonrelativistic situations. For α and β the elections are over, but they anxiously await the results, together with γ, for whom the elections are still in progress and undecided. So β cannot cause γ to experience the after-the-fact joy or disappointment about a race that for γ is still open; nor can α or β alleviate γ's concern that the elections were interrupted before the ballots closed. α and β think and speak of the closing of the ballots in the past tense, as an event the occurring and outcome of which are no longer in question, but, given their particular situation, they do not yet know that the elections terminated smoothly, and cannot alleviate γ's fears. Their condition is, in all relevant aspects, just like that of someone who voted in some ordinary, earthly elections but could not receive word of their conclusion until several hours after they were over (because he was on an airplane, or without electricity at home, etc.). Like the ordinary voter, α and β would hope the elections ended without interruption, and they would believe that, since what's done is done, the results cannot be influenced any more. But they would not be in a position to give assurances about any of this to γ, for whom the closing of the ballots is future.

The upshot of this is that, though the situation α, β, and γ are in is unquestionably peculiar, and very different from anything we experience, their apprehension of the situation, insofar as tense is concerned, is just like their apprehension of nonrelativistic situations. Their experiences are of tensely located events, and are accompanied by the familiar second layer of tense-sensitive sentiments and attitudes we have outlined in the previous sections. Tense figures in relativistic situations in exactly the way we are already familiar with. The only difference is that in relativistic situations different observers may find themselves situated differently, in tensed terms, with respect to a given event. But then again, in relativistic situations different observers find themselves situated differently with respect to many other features of reality as well.[39]

One of the outstanding features of the mathematical representations of physical systems is that the tenses are utterly absent from them. They tell us what the system's state is at t, but not whether t is past, present, or future. This is true, of course, not only of relativity theory, but of Newtonian physics as well. So the new question that supposedly arises with relativity theory is not whether the tenses are real even though they are not part of the way physics describes reality, but whether they can be accommodated satisfactorily into a relativistic description of reality. The arguments presented in section 2.3 were supposed to show us that any attempt to do so would end in contradiction. In this section we established that the fact that observers such as α, β, and γ differ with respect to the tensed location of a given event does not give rise to any contradictions. Contradictions arise only if this difference is taken to entail a *further* difference, a difference in the "ontological status" of the event.

Leaving these contradictions behind with the ontological assumption that generates them shows us how to incorporate tense into a relativistic conception of the world. We do so by retaining the tensed conceptions we are acquainted with from nonrelativistic situations, with one proviso, that copresentness may not be transitive. The nontransitivity of copresentness is a great discovery, which we owe first and foremost to relativity theory, but also to philosophy, which liberates us from ontological understandings of tense and from transitivity stipulations of the kind that are at work in Putnam's tenseless and Stein's tensed treatments of relativity.

6 Post-Post-Ontological Epilogue

6.1 Retrospective Overview

Our study of relativity theory and tense captures well the moral of the story we have been expounding about time, a story of which we can now outline a retrospective overview. This story begins with the intui-tion that "only the present is real." We have remarked on the origins, inescapability, and ubiquitousness of this intuition in section 1 of chapter 4. However, this intuition is seriously shaken by philosophical scrutiny. The tenseless arguments presented in chapter 2, which include the argument from relativity theory, do this shaking up. They are countered by attempts to salvage this intuition and ground it in metaphysical doctrines of the kind discussed in chapter 3. Thus, the tensed/tenseless debate emerges.

The next episode in our story concerns the fundamental metaphysical assumption, which underlies this debate—the ontological assumption. This is the assumption that the difference between past, present, and future concerns the *ontological status* of events, and that it is to be analyzed in terms of *reality claims*, claims to the effect that events are or are not *real*. This assumption constitutes the common turf on which the two sides of the debate meet. It is a natural assumption to make, but not one that can be sustained. Establishing this, and showing how it could be transcended, was the business of chapter 4.

Along the course from the initial tensed intuition to the ontological assumption and beyond, a variety of conceptual issues concerning time and tense were met. These were formulated and dealt with in chapter 5. The method consisted, in general, of two elements:

1. Tracing the issues' origins back to the ontological assumption, showing that they derive their potency from this assumption, and then, by referring back to the transcendence of the assumption, dissolving the problems.

2. Coming to appreciate as we do so the pivotal role experience plays in shaping our conception of time; replacing ontological distinctions by an analysis of this role; and focusing attention to those aspects of experience a detailed study of which enlightens our understanding of the same difficult issues that ontological distinctions were supposed to address.

We first employed this method to discuss and reject the persistent dogma that the present is pointlike (section 5.1). After establishing that the arguments supporting the pointlike present are grounded in the ontological assumption, we noted that phenomenologically, we never encounter "the present" as such, but only present things. This led to the conclusion that it makes no sense to speak of the duration of "the present," only of the duration of present events and states of affairs. Next (section 5.2) we took on the issue of the presence of experience. Our conclusion was that it is meaningless to deny that our experiences possess tensed locations, or to pose their locations as a phenomenon that needs to be explained. In particular, it is meaningless to seek an account for the presence of experience, or for the pastness of remembered experiences (section 5.3). Here again metaphysical theses that are grounded in the ontological assumption were superseded by a phenomenological assessment of the tensed properties of our firsthand experiences. We established that our firsthand experiences figure as quasi-standards, as that in relation to which we determine the tensed location of events, and also as that which grounds the tense terms of our language. By means of this notion of experiences as quasi-standards we could recover, this time *not as a thesis of the tensed view*, the basic apprehension that every event is either past, present, or future. We then (section 5.4) retrieved a conception of time's passage, which, again, is grounded not in metaphysical theories but in the phenomenology of time's passage, that is, in a study of the way time's passage figures in experience, thought, and language. The vexing conundrums concerning time's passage and truth were put to rest. Subsequently (section 5.5) we delved deeper into phenomenology by exploring the complex tensed-based sentiments that accompany our experiences. Examined from our post-ontological viewpoint, these offered further elucidations, not (merely) of our experience, but of the difference between the past, present, and future. Particular attention was paid (section 5.6) to the contrast between the past's fixity and the future's openness. Finally (section 5.7), we established that our conception of the difference between the past, present, and future holds good for relativistic situations as well.

The moral of our story is, then, that working through the metaphysical theories of time takes us beyond them to a point where a conception of tense is obtained that is not reducible to but that entirely derives from the phenomenology of tense, from a careful study of the way the differences between the past, present, and future figure in our experience and language. This phenomenology is not sustained by a metaphysical system but, to the contrary, emerges from the transcendence of the metaphysical enterprise. And it lays out before us the real differences between the past, present, and future, differences that have nothing to do with the original question of whether, depending on their temporal location, events and things are "real" or "not real."

6.2 Augustine's Confession

"What, then, is time?" Augustine asked, and famously confessed that, when confronted with this question, he could not answer it.[1] Are we in a better position than he was with respect to it? Can we, at the end of our voyage, say what time is? In an important sense, yes. We know how to address some key questions: is there a real difference between the past, the present, and the future? And what does the difference consist in? Does time really flow? Is the present pointlike? Do we really only experience what is present? Why can we remember the past but not the future? Why do we dread future pains but not past one? Is this rational? Is the past fixed and the future open? Our answers are not perfect, but we have acquired a method that enables us to approach these questions and perfect our answers. It consists in analyzing these questions from within the ontological framework, transcending this framework, and then deploying a phenomenological study. This method can help remove much of the confusion and obscurity that surround time, those expressed by the questions we have discussed, and those expressed by others questions, which were not broached, but which could also be handled by means of our method.

True, we do not possess a metaphysical theory of time, and so, insofar as *that* is what is expected from a philosophy of time, we may appear to have fallen short of the goal. But this impression is dispelled once we review the principled grounds we have for questioning the intelligibility of the very idea of such a theory. With this done, the post-ontological analysis we provide constitutes an adequate answer to the question "What is time?"

In fact, I believe this answer is in the spirit of the other part of Augustine's confession: "If no-one asks me what time is, I do know." As I take it, in confessing that if requested to explain what time is he is unable to do so, Augustine is asserting not that he does not know what time is, but— and now I'm switching to our language—that if we are asked for a metaphysical system that will explain time, we cannot give one. But if we think of time as we understand it, not from within a metaphysical system but from *life*, then we do know what time is. Put in our language, I read Augustine's claim to know what time is as saying that a close scrutiny of time as we know it from experience, language, and thought, that is, a meticulous and precise phenomenology of time, provides answers to all the questions that can be intelligibly posed with respect to it.

6.3   How to Continue

This would be a good point at which to end the book. But, we are countered by a sense that time is still a mystery to us. Like a mountaineer who has reached the summit, our sense of achievement is overshadowed by the apprehension that the sky remains far above. One reason for this sensation is, I believe, that there is a range of issues and activities (of "Vital Importance," to use Peirce's words) which place one before the mysteries of time, but which we have not discussed. Let me then before closing say something, if only sketchily, about these hitherto uncharted aspects of time, and about the role philosophy has with respect to them (it will be evident, I hope, that what I am about to say is in line with the promissory note entered above concerning the role of phenomenology).

We encounter the mysteries of time on various occasions. We encounter them in texts, philosophical and other, that allude to the timelessness of the soul or of God, or in texts that dare grapple with eternity. We find it in the elusive flow that strings together infinitesimal elements into a musical piece. There are also meditative activities, some of which are specifically designed to create encounters with the secrets of time. Perhaps the most hackneyed but, for many, the most intense encounter with time's hidden sides occurs through reflections on the end of one's personal time, on one's death. Indeed, Unamuno claims that such reflections are, more or less consciously, the primary fuel the work of every philosopher feeds on (Unamuno 1954, esp. ch. 1).

As I see it, the role of philosophy vis-à-vis the many manifestations of the mystery is not to eliminate them but to direct us toward them, and to help diminish the sense of restlessness that may accompany our encounters with them. This it can do by further enhancing our acquaintance with time. Phenomenology is a prime venue along which this familiarization process can progress. The phenomenological observations that figured prominently in the previous chapter were, it must be said, rudimentary. That we experience events as tensely located; that we fear future pains but not past ones; that we are uncertain with respect to if and how given future events will unfold but treat the past as fixed—these are but the preliminaries of a study of the temporal features of our experience. The world of our experience is endlessly rich and invites more and more creative descriptions of itself, descriptions by means of which we can delve into the intricacies of time and makes them less estranged.

Thus, to mention a popular example, a detailed and close examination of the temporal aspects of hearing a melody exposes abstruse relations between the past, present, and future, for the description of which Husserl introduces the notions of "retention" and "protention." Suppose we focus on individual beats of a musical piece (in the language of 5.1, individual beats constitute the context for the cognition of the tenses). Each beat is played at its turn, and while it is being played, those that precede it are past, and those that follow it are yet future. Yet, these past and future beats, though not present, must play a role in the present, for without them the beat being played would not be the musical event that it is.[2] Reflection on the "retention" of past beats and "protention" of future ones illuminates a dimension of tense that we have not touched upon—the "openness," as it were, of the present both backward and forward in time.

I'd rather refrain from further examples. The works of the leading figures of the phenomenological tradition, figures such as Husserl, Heidegger, and Levinas, are full of examples. But plucking them out of the texts

within which they are developed is bound to result in misrepresenta-
tions. Suffice it to say that a world of subtle and penetrating observations
concerning aspects of our consciousness of time is found therein. The
basic phenomenological excursions to which our analytic discussion
has led are a gateway to this world. And we enter it well prepared. Having
established the role of our firsthand experiences as quasi-standards through
which the temporal aspects of reality are given to us, we can be sure
that by means of such scrupulously crafted phenomenological observations we will attain a fuller grasp, not of our experiences, but of time and
tense themselves.

Moreover, having systematically superseded the metaphysical enterprise,
we can enjoy these insights without being distracted or misguided by either
the worries that lead to the analytic enterprise, or the metaphysics in
which many works of phenomenology are couched. For example, we do
not need to follow Husserl's reduction or his "bracketing" technique. Presumably, these methods are designed to facilitate a "pure phenomenology," one free of presuppositions and prejudices and so not grounded in
any pre-phenomenological metaphysics. However, as has been observed
by numerous commentators, these techniques themselves are replete
with metaphysical assumptions. Having set straight the ontological
issues related to time, we can enjoy the valuable descriptions Husserl
develops by means of these techniques while, as it were, "bracketing"
his "bracketing," thus realizing his aspirations and obtaining a truly de-
metaphysicalized exposition of our experiences and of time.[3]

Phenomenology is not the only philosophical school whose methods
and goals are principally descriptive. A descriptive strain dominates James's
pragmatism, as well as much of the work of the later Wittgenstein (and of
their followers). In this extensive literature we too can find further characterizations of the tensed features of our experiences. And we can venture
to explore time consciousness on our own.

With such an array of resources, our bank of characterizations of time
and of tense can grow indefinitely, and with it our conception of time, as
well as our appreciation of just how complex time is. Some of the mysteries of time may disperse along the way, and new ones may replace them.
But larger and larger segments of this terrain will become exposed before
us. To the extent that disquiet accompanies our encounter with the mys-

teries of time, this kind of philosophical exposure can be expected to calm it.

I have aimed in my discussion of time to place our experience at the center of our conception of time without rendering time "subjective," or experience dependent. This is tricky because our conception of time depends on our experience in a manner that is unique. Our conception of colors depends on our experience too (as does our conception of practically anything), but our experiences are not themselves colored and we do not have to analyze the color properties of our experiences to study colors. Nor do we study space by studying the spatial properties of experience. On the other hand, one of the keys to fathoming time is to carefully study the temporal features of experience. As I pointed out earlier, that our understanding depends in this distinct manner on an examination not of the subject of our understanding—time—but of our experience of time is one reason why time is so difficult to study.

But it also has this consequence: our conception of time will depend on the kinds of experiences we have. And again, I mean by this more than is contained in the observation that our conception of color depends on our perception of colors. To the extent that we have a say in fashioning, to some degree, our experiential world, the range and nature of the materials that go into the making of our conception of time will, to some degree, depend on choices we make. I have not touched upon this consequence in this book. The experiences we have been studying have been, for the most part, simple, ordinary experiences, such as going to the dentist. But when we move into other spheres of experience, especially those resulting from our choices, and more generally, from our conduct, we run into the suggestion that our moral character figures in how we apprehend time. This leads to the further conjecture, put forth by various phenomenologists, that our experiences are not only of time, but also constitutive of it. In the spirit of the approach I have been pursuing, what I think that means is not that time is a human fabrication, but that some experiences that bear on our understanding of time are so fundamentally *human* that it is impossible to weed out the human element from descriptions of time as it is met with in relation to them. In Levinas, for example, the morally charged encounter with the Other is crucial to the constitution of the deeper layers of one's comprehension of time. Take, more concretely (and as a last example given out of context) the human act of caressing: "The caress consists in seizing upon nothing, in soliciting what ceaselessly escapes its form toward a future never future enough, in soliciting what slips away as though it *were not yet*" (Levinas 1969, 257).

By analyzing such occurrences Levinas attempts to bring forth aspects of the future that are inextricably linked to the intersubjective relationship. I cannot here do justice to these difficult meditations. The point I wish to make is that the explorations of time we have been conducting are only a first step toward further investigations of it. The way we lead our lives determines *what* we experience and *how* we experience it. It therefore determines how time is given to us. Our moral profile, which shapes what and how we experience, will determine what we grasp of the subtler, more sublime facets of time, as well as how we grasp it.

In addition to the intersubjective components of our moral conduct, there are also activities around which, in some traditions, life is structured, whose subject is time itself. I am thinking, for example, of activities aimed at establishing a distinction between sacred and profane time, or of meditative practices in the description of whose products the term "timelessness" is employed.

I am aware that the last few paragraphs will invoke resistance and even irritation in some readers, and I am afraid that my attempts to make a case for rendering certain activities and experiences legitimate constituents in the stock of data on which our philosophical investigations of time feed may be counterproductive. I wish to insist on only one point: we cannot frame intelligible questions or claims concerning time without being highly attentive to our experiences. And for this matter, no type of experience can be ruled out in advance as irrelevant; nor is it possible to assume that all experiences are already familiar. Thus, any kind of activity has the potential of bringing forth unexpected insights.

The analytic school shuns obscurity and vagueness and champions rigor and clarity. But in its pursuit of these virtues it restricts itself to materials that readily offer themselves to clear and rigorous analysis. This means leaving out items that do not offer themselves to such analysis. And this omission of materials, of what can be called "empirical data," is antithetical to the empiricist and scientific tradition which analytic philosophy often models itself on. True, we may need to modify and adjust some of our attitudes before we are willing to treat caresses as "empirical data." But, once we realize that such items may be crucial for the exploration of the deeper, more hidden dimensions of time, we should at least become motivated to try.

Ideally, we should adopt and commit ourselves to the standards of rigor and clarity of analytic philosophy, and at the same time expand our horizons to include within the materials analyzed the boundless spectrum of experiences and activities that have been preoccupying the phenomenological tradition from its inception. Only this kind of synthesis of traditions can lead to a full and satisfactory understanding of time.

Notes

Preface and Acknowledgments

1. Queneau 1977. The quotations in this paragraph are from pp. 113, 118, 120. Raymond Queneau was a novelist, philosopher, and mathematician. *Le dimanche de la vie* was first published in 1952.

2. As I later explain, from the perspective of the present work, despite the multiplicity of titles, there are, basically, two camps: the presentist/tensed camp and the eternalist/tenseless camp.

Chapter 1

1. I say for the most part because there are exceptions. E.g., Tooley's *Time, Tense, and Causation* is an illuminating attempt to incorporate tensed elements into a theory that is essentially tenseless.

2. Early formulations of the tenseless view are found in the writings of, among others, Russell, Goodman, Quine, and Smart. Contemporary defenders of the view include Mellor (1981, 1998), Oaklander (2004), and Parfit (1996). Mellor and Parfit are discussed extensively in what follows. Forerunners of the tensed view include, among others, Broad, Prior, and Reichenbach. Two quite distinct contemporary renditions of the tensed view will occupy us, one of which I attribute to Dummett (1978, especially chapter 21, "The Reality of the Past") and another which is developed by Schlesinger (1980, 1982, 1991). Other defenders of the view include Bigelow (e.g., 1996), Craig (2000), Hinchliff (1996), and Markosian (e.g., 2004).

Chapter 2

1. See Calaprice 2000 (263) for the source of this quotation.

2. Of course Einstein's comment does not have to be read as denying the reality of time's passage; it could be understood as simply pertaining to how we experience this passage.

3. The argument appears again in *The Nature of Experience* (1927), vol. II, Bk. 5, ch. 33. The references I will be making are to the reprint of chapter 33 in Gale 1967.

4. What I call "the logical argument" is in fact only one segment of McTaggart's argument. The full course of McTaggart's reasoning aims at establishing a more radical thesis than that of present-day tenseless theorists, viz., that time itself is not real. Thus, while according to contemporary tenseless theorists all events and objects are in time (though they are not past, present, or future), and in particular, are before, cotemporal, or after each other, McTaggart concludes that "nothing is earlier than or later than anything else or temporally simultaneous with it. Nothing really changes. And nothing is really in time. Whenever we perceive anything in time . . . we are perceiving it more or less as it really is not" (Gale 1968, 97). McTaggart reaches this conclusion in two steps. First, he shows that "the distinction between past, present and future is essential to time" (Gale 1968, 87). In the second step he demonstrates that the tenses are not real. Together, the two claims yield the conclusion that time itself is not real. In this discussion I shall mean by the term "the logical argument" the second part of McTaggart's argument. That is the part of McTaggart's reasoning which is endorsed by those thinkers who base the tenseless view on his work. As we shall later see, there are thinkers, Dummett for example, who defend only the first element in McTaggart's argument. Accepting only this first part is bound to lead one toward the rival tensed view of time.

5. The term "token-reflexive" was first introduced by Reichenbach in his *Elements of Symbolic Logic*.

6. Besides the argument we are about to study, there is another line of reasoning one occasionally runs into, which also purports to make a case for the tenseless theory of time by appealing to relativity theory. The claim is that relativity theory obliterates the distinction between space and time, that it does not distinguish the time coordinate from spatial coordinates, and that, therefore, the "tenselessness" of space becomes that of time as well. This claim is groundless. Relativity theory clearly distinguishes space from time, conceptually and mathematically.

7. There is an exception to the claim that only what is present is perceptually accessible: very distant objects such as galaxies. But this exception does not mean we must withdraw the above observation about the manifestation of tense, only that we must qualify it: with the exception of very distant things, which form a minuscule subset of the things we actually perceive, things of the past are perceptually inaccessible.

Chapter 3

1. Some versions of the view (e.g., Broad's) place past events together with present ones as "ontologically endowed." I shall limit my discussion to those renditions of the tensed view that take only present things to be "real."

2. From Broad (1938), *An Examination of McTaggart's Philosophy*, vol. II, Part I.

3. Indeed, as mentioned, even tenseless theorists concede that time's passage plays an indispensable role in shaping and justifying many of our experiences and dispositions; they just think they can account for this fact tenselessly. But, again, our present interest is in how an examination of experience leads tensed theorists to their metaphysics of time, not in their debate with their tenseless rivals.

4. There are exceptions to this in mathematics. For example, the sentence "every real number is rational or irrational" is not true according to intuitionists.

5. This point needs some stressing. The phrase "is now or will subsequently be," as used by Dummett, does not have the meaning "is now or will subsequently be the case whether or not we can now show that this must happen," as it does in "classical" semantics and logic. For Dummett's central claim is that the "right" semantics and logic, metaphysically speaking, is intuitionist logic and semantics. (See his *The Logical Basis of Metaphysics* Dummett 1991). In intuitionist logic and semantics, to assert a disjunction, $p \vee q$, is to assert that we now know of a method by which we will be able to verify at least one disjunct—and that we now have a verification that the method has this property. Thus, it is now true that "the statement p is or will subsequently be verified" (i.e., "p is verified or p will be verified") only if we now have a verification that at least one of these disjuncts will be verified. But for this to be the case, we must have a verification—possibly an "indirect" one, in the sense of a "verification that there will be a direct verification"—that p. Thus there is no contradiction between Dummett's "is or will subsequently be" and his immediately following "we can now acknowledge." Dummett's metaphysics is one in which truth depends only on what is the case *now*; reference to future verifications are themselves understood, intuitionist fashion, in terms of *present* verification. This is important for understanding the argument that follows.

6. Perhaps this is the place to point out that, contrary to other tensed theorists, Dummett holds McTaggart's views in a positive light. This needs clarification, however, given that McTaggart is the author of one of the most famous arguments against the reality of tense. The first and highly significant point of agreement between McTaggart and Dummett concerns the conviction that tense is vital to our conception of time, or as it is sometimes stated, that tense is the essence of time: that to be in time just is to be past, present, or future. But McTaggart proceeds to argue that the tenses, and hence time, are not real. Dummett agrees that the tenses, as they are often conceived by tensed theorists, are vulnerable to McTaggart's argument. But he proposes his own conception of tense, and thus jumps off McTaggart's wagon just before it reaches the conclusion that time itself is unreal.

7. Let me also mention that it is usually tenseless theorists who are fond of treating passage talk as metaphorical because it seems to make that which is talked about less real. A tensed theorist who agrees with tenseless theorists on this crucial issue is making a costly concession. But this surrender seems inevitable if, like Craig, one

wants to uphold ontological differences between the past, present, and future and at the same time refuse to acknowledge some "moving Now" that makes these differences.

Chapter 4

1. It goes without saying that future-related phenomenology invites a parallel depiction. Here's one future-related illustration. I cannot see the desk my carpenter has begun building because it is not yet ready. Its completion is in the future. If I told the carpenter that I already want to take it home, he may angrily answer: "How can I give you something that doesn't even exist?" So like past things, future objects and actions are experienced not merely as out of reach, but as nonexistent. And here as well, this phenomenological inaccessibility points in the direction of ontology as the domain in which explanations ought to be sought.

2. Ovid: "The art of medicine is usually a matter of time" (*Temporis ars medicina fere est*).

3. "The loss of a spouse does not occur without sighs; The din of mourning is loud. But comfort comes one day: On wings of Time grief and sorrow fly off and away. Time brings back joys likewise." La Fontaine, from the fable "The Young Widow."

4. One popular saying describes time as "the great teacher."

5. It should be mentioned, in passing, that Parfit's labeling of the "are" in his articulation of his contention as "timeless" doesn't help, for it is an account of tenselessness that we are after; before we have one, the term "timeless" (which here means "tenseless") cannot be relied on for elucidating an otherwise incomprehensible use of "real."

6. Quoted from an anonymous referee for the *Philosophical Quarterly*.

7. The phrase "a fleeting product of one's cerebral processing" is used by H. H. Price in his *Perception* (1932), one of the books Austin critically discusses in *Sense and Sensibilia*.

8. Thus it is absurd to attribute to Wittgenstein the "theory of meaning as use," when a major aim of the *Investigations* is to establish that, when it comes to meanings, theories are exactly what we cannot and should not try to find.

9. I wish to register, in the margins, some astonishment at the fact that this simple argument against the possibility of reducing or eliminating tensed language escaped the giants of the first half of the previous century. I take this to be the consequence of a kind of blindness that zeitgeist can cast on those who shape it. Whether they took themselves to be positivists or not, the major figures of that era became spell-

bound with the positivist notion of an "ideal language," a quasi-scientific, formalized language, in which all the problems of metaphysics will either be solved or be made to vanish.

10. "[T]ense is not being banished altogether, merely replaced where it belongs—in our heads" (Mellor 1981, 92).

11. These terms derive from the classic "A-series" and "B-series" introduced by McTaggart (1908). The A-series gives the order in which events become present; the B-series arranges events according to how much earlier or later they are than each other.

12. For the same reason, Mellor's indexical theory (see his 1998, 32–34), which is a modification of his token-reflexive account, cannot constitute a theory of meaning for the tenseless view of time. It too turns on the idea of purely tenseless relations, differing from the token-reflexive account only in its conception of the terms that enter into these relations—events and times rather than events and tokens—but not in its reliance on a distinction we cannot draw between tenseless and tensed relations.

13. Sometimes anthropological findings such as Whorf's famous investigations of Hopi (Whorf 1950) are cited as evidence that tenseless languages actually exist. However, Whorf's claim that Hopi is temporally tenseless is not persuasive, for his very analysis of the language contains an elucidation of the manner in which Hopi *does* distinguish between the past, present, and future, and of how it conceives of time's passage.

14. Craig also points out that the indispensability and ineliminability of tense cannot be squared with the tenseless denial of the reality of tense. However, for Craig it is "ontological tense" that is indispensable and ineliminable. Thus, his criticism of the tenseless view is grounded in a thesis that is itself antithetical to the present project, namely, the thesis that tense is an ontological matter. Being grounded in the ontological assumption, Craig's criticism cannot reach the heart of the problem, which is the ontological assumption itself. Language does not merely resist the tenseless denial of the reality of tense; it resists framing tense in ontological terms altogether. The break with language does not occur when Mellor articulates his tenseless theses, but before that, when the ontological assumption is adopted, by either tenseless theorists such as Mellor, or defenders of tense such as Craig.

15. The quotation and its source can be found in Calaprice 2000, 75.

16. Even the claim that phlogiston does not exist is a rather uninteresting truism. A theory that reality is phlogiston-less would be worth defending only if, regardless of advancements in chemistry, we would not be able to escape cognizing reality as "phlogistoned."

17. This fact is the basis of Austin's adamant criticism (in his *Sense and Sensibilia*) of Ayer's attempt to draw from such cases the conclusion that all we ever perceive are sense data.

Chapter 5

1. That is, cannot be both past and present at the same time. McTaggart, as we know, puts forth the more radical claim that it is contradictory to attribute to a moment the properties of being past and present even successively. And his conclusion is likewise radical: not that the present is pointlike, but that there is no such thing as the present at all (or the past or the future).

2. Aristotle, *Phys.* vi. 3, 234^{a}9–19. In a seminar on time and identity (given at the Hebrew University in 2000) Kripke varied this argument a bit. If the present consists of intervals and not of points, then, unless we admit points in time that are never present, each of these intervals shares at least one instant with the intervals adjacent to it. Add to this the fact that presentness is transitive—if a and b are copresent and b and c are also copresent, then so are a and c—and any two adjacent presents merge into one, and so the present spans all of time. The only alternative to this everlasting present is a pointlike present. (This argument also assumes that the intervals are closed or that time is continuous.)

3. Westphal's only consideration of the differences between space and time concerns a rebuttal of G. E. L. Owen's explanation of why Aristotle did not put forth a spatial retrenchability argument. But time's passage does not figure in Owen's discussion, and so does not get attention from Westphal either.

4. In passing it should be mentioned that the same applies for the past and the future. Any talk of the past or the future is talk of past or future events or things or states of affairs. "Next year will be a hard one" says something about events, developments, or states of affairs that are expected next year. Even the general assertion that "the future is open" (cf. section 5.6), when unpacked, pertains to the status of future events, not to the future as such. E.g., one way of analyzing the future's openness (not the one endorsed in section 5.6) relies on the notion of future contingents, future-tense descriptive sentences that lack a truth-value. "It will rain in Vancouver on January 1, 2008," or "The winner of the next presidential race will be Al Gore," would be examples. Plainly, future weather conditions and presidents are involved, not simply "the future."

5. "Now" may even refer to events spanning thousands of years, as it actually does in the daily discourse of geologists, or even to eras orders of magnitude longer than that: when cosmologists, using a diagram to plot the change in the universe's size, indicate with their fine laser pointers where we are *now*, the beam covers a slice of time that is millions of years thick.

6. Note that this context is a rather artificial fabrication—it can only be described as the limit of some infinite series of intervals. And it is not obvious that an "event" can be associated with it. Perhaps there are examples of real pointlike events. The fusion of an electron and a positron may take less time than Plank time, in which case no duration can be attached to it. But in the absence of some independent description, talk of the *event* at the limit of the converging intervals is somewhat forced.

7. It should be noted that what has been said does not entail that the present is mind *in*dependent. Rejecting entirely the idea of a metaphysical mind–world interface, Putnam's point is that *any* talk of *dependence* is misguided. Of the present as well it should not be asserted either that it is mind dependent or that it is mind independent.

8. The term is a variation Mellor makes on McTaggart's A-series, "that series of positions that runs from the far past through the near past to the present, and then from the present through the near future to the far future" (Gale 1968, 87–88).

9. This last assertion is grossly inaccurate. We do not in fact refer back to S. We measure with whatever means are available to us. Still, there exist standards for units of lengths, and the credibility of the devices we use comes from their accordance with these standards. So, for the sake of the discussion, I will speak as though all length measurements are made by comparison with S.

10. Apprehending cotemporality in such a situation, as in many others, involves utilizing some background knowledge, e.g., knowing the broadcast is live, that the transmission signal travels at the speed of light, what the speed of light is, etc.

11. Complications that may arise from relativistic situations are discussed in section 5.7.

12. Some may want to say that, just as the intentional object of the experience of visiting the zoo was, among other things, i.e., the monkeys' cage, so that past experience is now the intentional object of the present experience of remembering the visit to the zoo. I disagree. As I explain at the end of this section, the intentional object of remembering the visit is the same intentional object of the past experience of visiting the zoo, i.e., the monkeys' cage. But this disagreement is beside the point. Even if we treat past experiences as the intentional objects of memory, these experiences can also be thought of as intentional states, and it is in their capacity as intentional states that they fulfill their function as anchors for our tense terms.

13. For an extensive study of these models see Sutton 1998.

14. A conjecture Russell famously presents in *The Analysis of Mind* (1921), pp. 159–160.

15. Sterelny uses this phrase in relation to perception, but it applies even more so to memory.

16. There is a question concerning the possibility of being in cognitive relations with objects that have not yet come into existence. If to be in cognitive relations with an object one has to be causally affected by that object—an idea that, insofar as material objects are concerned, is not implausible (though it calls for an accurate and detailed presentation, something I can not do here)—then one cannot be cognitively related to future objects. Still, one can envision future states of affairs involving past or present objects one *was or is* in cognitive relations with, and one can frame descriptions of future objects in terms of objects and properties of objects that one is acquainted with. These inputs provide all the materials that are needed for speaking and thinking about anticipated experiences and future events.

17. It will be useful to remember in the course of the discussion what McTaggart's argument is, and what it is not, meant to achieve: it does not aim at establishing the correctness of the tenseless view, but only at undermining the tensed view. As pointed out, achieving this second goal is usually conceived as tantamount to achieving the first. But that is because the choice between the tensed and tenseless views is conceived as inescapable. Once the impression that there is such a forced choice is dispelled, as I have tried to do, a solid argument against the tensed view can no longer serve as an argument in favor of the tenseless alternative.

18. It should be noted that Dummett's solipsism of the present moment is also immune to Mellor's argument. But the price here for escaping contradiction is the loss of any notion of time's passage. As will be discussed presently, given its ontological commitments, the view is truly a solipsism of the present moment: things that are not present are not part of the world at all. To paraphrase Dummett, the world just is the world as it is now. With nothing preceding or succeeding this solipsistic present, there is nothing from which or to which time can flow.

19. "Tanto brevius omne quanto felicious tempus." Pliny the Younger, *Epistles*.

20. There is an objection to these remarks that is worth mentioning. It may be argued that space, like time, is not tenseless. We can come to suspect that space is not tenseless by considering the idea that proper names such as "New York" *do not* furnish tenseless descriptions. The claim is that we do not understand the use of proper names of places independently of our understanding of the word "here." Imagine being given a map, or even a cosmic coordinate system that covers the entire universe, but never being told where you are. Such a map would be useless. If you can never indicate a point on the map and say "I'm here," then you cannot know what locations the names "New York," "Boston," etc., refer to. Be that as it may, it does not undermine the notion of spatially tenseless descriptions. The ability to understand locutions containing "here" is, if anything, a precondition for the everyday use of sentences such as "The Empire State Building is in New York," but

it is not an integral element of such uses. This sentence does not convey any spatially tensed content, and so can be used in abstraction of any such content—its truth is truly independent of where in space it is tokened.

21. Of course, as we've seen in section 5.2, "*e* occurs at *t*" is not tenseless and therefore not always true. For example, if it is true now, then, assuming *e* lasts less than a week, it will not be true a month from now.

22. See Mellor 1995. The elements of the theory needed in this context are summarized in Mellor 1998, section 12.2.

23. The existence of masochists does not undermine the validity of this claim. Concerning most pains, they too would agree that they are awful and to be avoided. In our arguments we focus on such pains, ignoring those that masochists voluntarily subject themselves to.

24. Another mark of the position's awkwardness is that, of course, the reasoning could be run in the opposite direction. If pain *is* unpleasant, and there is no difference between the past, present, and future, then *timeless* should abhor all pains all the time (assuming we abhor unpleasant sensations), regardless of their temporal location. Why should the pain at t_1 matter more than the pain at t_2? To state that at t_1 the pain at t_1 matters but not the pain at t_2 seems arbitrary. Why shouldn't it be the other way around?

25. Perhaps not all unpleasant experiences prompt fear. But let us assume that acute, unfamiliar pains do, and focus on them. And again, to circumvent the objection from masochism, let us focus on pains that all masochists would abhor as well.

26. Needless to say, "epistemic" uncertainty of this latter kind, uncertainty as to whether something will happen and if so how, is different from, for example, the dread we discussed in the previous section. We can dread an upcoming experience about which we have no doubt that it will take place (e.g., a dental treatment that is about to commence in a few minutes), and we may be in doubt as to whether something will happen without dreading it (we may be unsure what the magician's next trick will be, but know we will enjoy it, whatever it is).

27. David Albert also comments that "there is a vast physical and philosophical literature nowadays about the alleged difficulty of specifying exactly *what that difference is*" (2000, 113).

28. I am not suggesting that for every statement about the future there is a context in which that statement expresses *knowledge*. There is no context in which our conjectures concerning the weather in New York on January 1, 2010 can count as anything more than an educated guess.

29. Were we to delve into this terrain, one consequence we'd draw is that it is far from clear that we can always intelligibly doubt our knowledge about the future.

We can doubt that our friend will stay until the chess match is over, and even that the door will open when he pushes it to go out. Doubting that the moon will still be orbiting around earth is more difficult, and that the solar system will exist in five minutes even more so. At some point it ceases to be evident that our doubting still makes sense.

30. Someone may object and claim that if New York will no longer exist at some future time t then the sentence "It will rain in New York at t" is not false (and is certainly not true). For a sentence about New York to be true or false, it may be claimed, New York has to exist. But then it is also the case that "It rained in New York at t," when t precedes the creation of New York, is neither true nor false. So the attempt to spell out a contrast between the past and the future in terms of truth-values fails.

31. Dummett suggests that in the past-tense case, the "or" in "p or $\sim p$" is "selective," whereas the future tense "or" is "non-selective," by which he means that "p or $\sim p$" is true even though neither disjunct is "determinately" true. But this conception of future contingents relies on a metaphysical distinction between "selective" and "non-selective" disjunctions that we are not told how to draw.

32. I am not claiming that all descriptive future-tense sentences have a truth-value. As commented in note 29, there may be cases in which we may not want to say that. If someone says, "In a week's time the milk will no longer be fresh," she is speaking truthfully if in a week's time the milk will have gone sour. But would we say her utterance is true if in a week's time the milk will have been drunk? Would we say the milk is no longer fresh because it no longer exists? Perhaps not, at least not in any context. So a sentence about the state at a future time t of milk that will no longer exist at t may not have a truth-value. That does not contradict my claim that many statements about the future do possess a truth-value and that therefore we cannot explicate the future's openness by claiming that statements about the future lack a truth-value. Moreover, there are contexts in which it is not straightforwardly obvious that descriptive past tense sentences possess a truth-value. Wouldn't it be odd to say that "the milk was not fresh a week ago" is true because the milk did not exist then? If so, then the contrast between the future's openness and the past's fixity cannot be elucidated by claims about truth.

33. Stein borrows these formulations from Maxwell (1985).

34. More technically, with "Rab signifying that the state at b is definite as of a," then, "if R is a reflexive, transitive relation on a Minkowski space, invariant under automorphisms that preserve the time-orientation, and if Rab holds for some pair of points (a, b) such that ab is a past-pointing (time-like or null) nonzero vector, then for any pair of points (x, y), Rxy holds if and only if xy is a past-pointing vector" (Stein 1991, 149).

35. Stein's proposal is further developed by Clifton and Hogarth (1995).

36. Here we ignore past horizons and the possibility of future horizons.

37. There is the view that events that are space-like separated are not temporally ordered. I find this view unattractive. In what sense are events that are not temporally ordered, and not tensely located, in time at all? Without any temporal attributes, which is it seems forced to say of such events that they are in time. One could say their temporality comes to light in other contexts, when they are considered in relation to other events that are not space-like separated from them. But that still leaves contexts in which events lack all temporal attributes, which is not something we know how to take. A better solution is to maintain the ordinary conception according to which events have the temporal properties we always knew they had, but to realize these have to be relativized to a frame of reference.

38. Not that it is really tenseless—there are no such sentences. But it would count as tenseless by tenseless theorists. Thus, in the paper we are discussing, Putnam himself identifies disjuncts of this type as "tenseless": "the 'tenseless' notion of existence (i.e., the notion that amounts to 'will exist, or has existed, or exists right now') is perfectly well-defined" (1975a, 204). So the argument is circular, employing formulations that in the context of the argument are counted as "tenseless" for the sake of establishing "tenseless" conclusions.

39. It is worth noting that further relativizations of time relations to the situation of the observer could conceivably be required by physics. For example, if "closed time-like world-lines" turn out to exist in our space-time (Gödel 1949, showed that this is compatible with general relativity), then, as Putnam (1975b) pointed out, "earlier" and "later" might have to be relativized to *parts* of world lines. Undoubtedly, this would have far-reaching implications for our conception of time.

Chapter 6

1. "What, then, is time? If no one asks me, I know; but if I am asked what it is and try to explain, I know not." Augustine, *Confessions*, bk. XI, 14.

2. See Husserl 1964, for example, §14.

3. In reading Heidegger as well, it is difficult not to get distracted by the metaphysics that permeates his phenomenology. In the case of Levinas, a positively antimetaphysical sensibility seems to guide his work, so the worry is less acute. Here the challenge is to penetrate his highly specialized language and succeed in mastering it as a means for transcending metaphysics rather than a means for developing one.

References

Albert, D. (2000). *Time and Chance*. Cambridge, Mass.: Harvard University Press.

Aristotle (1930). *Physics*. In *The Works of Aristotle*, vol. II. Trans. W. D. Ross. Oxford: Clarendon Press.

Augustine (1991). *Confessions*. Oxford and New York: Oxford University Press.

Austin, J. L. (1962). *Sense and Sensibilia*. Oxford: Oxford University Press.

Austin, J. L. (1979). *Philosophical Papers*, 3rd ed. Oxford University Press.

Bigelow, J. (1996). "Presentism and Properties." *Philosophical Perspectives* 10: 35–52.

Broad, C. D. (1923). *Scientific Thought*. London: Kegan Paul.

Broad, C. D. (1938). *An Examination of McTaggart's Philosophy*. Vol. II, part I. Cambridge: Cambridge University Press.

Calaprice, A. (ed.) (2000). *The Expanded Quotable Einstein*. Princeton: Princeton University Press.

Clifton, R., and Hogarth, M. (1995). "The Definability of Objective Becoming in Minkowski Spacetime." *Synthese* 103: 355–387.

Craig, W. L. (2000). *The Tensed Theory of Time: A Critical Examination*. Boston: Kluwer Academic.

Davies, P. (1984). *God and the New Physics*. London: Penguin Books.

Descartes, R. (1996). *Meditations on First Philosophy*. Cambridge: Cambridge University Press.

Dieks, D. (ed.) (2006). *The Ontology of Spacetime*. Amsterdam: Elsevier.

Dummett, M. (1978). *Truth and Other Enigmas*. Cambridge, Mass.: Harvard University Press.

Dummett, M. (1991). *The Logical Basis of Metaphysics*. Cambridge, Mass.: Harvard University Press.

Dummett, M. (2003). *Truth and the Past*. New York: Columbia University Press.

Gale, R. (ed.) (1968). *The Philosophy of Time*. Garden City, N.Y.: Anchor Books.

Gellner, E. (1959). *Words and Things*. London: Gollancz.

Gödel, K. (1949). "A Remark about the Relationship between Relativity Theory and Idealistic Philosophy." In *Albert Einstein: Philosopher, Scientist*, ed. P. A. Schilpp. La Salle, Ill.: Open Court.

Goodman, N. (1951). *The Structure of Appearance*. Cambridge, Mass.: Harvard University Press.

Heidegger, M. (1962). *Being and Time*. New York: Harper and Row.

Hinchliff, M. (1996). "The Puzzle of Change." *Philosophical Perspectives* 10: 119–136.

Husserl, E. (1964). *The Phenomenology of Internal Time-Consciousness*. Bloomington: Indiana University Press.

Jaques, E. (1982). *The Form of Time*. New York: Crane, Russak.

Kierkegaard, S. (1972). *The Concept of Anxiety*. Princeton: Princeton University Press.

Kripke, S. (1980). *Naming and Necessity*. Cambridge, Mass.: Harvard University Press.

Le Poidevin, R., and M. MacBeath (eds.) (1993). *The Philosophy of Time*. Oxford and New York: Oxford University Press.

Levinas, E. (1969). *Totality and Infinity*. Pittsburgh: Duquesne University Press.

Markosian, N. (1993). "How Fast Does Time Pass?" *Philosophy and Phenomenological Research* 53 (4): 829–844.

Markosian, N. (2004). "A Defense of Presentism." In *Oxford Studies in Metaphysics*, vol. 1, ed. D. Zimmerman. Oxford: Clarendon Press; New York: Oxford University Press.

Maxwell, N. (1985). "Are Probabilism and Special Relativity Incompatible?" *Philosophy of Science* 52: 24–43.

McTaggart, J. M. E. (1908). "The Unreality of Time." *Mind* 17: 457–474.

McTaggart, J. M. E. (1927). *The Nature of Experience*. Cambridge: Cambridge University Press.

Mellor, D. H. (1981). *Real Time*. Cambridge: Cambridge University Press.

Mellor, D. H. (1995). *The Facts of Causation*. New York: Routledge.

Mellor, D. H. (1998). *Real Time II*. London and New York: Routledge.

Merleau-Ponty, M. (1962). *Phenomenology of Perception*. London and New York: Routledge.

Oaklander, N. (2004). *The Ontology of Time*. Amherst, N.Y.: Prometheus Books.

Parfit, D. (1996). "Rationality and the Metaphysics of Time." Unpublished draft.

Price, H. H. (1932). *Perception*. London: Methuen.

Prior, A. N. (1959). "Thank Goodness That's Over." *Philosophy* 34: 12–17.

Prior, A. N. (1993). "Changes in Events and Changes in Things." In *The Philosophy of Time*, ed. Robin Le Poidevin and Murray MacBeath, pp. 35–46. Oxford Readings in Philosophy. Oxford: Oxford University Press. First published 1962.

Putnam, H. (1975a). "Time and Physical Geometry." In *Mathematics, Matter, and Method*. Cambridge: Cambridge University Press. First published in *Journal of Philosophy* 64 (8).

Putnam, H. (1975b). "It Ain't Necessarily So." In *Mathematics, Matter, and Method*. Cambridge: Cambridge University Press. First published in *Journal of Philosophy* 64 (8).

Putnam, H. (1990). *Realism with a Human Face*. Cambridge, Mass.: Harvard University Press.

Queneau, R. (1977). *The Sunday of Life*. New York: New Directions.

Reichenbach, H. (1957). *The Philosophy of Space and Time*. New York: Dover.

Reichenbach, H. (1966). *Elements of Symbolic Logic*. New York: Free Press.

Russell, R. (1921). *The Analysis of Mind*. New York: Macmillan.

Russell, R. (1991). *The Problems of Philosophy*. Oxford: Oxford University Press.

Schlesinger, G. N. (1980). *Aspects of Time*. Indianapolis: Hackett.

Schlesinger, G. N. (1982). "How Time Flies." *Mind* 91: 501–523.

Schlesinger, G. N. (1991). "E PUR SI MOUVE." *Philosophical Quarterly* 41: 427–441.

Seddon, K. (1987). *Time: A Philosophical Treatment*. London: Helm.

Smart, J. J. C. (1980). "Time and Becoming." In *Time and Cause*, ed. P. van Inwagen. Dordrecht/Boston: Reidel.

Sorabji, R. (1983). "Is Time Real? Responses to an Unageing Paradox." In Proceedings of The British Academy, vol. 68, 189–213.

Stein, H. (1968). "On Einstein-Minkowski Space-Time." *Journal of Philosophy* 65 (1): 5–23.

Stein, H. (1991). "On Relativity Theory and the Openness of the Future." *Philosophy of Science* 58: 147–167.

Sterelny, K. (1991). *The Representational Theory of Mind*. Cambridge, Mass.: Basil Blackwell.

Sutton, J. (1998). *Philosophy and Memory Traces: Descartes to Connectionism*. Cambridge: Cambridge University Press.

Tooley, M. (1996). *Time, Tense, and Causation*. Oxford: Clarendon Press.

Unamuno, M. De (1954). *Tragic Sense of Life*. New York: Dover.

Westphal, J., and C. Levenson (eds.) (1993). *Time*. Indianapolis/Cambridge: Hackett.

Westphal, J. (2002). "The Retrenchability of 'the Present.'" *Analysis* 62 (1): 4–10.

Whorf, B. (1950). "An American Indian Model of the Universe." *International Journal of Ameican Linguistics* 16: 67–72.

Wittgenstein, L. (1958). *Philosophical Investigations*. Oxford: Basil Blackwell.

Wittgenstein, L. (1969). *On Certainty*. New York: Harper and Row.

Wittgenstein, L. (1993). *Philosophical Occasions*. Indianapolis/Cambridge: Hackett.

Index

Analogy with colors, 4, 98, 146, 215
Analogy with space, 23, 32–33, 61, 99, 120, 144, 146, 167–170
Analytic/continental divide, viii–ix, 2–3, 14–15, 214–217
Aristotle, 69, 70, 117–120, 124, 204
A-time, 87, 129, 131–132
Augustine, 118–120, 123, 211–212
Austin, J. L., 69–76, 78
Ayer, A. J., 80, 101

Becoming, 43, 58, 197–202
Broad, C. D., 38, 74, 75, 132
B-time, 87

Causal inaccessibility of the past, 14, 63–64. *See also* Past, inaccessibility of
Causal order, 148, 176, 189
Colors. *See* Analogy with colors
Complete description of the world, 23–25, 161, 167–170
Continental philosophy. *See* Analytic/continental divide
Continuity of time, 1, 119, 121–122, 224n2
Counterfactuals, 135, 138–139, 181, 192
Craig, W. L., 58, 221n7, 223n14

Damascius, 121
Death, 1, 173, 177, 213

Descartes, R., 101, 129
Determinism, 184, 188, 192
Dieks, D., 26
Diodorus Chronus, 121
Divine preordination, 184, 199, 191
Dummett, M., 7, 16, 19, 23, 44–58, 75, 77, 102–109, 110, 149, 160–162, 164, 186, 220n4, 221n5, 221n6, 226n18, 228n31

Earlier/later relations, 4–5, 20–22, 34, 38, 40, 43, 81, 87, 110–112, 168, 171–172, 190, 202. *See also* Succession
Einstein, A., 2, 4, 17, 26, 95–96, 196, 219n2
Eternalism, 6
Eternity, 1–2, 212
Experiences as quasi-standards, 139–144, 146, 171, 210, 214

Fatalism, 188, 191–192
Fear of death. *See* Death
Fixity of the past, 10–11, 13, 28–29, 33–34, 183–195, 196, 203–204, 211, 213, 228n30
Future, openness of, 11, 13, 26, 28–29, 33–34, 183–195, 196, 203–205, 211, 224n4, 228n32
Future contingents, 186

Gale, R. M., 118–119, 123
Gellner, E., 78
Goodman, N., 80–82

Husserl, E., 15, 213–214

James, W., 3, 214
Jaques, E., 149–150

Kierkegaard, S., 2
Kripke, S., 7, 134–135, 138–139, 224n2

Levinas, E., 2, 213, 215–216, 229n3

McTaggart, J. M. E., 6,18–22, 43, 56–57,
  110, 156–164, 220n4, 221n5,
  223n11, 224n1, 225n8, 226n17
Meaning, theory of, 38, 57, 69, 77,
  78–79, 84, 94–95, 136, 222n8,
  223n12
Mellor, D. H., 2, 20–22, 31, 34, 73, 74,
  77, 82–95, 96, 97, 100, 129–146,
  147–148, 156–159, 174, 189–190,
  223n12
Memory, 32, 49, 66, 97–98, 131–132,
  146–154, 163, 171, 210, 211,
  225n12, 226n15
Merleau-Ponty, M., 147–148
Metaphor. See Time's passage as
  metaphor
Moral conduct, 15, 215–216
Moving Now, 7, 12, 37, 38–43, 57–58,
  66, 68, 109 – 112, 157, 164, 165–166

Newton, I., 207

Ontological assumption, definition
  and role, viii-ix, 8–11, 13–15,
  209–210
Ontological status of the present, viii,
  6, 24, 38–39, 42–43, 57, 58, 61,
  64–66, 68, 107–108, 112–113,
  121–123, 157, 170

Openness of the future. See Future,
  openness of
Ordinary language, 13, 43, 63, 65, 67,
  69–70, 75–76, 80–81, 93, 111, 114,
  134, 155, 181

Parfit, D., 15, 23–25, 63, 64, 69, 72–73,
  74, 167–169, 172–178, 180, 222n5
Past, inaccessibility of, 10, 14, 31–32,
  57, 61–62, 63–64, 162, 220n7,
  222n1
Past's fixity. See Fixity of the past
Phenomenology, as a method, viii–ix,
  3, 10–11, 14–15, 210–211, 214
Presence of experience, 15, 66,
  129–146, 210
Present
  pointlike-ness of, 13, 66, 141,
  117–129, 210, 211
  spatial restriction of, 198–200
Presentism, 6
Prior, A. N., 33, 39–40, 165, 172
Putnam, H., 25–26, 28, 126, 128, 196,
  200, 203–205, 207, 225n7, 229n38,
  229n39

Quine, W. V. O., 80, 82

Rationality/irrationality, 172, 211
"Real" differences vs. "ontological"
  differences, 13
Reality claims, 8, 12, 62–65, 67, 74,
  114–115, 159, 161, 200, 209
Reichenbach, H., 38, 135, 220n5
Relativity theory, 7, 14, 17, 25–29, 77,
  195–207, 220n6, 229n37, 229n38,
  229n39
Russell, B., 80, 82, 130, 225n14

Sacred/profane time, 216
Schlesinger, G. N., 15, 38, 40–43, 58,
  74, 75, 110–112, 165, 173, 174,
  176–177

Scientific language, 13, 14, 67, 114, 181

Seddon, K., 175–176

Simultaneity, 5, 27, 30, 76, 77, 79, 80, 196, 201–203

Smart, J. J. C., 69, 174, 176–177, 180

Spatial analogy. *See* Analogy with space

Stein, H., 197–200, 207

Succession, 4, 6, 42–43, 65, 79, 92, 93, 110, 112, 119, 123, 157, 224n1. *See also* Earlier/later relations

Temporal neutrality, 175–181

Temporal order, 43, 189, 202

Tense
 beliefs, 2, 34–35, 41, 79, 84, 87, 97–100, 131, 140, 174, 177
 biases related to, 13, 33, 34–35, 39, 171–183, 211, 213
 indispensability of, 4, 39, 68–69, 82, 84, 91, 96, 98
 inescapability of, 31, 96–99, 102, 199

Tensed relations, definition of, 4–5, 79

Tenseless relations, definition of, 4–5, 79

Tenseless/tensed debate, common grounds of, viii–ix, 8–9, 14–15, 16, 67–68, 190–191, 209

Time's passage
 change and, 33, 61
 claims concerning the nature of, viii, 1–3, 6, 13, 26, 59, 61, 65–66, 110–113, 120–122, 144, 154, 155–170, 197–198, 210–212, 226n18
 experience of, 2, 34–35, 39–42, 49, 69, 120, 172, 174, 180, 221n3
 as an illusion, vii, 1–2, 17, 25, 26, 28–31, 37, 65, 80, 96, 113, 155–156, 164, 168, 170, 196
 as metaphor, 58, 166–167, 221n7
 rate of, 17, 43, 61, 66, 156, 165–167, 170

truth and, 21, 53–57, 109, 156–164, 210 (*see also* Dummett, M.)

Token reflexive account, 20, 22, 25, 34–35, 69, 77, 79, 87–95, 223n12

Transitivity of copresentness, 197, 199–203, 207

Truth conditions, 158–164, 204
 tensed, 21, 48–49, 53–58, 69, 75, 85, 103, 109, 157–158, 164, 170
 tenseless, 2, 6, 21, 34, 48, 69, 77, 79, 82–83, 85–89, 164

Westphal, J., 119, 120, 123, 224n3

Wittgenstein, L., 3, 15, 76, 89, 133–136, 139, 186, 214, 222n8